The IEBM Dictionary of
Business and Management

Titles from the International Encyclopedia of Business and Management Series

International Encyclopedia of Business and Management
6 volume set, hardback, 0-415-07399-5

Concise International Encyclopedia of Business and Management
1 volume edition, hardback, 1-86152-114-6

Pocket International Encyclopedia of Business and Management
Paperback, 1-86152-113-8

IEBM Handbook Series

The IEBM Handbook of Human Resource Management
Edited by Michael Poole and Malcolm Warner
Hardback, 1-86152-166-9

The IEBM Handbook of Management Thinking
Edited by Malcolm Warner
Hardback, 1-86152-162-6

The IEBM Handbook of Organizational Behaviour
Edited by Arndt Sorge and Malcolm Warner
Hardback, 1-86152-157-X

The IEBM Handbook of International Business
Edited by Rosalie L. Tung
Hardback, 1-86152-216-9

The IEBM Dictionary of Business and Management

Edited by
Morgen Witzel

INTERNATIONAL THOMSON BUSINESS PRESS
I(T)P An International Thomson Publishing Company

London • Bonn • Boston • Johannesburg • Madrid • Melbourne • Mexico City • New York • Paris
Singapore • Tokyo • Toronto • Albany, NY • Belmont, CA • Cincinnati, OH • Detroit, MI

The IEBM Dictionary of Business and Management

Copyright © 1999 International Thomson Business Press

First edition published by International Thomson Business Press

I(T)P   A divison of International Thomson Publishing Inc.
The ITP logo is a trademark under licence

Whilst the Publisher has taken all reasonable care in the preparation of this
book the Publisher makes no representation, express or implied, with
regard to the accuracy of the information contained in this book and cannot accept any legal responsibility or liability for any errors or omissions
from the book or the consequences thereof.

Products and services that are referred to in this book may be either trademarks and/or registered trademarks of their respective owners. The
Publisher/s and Author/s make no claim to these trademarks.

British Library Cataloguing-in-Publication Data
A catalogue record for this book is available from the British Library

Typeset by Helen Skelton, London
Printed in the UK by Clays Ltd, Bungay, Suffolk

ISBN 1 86152 218 5

International Thomson Business Press
Berkshire House
168–173 High Holborn
London WC1V 7AA
UK

http://www.itbp.com

Introduction

Business and management is a complex discipline, or rather, collection of disciplines. As such, it has developed a rich, varied and elaborate vocabulary, the sources of which are as varied as the concepts they describe. Business and management has successfully imported terms and concepts from most of the social and physical sciences – anthropology, sociology, psychology, physics, engineering and biology, to name just a few – and has adapted them to fit business situations. It is small wonder that students, and even sometimes experienced managers, are often baffled by the complexities of the language they are required to use and understand.

A few words should be said about what the Dictionary does not contain. First, we have eschewed jargon wherever possible. Management jargon tends to change rapidly, and it is impossible to be fully current; we chose not to use terms which are likely to go out of favour quickly, only including jargon where it has become an accepted part of the relevant disciplines. We have not included large numbers of organizational names and acronyms. Many of these are parochial, only relevant to managers in a certain sector or country; in line with the general philosophy of the IEBM, we have sought to include terms of international importance only.

We have also focused on business and management terms only (though, as noted, many of these have their origins in other disciplines). There are two exceptions: economics and information technology. Some common economics terms have been defined, as they are concepts which are relevant to international management, in particular. IT is now such a part and parcel of daily business life, and yet its concepts are often so ill-defined, that we felt it would be useful and relevant to include some basic terms here.

The IEBM Dictionary of Business and Management is designed as a reference for students, managers and lay people in general who need to understand the language of business. The project is an offshoot of the *International Encyclopedia of Business and Management* (ITBP, 1996), a six-volume, major international reference work which explores issues in management, marketing, organization behaviour, operations management and research, business economics, information management, strategy, among others. This dictionary provides a reference tool for use with the

Encyclopedia. However, not every term which appears in the former also appears in the latter. One of the strengths of the Encyclopedia is its comprehensive annotated bibliographies which accompany each article. As well as being a reference work in its own right, then, the Encyclopedia serves as a guide to further reading and exploration of its topics. This dictionary is designed to accompany such further reading, and to assist novice readers in understanding the often complex language which they will encounter.

However, it must be added that we cannot make any claims to completeness. Although this is one of the largest dictionaries in the subject area ever compiled, with over 7500 terms, some material has inevitably been left out. These omissions for the most part include terms relevant to specific sectors or national economies/markets. There have too been omissions in economics and IT terminology, but we have supplied enough to help novices in these fields come to terms with the basics. (On this note, I should add that, despite the disclaimers above, all responsibility for errors and omissions is my own.) Finally, we have not attempted to define terms so strictly as to account for nuances of meaning in very specific contexts; rather, we have provided broad meanings which indicate the kinds of specific concepts these terms can represent. This is necessary because the language of business and management is still growing and evolving; some terms can be employed in many subtly different ways.

Within the dictionary, terms are given in the strict alphabetical order of the first word. We tend to present terms in their normal word order, thus direct marketing rather than marketing, direct; relational database rather than database, relational. In some cases, however, we have chosen to group terms by common key concepts; thus bond, government and bond, indemnity rather than government bond or indemnity bond. If you do not find a term where you expect, try looking under a variant word order as in the previous example. We have included a limited number of dummy headwords in obvious instances, which will help guide the reader to the appropriate definition. We have also provided cross-references where terms are closely linked; these appear at the end of the relevant definitions.

On a personal note, I would like to thank a number of people who have helped make this book possible: Malcolm Warner, general editor of the *International Encyclopedia of Business and Management*, for his encouragement and guidance over the years; Tara Montgomery, the original project manager who got me involved with the Encyclopedia in the first place; and Kay Larkin, for asking me to take on the challenging and fascinating task of compiling and editing the Dictionary. So-Shan Au, Sophie Durlacher, Helen Skelton and Kim Allen worked on the text and helped it to reach readability; Marilyn Livingstone provided feedback on my definitions and general moral support; and Janette Lee came up with a comprehensible definition of relational database. To all of them, my thanks.

Morgen Witzel, London, 1998

A-scores a credit risk management system for predicting company failure; subject companies are scored on three scales, measuring defects, symptoms and mistakes.

abandonment the relinquishment of goods or assets to another party, either without compensation or, in the case of insurance, in exchange for a total loss settlement.

abandonment stage the final stage in the product life cycle, when profits have declined and the selling firm discontinues the product.

abatement cancellation or reduction of an expenditure, debit or tax; also more generally reducing, as in abatement of nuisance.

ABC *see* activity-based costing.

ability to pay **1** generally, the concept that charges levied on an individual or organization should reflect the latter's financial resources and therefore ability to meet those charges; **2** in wage negotiations, the concept that wage and salary levels should be based on the employer's ability to pay.

Abitur in Germany, the final school-leaving exam, a prerequisite for entering university.

above normal loss loss greater than might usually be expected, often caused by weather or unforeseeable accidents.

above par above the face value of a stock or bond.

above the line promotion advertising in the press or broadcast media; *see also* below the line promotion.

abrogation the cancellation of a contract or agreement.

absence an absent employee is one who is not present in the workplace when normally expected to be so.

absence of demand in marketing, when there is insufficient demand for a product to make that product financially viable.

absentee an employee who is absent; *see* absence.

absenteeism general term to describe the condition of absence by employees; rates of absenteeism measure the overall incidence of absence.

absolute advantage trade theory non-replicable advantage enjoyed by a country over its trade rivals in terms of manufacturing capability or natural resources, first defined by Adam Smith.

absolute cost barriers barriers to entry that are fixed in nature; tending to favour established firms over new entrants, and large firms over small ones.

absolute frequency research term, meaning the frequency of appearance of a given data point in a particular data set; often referred to in marketing research.

absolute sale sale where no conditions are required for completion.

absorb 1 the process of transferring costs from one account to another; **2** the merger of one account into another.

absorption costing accounting procedure for assigning indirect or overhead costs as part of the product cost for each unit produced; also known as contribution costing.

absorption point in securities markets, equivalent to saturation; the point at which the market rejects further offerings of the same security at the same price.

absorptive capacity the ability of firms to adopt new ideas, often based on their ability to scan and integrate external knowledge.

abstract brief summary of a longer document.

abstract of title legal document setting out the previous ownership of property, used to determine present title.

accelerated depreciation depreciation of capital goods at a faster than expected rate.

acceleration principle in marketing, the phenomenon whereby sales of a good to end consumers can result in an even larger increase in overall sales.

accelerator the concept whereby an increase/decrease in consumption spending will result in a still larger increase/decrease in investment; *see also* marginal propensity to invest.

acceptability the extent to which a particular currency is accepted in a given market.

acceptable quality level quality standard, expressed as the maximum number of defects or minimum number of non-defective units in a particular lot.

acceptable usage policies (AUPs) self-regulation mechanism for Internet users, requiring that users not hamper or hinder other users, for example, by occupying excessive bandwidth or flooding their portion of the Internet with large amounts of data.

acceptance 1 generally, the receipt of a consignment of goods by one party in the supply chain from another; **2** in banking, acceptance is the process whereby a third party guarantees a bill of exchange, usually on the basis of proof of title to merchandise; *see* acceptance house.

acceptance financing short-term financing whereby credit is advanced on the basis of proof of title to merchandise; *see* acceptance, acceptance house.

acceptance house financial institution specializing in acceptance financing.

acceptance number the maximum number of allowable defects in a lot or order; *see* acceptable quality level.

acceptance time time required for new ideas to become used and accepted.

acceptor the party drawing a note, and who will pay that note when due; *see* bill of exchange.

access controls measures such as locks, codes, etc. which define who has access to physical sites or computer systems.

accession the act of a new employee joining the firm; the promotion of an employee or manager to a more senior position.

accession rate total or average numbers of employees joining the firm over a given period; *see also* accession.

accessory person, system or instrument which assists in the completion of a task.

access time the time required for a computer user to gain entry to a particular file or application.

accident an event that occurs unintentionally and not by design.

accidental death benefit insurance benefit payable in the event of the insured dying by accident.

accident insurance insurance against the possibility of an accident affecting persons, systems or equipment.

accident severity a measure of the effects of an accident, most commonly expressed in terms of time/money lost as a result.

accommodation the pledging by one party of their reputation or credit so as to allow a second party to borrow money; no other collateral is involved.

accommodation note promissory note or other document in which one party provides accommodation to another to allow the latter to borrow money; *see* accommodation.

accommodation paper *see* accommodation note.

accommodation party the party who signs the accommodation note, thereby serving as guarantor for another party; *see* accommodation, accommodation note.

account 1 a record of the financial transactions of the business or a particular business operation, showing the date and financial value of each transaction; **2** also, in sales, refers to each client, i.e. in advertising, an 'account' is a client of an advertising agency; **3** also, in finance, funds deposited in a bank or other financial institution on behalf of a person or organization.

accountability the concept that employees, managers and organizations are responsible for their decisions and actions, and can be affected by the consequences.

accountability, corporate *see* corporate accountability.

accountant a person who works in accounting, and has reached a certain level of professional qualification; *see also* certified accountant, chartered accountant.

account balance the net of credit or debit in a specific account.

account classification in sales, a method whereby selling agents rank clients according to business potential.

account debtor an individual or organization that owes money to a specific account is a debtor to that account.

account executive term used most commonly in advertising and public relations, denoting the manager responsible for managing the service provided to a particular account (client).

accounting the process of establishing and keeping accounts; the recording and analysis of all the company's financial transactions and summary of the present financial position, and the reporting of such to the company's managers and shareholders, tax and other government authorities, and all other relevant parties; *see also* cost accounting, equity accounting, financial accounting, international accounting, management accounting, public accounting.

accounting code code used by accountants to identify particular expenditures or incomes so that these are debited/credit to the appropriate account.

accounting, consolidated the preparation of consolidated financial statements; *see* consolidated financial statement.

accounting controls **1** procedures for monitoring the accounting process, and for ensuring the accuracy and integrity of the accounts; **2** also, procedures for comparing actual financial performance with project performance, so as to determine whether the company or business unit is meeting financial targets.

accounting, creative *see* creative accounting.

accounting, current cost procedure developed by Theodore Limperg, according to which value is equal to either current cost or net replaceable value, whichever is smaller; accounts should be based on the theoretically correct measure of value.

accounting cycle accounting activities which occur over the course of an accounting period; see accounting period.

accounting environment political, legal and business factors which determines accounting practices and procedures in different countries.

accounting, equity *see* equity accounting

accounting exposure the risk of foreign exchange currency appreciation or depreciation affecting an account. Accounting exposure includes both translation risk and transaction risk.

accounting, financial *see* financial accounting.

accounting, full cost in environmental reporting, a term which indicates that the environmental, social and economic aspects of corporate performance are linked together.

accounting, historical cost *see* historical cost accounting.

accounting information system information system which collects and processes financial data from accounts, generating a report on those accounts for management use.

accounting, management *see* management accounting.

accounting period time between each summary or statement of accounts. Each accounting period contains a complete accounting cycle, beginning with the statement of the account balance at the start of the period, a series of transactions which are recorded and their effects determined, and then the closure of the record and the preparation of a financial report or statement. Accounting periods are typically one month, sometimes less.

accounting procedure the procedures by which accounts are kept and analysed and reports created, and which determine their accuracy and integrity; *see* accounting controls.

accounting process the recording and analysis of financial transactions and the preparation of accounting reports. The accounting process results in a complete accounting cycle.

accounting profit the net of gross revenue minus explicit costs.

accounting rate of return method of capital investment appraisal which relates the projected accounting profit from a project to the cash investment or other assets required; also known as unadjusted rate of return.

accounting ratio *see* management ratio; also known as financial ratio.

accounting regulation the setting and maintaining of standards for the accounting profession, either through self-regulation by industry bodies or by governments through statute.

accounting report the summary of accounts at the end of each accounting cycle, which states the closing account balance and summarizes financial activity leading up to that balance.

accounting standardization **1** the harmonization of accounting procedures across an organization; **2** also, the harmonization of accounting procedures between countries; *see* accounting standards.

accounting standards standards to which members of the accounting profession are expected to work in terms of the reporting and presentation of data. National standards are increasingly being supplanted by international standards.

account period *see* accounting period.

accounts payable also known as creditors; liabilities, where the account owes money to another party for goods or services received.

accounts receivable also known as debtors; assets, where the account is owed money by another party for goods or services provided.

accounts-receivable financing short-term credit where accounts receivable are used as collateral for a loan, or are transferred to the lender in exchange for the loan.

accreditation **1** a form of formal qualification; **2** alternatively, the granting of credentials to another party to operate on the firm's behalf; see accredited agent.

accredited agent a third party licensed by a firm to operate on its behalf in a particular location or market.

accredited list persons accredited to act as agents for the firm; in distribution, accredited agents are empowered to collect and transport goods without specific authority in each case.

accretion **1** the growth of funds deposited in a bank account, pension fund, etc., usually through a combination of new deposits and interest or income accruing to funds already deposited; **2** more generally, the increase in the value of an investment.

accretion account record of the increase in value of an investment, comparing the original sum invested with the present value of the investment.

accruals amounts owing but not yet recorded in the balance sheet.

accruals principle in financial accounting, the recognition of revenues when they are earned and expenses when they are incurred.

accrue **1** to accumulate or add funds to an existing account or investment; **2** more generally, to gain or to profit; in legal terms, to become eligible for a right or claim which has been passed on from another party.

accrued assets income or revenue which has been earned but not yet received.

accrued charges payments to be made, where services have been received in advance of payment and where payment itself is not yet due (for example, hire charges which are paid on a monthly basis).

accrued dividend a dividend which has been earned but has not yet been declared or paid; *see* accrued revenue.

accrued expense expenditure which has been incurred but not yet paid; *see* accrued charges.

accrued liabilities debt incurred from accumulated expenses or charges.

accrued revenue income which has been earned but is not yet due or received; for example, wages paid at the end of the month for work performed during that month.

acculturation the process of assimilating portions of another culture, preferably without diluting or diminishing one's original culture.

accumulated dividend a dividend which is due and declared but not yet paid.

accumulated earnings earnings which are due, but have not yet been paid.

accumulated leave leave or time off due to an employee but not yet used.

accumulated profit tax specific tax measure directed by authorities at companies that delay announcing dividends.

accumulation 1 addition of income to a principal amount in a fund or account; **2** also, in securities, the building up of a single holding with a large number of shares in a particular company.

accumulation factor the difference between the present cash value and the terminal value or disposal value of an asset.

achieved penetration marketing term for the extent to which a particular product or service has been taken up in the target market; usually expressed as a percentage or ratio of actual customers to potential customers.

achievement test US technique for measuring an employee's actual achievement, as opposed to aptitude or potential.

acid test ratio technique for determining the creditworthiness of a firm by expressing a ratio of total disposable assets (including cash and receivables) to total current liabilities. A ratio of 1:1 is considered satisfactory.

ACORN acronym for A Classification of Residential Neighbourhoods; lifestyles classification used by UK marketers, a form of psychographic profiling based on postal codes; used by direct mailers and other marketers.

acquisition generally, the purchase of equity or assets belonging to one company by another; often used to mean the complete acquisition of one firm by another.

acquisition cost the costs involved in acquisitions, including legal fees and commissions to third parties involved in the acquisition, such as brokers.

acquisition method in consolidated financial accounting, where the cost of an acquisition is calculated as the sum of the payment made by the acquirer for the acquisition.

acquittance discharge from any debt or other obligation.

across the board 1 generally, applying to all those involved in a uniform fashion; **2** more specifically, a pay increase giving an equal increase to all employees of a given grade or rank.

ACT *see* advance corporation tax.

action 1 steps taken to implement a particular plan or strategy; **2** in securities, the performance of a particular stock.

action research research which attempts to combine the investigation of a specific problem with recommendations for and implementation of a solution.

action science research and intervention designed to understand and alter the reasoning and learning processes of individuals and organizations.

activation probabilities in a habitual domain, the probabilities of ideas or actions that are actually activated or in the actual domain.

active account an account which features a high level of activity, either frequent withdrawals and deposits (bank accounts) or frequent purchases (sales accounts).

active investor describes an investor who not only invests capital but who is actively involved in the management of that investment.

active market 1 any market which has a large number of transactions and high levels of trading; **2** numerous transactions in securities trading.

active money money in current circulation.

active trade balance a favourable balance of trade.

activism, shareholder positive initiatives on the part of a company's shareholders to control or counter management policy.

activity a particular task or operation; *see also* action, process.

activity-based budgeting *see* activity-based costing.

activity-based costing (ABC) a system of costing where costs are based on actual resource consumption involved in a particular activity or process.

activity-based cost management *see* activity-based costing.

activity charge service charge imposed by banks on accounts for each withdrawal or deposit; often imposed on accounts with low balances.

activity chart map or diagram showing the individual operations and activities involved in a particular process, in the actual order in which they are carried out.

activity ratio a comparison of actual work output with planned or forecasted output.

act of God legal term for event outside the scope of human control, such as an earthquake or tornado.

actual cash value the replacement cost of an item, less depreciation; in other words, the cost of replacing that item with a similar item in similar physical condition.

actual costing method of costing which allocates costs to products according to materials, labour and overheads required directly to produce that product.

actual domain (AD) in habitual domains, the set of events and actions that are actually activated.

actual investment money invested in facilities and equipment.

actualization–atmosphere factors factors combining to make up motivation to work; actualization factors are work and all forms of gratitude achieved through work; atmosphere factors are remuneration, job security, management policy in the company and relations between colleagues.

actuals goods or services that are immediately available and are handed over to the customer directly upon purchase, as opposed to futures.

actual total loss insurance term for an item which is destroyed or so badly damaged as to be unusable.

actual valuation value of an item or lot at time of delivery.

actuarial calculation in insurance and pensions, used to determine what contribution will be paid into a particular scheme; based on estimates of what benefit would be paid given any particular contingency, and the likelihood of that contingency occurring.

actuarial return return on investment as measured by discounted cash flow analysis; also known as internal rate of return.

actuary insurance risk measurement specialist, who makes actuarial calculations.

AD *see* actual domain.

ad short for advertisement.

adaptability ability of a person, system or organization to adjust to change, to acquire and integrate new information, and to change modes of operation to reflect these.

adaptability screening in human resources, a method of testing the ability of managers to adapt to different cultures, used particularly when managers are being considered for overseas assignments.

adaptation the process whereby people, systems and organizations adapt, either by building on existing competences or acquiring new ones.

adaptive isomorphism phenomenon whereby firms experiment with new products and processes in order to cope with new technological, marketing or organizational problems.

adaptive management the relation of an organization to its environment by adapting the organization to meet changes in that environment.

adaptive programme a mode of instruction or training, where the sequence of the programme is controlled by the trainee and can vary from person to person.

addback in accounting, the process of working backwards from a statement of net income and then adding or deducting income statement items.

added value the value to the customer or end-user of a product or service, which is added to the basic product during production or service processes; *see also* value added.

additional insured in insurance, persons insured under a particular policy additional to the actual policy-holder.

additional mark-on a retailer's increase in the price of merchandise over and above the manufacturer's recommended price.

adhocracy a form of organization structure where production and administrative staff work together on an informal basis to achieve goals.

adjournment termination, temporary or permanent, of a formal meeting;

sometimes used to mean the reconvening of that meeting in the same or a different location at a later time.

adjudication the resolution of a dispute by a third party, typically a court or a tribunal.

adjunct account temporary account used to hold transfers from existing accounts.

adjustable peg form of fixed exchange rate which allows for regular adjustments of the rate.

adjusted earned income earned income which is subject to tax.

adjusted gross income gross income less expenses and losses.

adjuster insurance company employee who checks on insurance claims, evaluates their validity and makes recommendations as to the amount of compensation due to the insured.

adjustment in insurance, the process of determining the amount of compensation to be paid; in accounting, a change to an existing account.

adjustment policies government policies aimed at rectifying negative trade balances.

adjustment preferred securities preferred stock created by the restructuring of a company.

ad men colloquial term for professionals working in advertising.

administered price price set by the seller independent of market conditions.

administration management activities which focus on the efficient running of an organization, including such tasks as control and record keeping; alternatively, the management of a bankrupt business by a third party called in to run the business.

administration costs costs incurred in the administration of a department or business unit, through managerial and administrative activities.

administration, public sector *see* public sector administration.

administrative control managerial control over the people and processes within an organization, ensuring that all are focused on meeting the organization's goals.

administrative discretion *see* management discretion.

administrative expenses *see* administration costs.

administrative inflation created when administered prices are employed, caused by the fall of output and the relative stability of prices.

administrative management organization structure-oriented principles of general management, developed by Henri Fayol.

administrative reorganization restructuring of the administrative processes and personnel of a company so as to make administration functions more efficient and effective.

administrative science 1 application of scientific principles of administration (*see also* management science); **2** general term for theories of public sector administration developed in Europe early in the twentieth century.

administrative services services provided by administration to the rest of the company or organization, including accounting, record keeping, planning, control and so on.

administrative unit any unit within the organization recognized as an administrative entity, for example, as a cost centre or profit centre.

admiralty court any court which hears cases covered by maritime law.

admonition warning or reprimand delivered verbally.

adopter customer who, buys a product or brand for the first time, and continues to buy the same one on a steady basis.

adoption process in marketing research, the procedure by which a customer decides to purchase and use a product.

ad valorem tax or duty which varies according to the value of the thing being taxed.

ad valorem **tariff** tariff based on the value of the goods being imported or exported.

advance 1 payment made prior to the due date; **2** increase in price, value or cost; loan made by a bank to cover business expenditures.

advance against documents loan using written documents such as sales contracts or bills of lading as collateral.

advance bill bill or invoice presented to the customer prior to the delivery of the goods being purchased.

advance commitment prior agreement by a lender to make a loan for a given amount.

advance corporation tax (ACT) tax levied when a company pays out dividends; the amount paid is deducted from the total of corporation tax when this is assessed.

advanced manufacturing technologies (AMTs) general term for high technology applied to manufacturing processes, including for example computer-assisted design and manufacturing systems.

advance import deposit downpayment made to government to secure an import licence, refundable once the import has been made.

advance on wages payment of wages prior to the normal payment date, sometimes in advance of when the work is carried out.

advantage favourable condition which gives a business or country the ability to compete successfully; superiority over a competitor.

adventure a speculative undertaking.

advertisement a public announcement concerning a product, service or brand that is offered for sale, placed with one or more available media such as newspapers, radio, television, billboards and so on; *see also* advertising.

advertising the promotion of goods and services using printed or broadcast material.

advertising agency professional agency which specializes in the design and placing of advertisements.

advertising allowance price reduction given by the manufacturer to retailers when the latter have incurred large expenses in advertising the manufacturer's products.

advertising campaign promotional campaign involving the placing of advertisements in a variety of media, designed to support a particular product, service or brand.

advertising credit mention of the name of another brand, or of a retailer, in an advertisement paid for by the manufacturer.

advertising effectiveness measure of the extent to which an advertisement or campaign has increased sales and profits.

advertising, international advertising campaigns directed at more than one national market.

advertising localization the development of advertising campaigns directed at specific local or cultural markets; as opposed to advertising standardization.

advertising media general term for newspapers, journals, radio, television, billboards and other channels of communication that can be used to carry advertisements.

advertising planning the planning and budgeting of advertising campaigns.

advertising platform the product or service features and selling points which form the principal focus of an advertising campaign.

advertising standardization the use of common advertising campaigns, or campaigns with common elements, across more than one national market; as opposed to advertising localization.

advertising strategy a company's overall approach to advertising, which sets out the level and nature of advertising needed to help the company meet its goals.

advice note document sent by a seller to a buyer listing goods which have been shipped to the latter.

affidavit sworn statement of fact.

affiliate 1 company which is associated with another company, usually through common ownership; **2** in media broadcasting, a local station which carries the programmes of a national network.

affiliation 1 association or relationship; **2** membership of a trade union; **3** membership of a union in an association of trade unions

affiliation needs human need for acceptance into a peer group.

affinity card credit card offered to a group of people who belong to a common group or association, in effect creating a club of credit card users; in the UK, the term is most commonly used for credit cards issued by banks in association with charities.

affirmative action legislation or employment policies aimed at recruiting and employing people from minority groups.

aftersight the determining of the date when a bill is due for payment once the bill has been presented for acceptance.

AG abbreviation for *Aktiengesellschaft*, the German term for corporation; these initials usually appear after the corporation's name on official documents.

ageing trends trend, especially visible in developed countries, for the average age of the population to increase.

agency 1 business relationship whereby one party, the principal, delegates authority to another party, the agent, to conduct business on behalf of the former (*see also* agent); **2** the business operations of an agent.

agency agreement contract between a company and an agent.

agency costs costs of using an agent, both in terms of direct payment to the agent and the opportunity costs compared with handling business directly.

agency, markets and hierarchies subset of economics which looks at different ways of coordinating economic activity.

agency shop workplace agreement where the union permits non-union workers to be employed, but the latter must pay the union (usually a sum equivalent to union dues).

agency–structure relationship the relationship between the people, or agents, in an organization and the structure of the organization.

agency theory theoretical conceptualization between principals and agents in different circumstances.

agenda schedule of subjects to be discussed at a meeting.

agent 1 person or company who acts on behalf of another, most commonly as a buyer and/or seller, or other recognized representative; **2** more generally, any person or force which creates and carries out an action (as in 'agent of change').

agent, direct salesperson or agent who is directly employed by a company.

agent, exclusive agent or salesperson who represents only one client company, but is not directly employed by the latter.

agent, free *see* agent, independent; more generally, a person who is able to act without hindrance, free of any contractual obligations.

agentic state the condition of persons in an organization or hierarchy; as opposed to autonomy.

agent, independent agent who freely represents two or more clients in a similar capacity.

agglomeration collection of individual units into a mass.

aggregate total or sum.

aggregate consumption total consumption within an economy over a given time period.

aggregate demand total spending within an economy over a given time period.

aggregate income total income within an economy over a given time period.

aggregate real demand total spending within an economy over a given time period, expressed in real money terms.

aggregate supply total labour supply within an economy over a given time period.

aggregation the process of adding figures or amounts together to reach a total or sum.

aggressive portfolio investment portfolio which is held on the assumption that its value will increase

AGM *see* annual general meeting.

agreed procedure 1 procedure for carrying out certain tasks which is laid down and accepted by all parties in advance; **2** procedures accepted by both unions and employers setting out actions to be taken to resolve industrial disputes.

agreement mutual understanding between two or more parties, not necessarily legally binding on its own.

agribusiness general term for the agricultural sector and all industries connected with it.

agricultural revolution sudden, rapid increase in agricultural productivity.

AI *see* artificial intelligence.

aid money, goods and services provided to developing countries to assist their development, either without condition or in exchange for trading concessions or other benefits.

AIDA model acronym for Attention, Interest, Desire, Action, considered to be the four behavioural stages consumers go through in response to sales promotions.

aided recall in market research, technique used to help interviewees remember or recall certain events or things.

aim goal or objective.

airline management management techniques and skills required to run an airline.

algebraic manipulation altering the values of variables in an equation.

aliases in systems design, other names by which a data item or system component may be known by various users.

alien company company which is domiciled in a foreign country.

alienation disposal of property or assets, including all rights over the latter.

all-commodity distribution method of measuring distribution which looks at the number of retail outlets responsible for a given percentage of total sales.

all-commodity rate uniform transportation charge levied on all goods carried.

alliance formal arrangement whereby two or more companies agree to work towards a common goal.

allocation 1 decisions as to the level of resources to be devoted to different projects and operations, given the constraints of total resources available; **2** in costing, the decision as to how overhead costs will be apportioned among cost centres.

allonge document attached to a bill of exchange for recording additional endorsements.

allotment *see* allocation.

allowable depreciation the maximum amount that can be deducted to account for asset depreciation each year.

allowance 1 money set aside for a specific purpose; **2** money paid to another to help the other party cover costs.

allowance method accounting technique used for the recording of bad debts.

allowed time *see* standard time.

all-risks insurance insurance policy that protects the insured against a wide variety of potential risks.

alpha stocks class of stocks traded on the London stock market, composing the leading 100 stocks.

alternating shift system of shift work where workers change shift on a regular basis.

alternative budget budget which sets different levels of expenditure for different alternative levels of activity.

alternative cost cost that will be incurred if an alternative action is taken, rather than the one currently planned or contemplated (*see also* opportunity cost).

AMTs *see* advanced manufacturing technologies.

amalgamation *see* merger.

amendment in meetings, a form of secondary motion which proposes an alteration to the motion currently being discussed.

amenity any feature which serves to make a product, service or other good more attractive or useful.

AMI *see* application of metrics in industry.

amortization 1 paying off a debt in installments over time; **2** also, synonym for depreciation.

amortized loan loan which is repaid in regular installments.

analysis examination of an issue and its component parts, usually using numerical or mathematical techniques, in order to understand its nature and implications.

analyst researcher who conducts analysis of data or information, particularly of share prices and movements.

analytical forecasting prediction of future economic performance using analytical techniques.

analytical procedures auditing techniques which involve setting expectations as to what account balances, financial ratios and so on should read, comparing these with the actual results, and investigating any overly large variations; more generally, any procedure involving the analysis of data or information.

annual capital cost assessment of the cost of capital, reached by comparing annual cash flow with capital charges over the same period, *see also* capital, cost of.

annual earnings total earnings or revenue over the course of a year.

annual general meeting (AGM) meeting of all shareholders held once per year, which receives reports from the board of directors and votes on outstanding issues.

annual hours the number of hours per year that an employee is required to work.

annual improvement factor in wage agreements, principle whereby wages will increase annually by an amount linked to the increased productivity of the firm.

annual percentage rate (APR) rate of interest charged on a loan over the course of a year.

annual premium cost pension plan, insurance policy or similar where the beneficiaries pay premiums on an annual basis until the plan or policy matures; as opposed to single premium costing.

annual report report on the financial and strategic position of a company, prepared each year by the directors for shareholders.

annual return **1** rate of return on investment over the course of a year; **2** document which must be provided to tax authorities stating total income and taxable income for a year.

annual statement *see* annual report.

annual wage total wage paid to an employee each year.

annual wage plan wage scheme which totals the annual wage paid to an employee and then divides this into equal installments which are paid at intervals through the year.

annuitant person receiving an annuity.

annuity regular payment made to a beneficiary, used most commonly to describe payments made under pension plans to retired employees.

annuity accumulation period in pensions, the time between the point when the beneficiary first makes a deposit or pays a premium and the point when the annuity begins to be paid.

annuity accumulation value in pensions, the increase in value of deposited premiums which is used to calculate the value of any annuity to be paid.

annuity period the period after the payment of annuities begins.

antagonistic cooperation temporary cooperation between two parties who are ordinarily rivals.

anticipated balance forecasted balance of an account at the end of an accounting period, taking into account all known future deposits and withdrawals.

anticipated interest forecast interest earnings on an account or investment.

anticipation payment of an account or debt before it is due; this may permit the debtor to receive a discount or rebate.

anti-competitive any action which will prevent or impede free competition.

anti-dumping laws laws designed to prevent dumping of products from one country into another country's markets.

antitrust policies government policies aimed at the prevention of monopolies and the maintenance of competition in the market.

anti-usury laws laws intended to prevent the charging of excessive rates of interest.

appeal the aim of promotional activities, to 'appeal' to customers to evaluate and purchase the good being advertised.

applicant person applying for a job or position.

application of funds in annual financial reporting, a statement showing the origin of funds and how they were employed.

application of metrics in industry (AMI) performance measurement system used in software development.

applied economics the use of economic theory to understand and solve practical economic problems.

applied overhead overhead costs which are assigned to cost centres at a predetermined rate.

applied psychology the use of theories of psychology to understand and solve the practical problems involved in managing and working with people.

applied research general term for putting research into practice, or for using the results of research to understand real issues and solve real problems.

apportion the apportionment or allocation of costs, goods, resources, etc.

apportionment *see* allocation.

appraisal the determination of the value of an asset or good, or of the performance of a person, organization, system, etc.

appraisal method method of calculating depreciation, in which an appraisal is made at the start and finish of the accounting period and the resulting values compared.

appreciation the increase in value of an investment over time.

apprentice junior employee in training for a particular trade or occupation.

apprenticeship formal training programme for apprentices.

approach phase in personal selling, the initial description by the salesperson of his or her firm and the product or service being sold.

appropriation setting aside money for specific future needs; *see also* allocation.

approximation method mathematically based method used for setting interest rates.

APR *see* annual percentage rate.

APT *see* arbitrage pricing theory.

aptitude test tests which measure a person's ability or aptitude for a specific task.

arbitrage simultaneous buying and selling of securities, currency, etc. in different markets.

arbitrage pricing theory (APT) derivative form of the capital asset pricing model, used in portfolio theory.

arbitrageur trader who makes a profit by buying and selling securities, currency and so on in one market and then selling them on in another market, making a profit on the different prices available.

arbitration method of dispute resolution where both parties put their case before a neutral third party (an arbitrator) who then makes a ruling (*see also* binding arbitration).

arbitration agreement agreement between two parties that any disputes between them will be referred to an arbitrator.

arbitrator neutral third party who agrees to arbitrate disputes.

architecture 1 in organizations, term for the organizational structure or hierarchy of the organization; **2** in systems design, general term for the overall structure of the system.

archive computer storage facility for storing inactive files.

area agreement collective agreement covering all workers and employers in a particular industry or region.

area concentration concentration of marketing and promotional effort on a particular geographical area and market.

arm's length relationship relationship where the two parties are not directly connected, usually employing an agent or go-between.

arrangement agreed schedule for the repayment of unsecured debts.

array arrangement of different values by magnitude, usually from smallest to largest.

arrears money which is due but has not been paid; loan or mortgage repayments which are overdue and are not yet paid.

arrow method in process mapping, diagrammatic method of representing the sequence of activities required to complete a process.

articles of agreement *see* contract.

articles of association formal statement of a company's structure, its legal framework and the powers of the directors (*see also* memorandum of association).

articles of incorporation formal registration of a corporation, which must be registered with government authorities.

artificial currency unit monetary unit which exists for accounting purposes only, and is not actually in circulation.

artificial intelligence (AI) computer systems or programs which mimic some aspects of human intelligence, in particular logical reasoning.

artificial neural network *see* neural network.

ASCII in computing, acronym for American Standard Code for Information Interchange; standard method of assigning bit patterns to letters, numbers and symbols.

ascribed status status which a person enjoys in their personal life or social setting outside the workplace.

ASEAN *see* Association of South East Asian Nations.

as is condition of sale whereby the buyer accepts goods in their present condition.

aspirational group in marketing research, a type of reference group composed of people who wish to belong to a particular social group or achieve a particular social status.

ASR *see* automatic speech recognition.

assembling putting together components to make a finished product.

assembly chart graphic depiction of an assembly process showing how components are brought together to form the finished product.

assembly line continuous production line in a factory, composed of a number of different work stations each manned by workers responsible for a small group of subordinate tasks within the overall assembly process.

assembly-line balancing the allocation of tasks to work stations in order to achieve an efficient and even work flow.

assembly-line production mass production using assembly lines to produce highly standardized products.

assented securities securities whose owners have agreed to a change in status.

assessment **1** a tax, levy or charge; **2** an analysis of the effectiveness, efficiency, profitability, etc. of a system, person or organization.

assessment centre organization which provides assessment services, particularly in relation to assessing employee and management performance and abilities.

asset any thing which has value, as opposed to liability; property owned by a company or individual, *see also* current assets; fixed assets; tangible assets.

asset approach accounting method where expenses are first charged to an asset account.

asset management management techniques which aim to maximize the use of a company's assets.

asset stripping selling off of a company's assets for immediate profit.

asset substitution effect phenomenon whereby, when a company undertakes risky investments, the major portion of the risk is born by bondholders rather than shareholders.

asset turnover ratio of total sales to total assets.

assign to designate a particular employee or group of employees as having responsibility for performing a stated task; to transfer property or rights to another party.

assigned risk type of risk which insurers are legally obliged to cover.

assignee person to whom a property or right is assigned.

assignment 1 a task which has been given to an employee or manager by his or her subordinate; **2** the process of transferring property or rights.

assignor person assigning a property or right to the assignee.

assimilation 1 the integration of new components into an existing system; **2** the complete distribution of a securities issue to investors.

associate partner or colleague; to engage in similar work on a collaborative basis.

association group of people or institutions who come together to advance their mutual interests.

Association of South East Asian Nations (ASEAN) political and economic association of South East Asian countries, including the Tiger economies.

assumed liability debt or liability which is accepted by a party other than the one who originally contracted it.

assumption the process of assuming a debt or liability owed by another.

assumption of risk legal condition whereby one party is fully aware of the risks inherent in a situation and cannot transfer liability to another.

assurance 1 similar to insurance, but an assurance covers events which will definitely happen but at an unknown point in time; **2** alternatively, a promise made by one party to another.

asymmetrical contract contract where one party gains much more benefit than the others involved.

asymmetric information market condition where some parties in the market have access to more information than others.

asynchronous transfer mode (ATM) communications technology which makes it possible to send different types of signal down the same path.

ATM 1 *see* asynchronous transfer mode; **2** *see* automated teller machines.

at or better selling condition where the seller will accept any offer which meets or exceeds the stated minimum price.

at par security which sells for the same price as its face value.

at sight bill of exchange which is payable immediately on presentation.

attachment legal process granting a lien on the property of a debtor.

attainment achievement of a certain standard or level.

attendance presence of an employee at work.

attendance management subset of human resources management which focuses on ensuring that employees are present for work at the right time, including scheduling, flexible working practices and so on.

attest to witness a signature.

attest function US term for a statement by an auditor that the company's books have been examined and are correct.

attitude previously formed view of an issue, person, organization, good, etc., which influences subsequent behaviour.

attitude scale evaluation of personal attitudes, where individuals' attitudes can be plotted to ascertain how far they conform to or deviate from group attitudes.

attitude survey survey technique used to determine people's attitudes to given subjects.

attorney US term for lawyer.

attorney, power of *see* power of attorney.

attribute 1 specific quality or feature; **2** to assign to a particular cause or agent.

attrition 1 gradual decline through wear and tear or natural causes; **2** long-term decline of average salary levels.

auction trading situation in which a single seller offers goods to buyers, usually selling to the buyer who makes the most favourable bid.

auction design in gaming theory, games that model auction situations with more than one bidder competing.

audience the total population which can receive or understand a particular communication or are receptive to a particular communications medium.

audience flow in media broadcasting, the movement of audience members between channels.

audience measurement survey techniques which gauge the number of people who see or hear a particular communications medium.

audiovisual aids sound and video technology used in learning and training.

audit 1 assessment of a current position; **2** verification that a set of stated facts (such as financial accounts) are in fact true and correct.

audit cycle 1 period of time between audits; **2** period during which all departments of a company are audited from first to last.

audited net sales total of net sales as verified by an audit.

auditing the process of conducting an audit.

auditing standards codes of conduct and behaviour to which auditors are expected to conform.

auditor person who conducts an audit.

audit trail record of transactions or activities which is checked by an auditor to ensure that the stated summaries correspond to actual activity.

AUP *see* acceptable usage policies.

authentication verification that an item, good or statement is true and genuine.

automated data processing data processing functions carried out mechanically or, most commonly, by computers.

automated programmed instruction programmed instruction which is carried out by computers, in effect allowing a form of self-learning whereby the computer delivers the learning programme to the trainee in a preset fashion.

automated teller machine (ATM) computerized self-service point which offers banking facilities, particularly withdrawals, to bank customers.

automatic progression pay increases which automatically come into effect at intervals.

automatic selling selling from automated machines or systems which dispense goods or services on instruction from the buyer (*see also* vending machine).

automatic speech recognition (ASR) *see* speech processing system; voice recognition system.

automatic stabilizer fiscal or monetary policy measure which is activated automatically in certain economic conditions.

automation the independent performance by machines of tasks formerly done by hand.

automation engineering branch of engineering which applies the concepts of automation to production and distribution processes.

automatization replacement and/or extension of human control by machines.

autonomous bargaining process where the local union and the employer engage in collective bargaining independently of outside interference.

autonomous consumption consumption that bears no relation to income.

autonomous transactions forms of trade between nations that are not directly related to the balance of payments.

autonomous work groups work groups which, once established, have a large degree of autonomy in determining how they will meet the goals set for them and which worker will perform which required task.

autonomy independence or freedom from control.

authoritarian leadership style of leadership that is strongly directive and focuses on top-down direction and control.

authoritarian theory conceptualization of human behaviour based on the view that people are naturally dependent and selfish, and therefore require high levels of direction and control.

authority **1** power which a manager can exercise over juniors and subordinates; **2** more generally, the ability to cause things to happen.

authority to purchase authority given by a principal to an agent to make purchases on behalf of the former.

authorization granting of authority from one party to another.

authorization card card signed by unionized workers, granting the union the authority to bargain on the worker's behalf.

authorized capital share capital which a company is allowed to issue according to the terms of its articles of association.

authorized dealer dealer or trader who is authorized to act as an agent and trade on behalf of the principal.

authorized stock *see* authorized capital.

auxiliary subordinate or support organization, not directly linked to its main functions.

availability extent to which a product is physically present and can be sold.

average 1 arithmetical mean, or central tendency, obtained by dividing the total value of all units in a set by the total number of all units in a set; **2** generally prevailing rate; **3** in maritime insurance, damage caused to goods being shipped by sea.

average cost cost of each item divided by the number of units of that item in stock or sold.

average cost pricing pricing strategy based on the calculation of the average cost of goods being sold.

average credit ratios of debtors to stock (for credit given) or purchases to creditors (for credit taken).

average daily balance average money on deposit in a bank account.

average due date average of the due dates of several required payments.

average fixed costs total of fixed costs divided by the volume of production.

average gross sales total of gross sales divided by the number of customers.

average load average quantity or weight of cargo carried per vehicle.

average mark-up pricing technique which calculates the costs of several similar products, averages these, and bases the retail price on this average.

average revenue *see* average gross sales.

average salary pension scheme pension plan where the pension benefit is based on an average of the employee's annual salary over a given period of time.

average straight time hourly earnings average hourly earnings for ordinary working time, excluding overtime and bonuses.

average total cost *see* average cost.

average variable cost total variable costs divided by volume of production (*see also* unit cost).

average wage average of wages paid across a particular sector for a particular type of job.

averaging the process of finding an average.

avoidable cost 1 costs incurred which could have been avoided had those responsible chosen a different strategy or method; **2** costs which will disappear if a certain action or strategy is discontinued.

avoidance *see* tax avoidance.

award benefit obtained from the settlement of a dispute or legal case.

awareness condition where a customer is aware of the existence of a product, service or brand but has yet to exhibit any interest in it.

B

back to support or invest in a project.

backdating dating a document prior to the actual date when it was drawn up.

backdoor financing practice whereby US government agencies borrow directly from the Treasury.

backer someone who supports a project; typically, an investor.

backflush costing production costing system whereby costs flow backwards from outputs to various inputs; used to assign specific costs, not to determine product cost.

background circumstances surrounding or leading up to a particular issue or event; *see also* environment.

backlog accumulated orders which have not yet been filled.

back office functions in service operations which do not require direct customer contact; typically, these are support and administration functions.

back orders items previously ordered but not yet sent.

back pay wages due for work which has already been carried out; where pay is given in arrears, back pay is usually pay owed beyond the normal period of arrears.

back selling sales promotions by manufacturers or wholesalers aimed directly at consumers so as to stimulate retail sales.

back-to-back credit type of credit allowed to an exporter by a finance house or bank acting as a go-between with a buyer in an export market.

backtracking *see* bumping.

backward integration expansion by a distributor or retailer up the product chain to acquire manufacturing or materials supplies facilities.

backwardation system whereby commodity futures which are to be delivered in the near future cost more than those whose delivery date is some way off.

backwash effect refers to the inherent differences in productivity between developed and under-developed countries.

bad cheque cheque written on an account where there are not sufficient funds to cover it.

bad debt arrears or money owed which cannot be collected or recovered.

bad debt expense the cost of attempting to collect or recover a bad debt.

bad debt write-off occurs when bad debts are treated as a loss and written off the company's accounts.

bad delivery when the item delivered does not conform to the specified order.

bad faith a negotiation or sale where one or both parties sets out to mislead the other is said to be made in bad faith.

bail out 1 the use of corporate funds to make payments to shareholders at favourable capital gains tax rates (illegal in many jurisdictions); **2** loans or subsidies made to a company to prevent it from going bankrupt.

bait and switch selling technique where a low-priced product is offered in hope of inducing the customer to purchase another higher priced product.

balanced budget budget in which expenditures match revenues.

balanced economy when a country's exports and imports are equal in value; *see also* balance of trade.

balanced growth growth which occurs at the same rate in all parts of the economy.

balance due amount owing on an account.

balance of payments balance sheet of transactions between a country and its trading partners; *see* current account; capital account.

balance of trade the difference between a country's imports and exports.

balance sheet itemized statement of a company's financial position, showing assets and liabilities of the business at a given point in time.

balance sheet ratios performance measures which can be taken from the balance sheet, such as profit to sales or assets to liabilities.

balance theory communications theory, that the effectiveness of communications depends on the attitudes of sender and receiver.

balancing allowance deduction from taxable profits when an asset is sold for a price greater than its depreciation allowance.

balancing charge addition to taxable profits when an asset is sold for a price greater than its depreciation allowance.

balancing time altering working hours but without altering the number of hours worked.

ballooning sudden and above-normal increase in price.

balloon loan loan requiring only small payments, the larger part of which is paid off in a single payment.

balloon note note requiring only small payments, the larger part of which is paid off in a single payment.

band curve chart breakdown chart showing various components plotted on a graph one above the other.

banding segmenting subjects in layers of value, complexity, etc. from lowest to highest.

bandwagon tendency in groups for members to conform to the ideas that appear to represent the group's values, for fear of being left on their own.

bandwidth 1 in information technology, the capacity of a system to carry electronic messages; **2** also used in flexible working hour schemes to denote times when all employees must be present.

bank general term for a financial institution which accepts deposits and makes loans.

bank accommodation short-term bank loan.

bank call government regulator's demand for a bank's balance sheet.

bank clearing *see* clearing and settlement.

bank credit credit granted by lending banks through loans or other instruments.

bank debits debits drawn against deposited funds.

bank discount bank charge for discounting a bill or note.

bank draft paper or note issued by a bank against funds held in an account; *see also* cheque.

banker's acceptance bill of exchange accepted by a bank in order to pay specific sums on behalf of a customer.

banker's cheque cheque issued by a bank.

bank holiday UK term for public holiday.

banking business conducted by financial institutions that accept deposits and provide loans, often along with other financial services.

banking controls procedures for controlling the activities of banks to ensure financial stability and probity, enacted by banks themselves and/or government regulators.

banking lending *see* bank lending.

bank lending the issuing of loans and other forms of credit by banks.

bank note legally, a promissory note issued by a bank and payable on demand to the bearer; in practice, currency or cash.

Bank of England the central bank of the UK; *see also* central bank.

bank of issue any bank authorized to issue its own bank notes which then circulate as currency.

bank overdraft amount owed on a bank account by a bank customer; occurs when withdrawals exceed deposits in the specific account.

bank rate rate of interest or charging rate at which a central bank lends money to other banks.

bank reconciliation comparison of a company's own books with bank records of financial activity.

bank reserve money which a bank is obliged to hold as a contingency to meet the needs of depositors.

bank run rapid withdrawals of large sums of money from a bank, usually precipitated by fears that the bank will fail.

bankrupt a company or person in a state of bankruptcy.

bankruptcy when a company or person is no longer able to pay debts owing; *see also* insolvency.

bank service charge fees charged by banks for services such as maintaining accounts or granting credit.

bank statement statement of account rendered by banks to account-holding customers.

bar chart diagrams in which a range of frequencies are represented in separate columns.

bar code computer code on a product that is scanned at the point of sale, used for both pricing and stock control; *see* electronic point of sale.

bargain any negotiated sale or contract; a good or service bought at a lower than usual price.

bargain counter 1 area where goods are sold at bargain prices; **2** in stock markets, stocks which are offered for sale at below current market value.

bargaining 1 negotiations leading to the final price for a good or service; **2** negotiations over pay and working conditions; *see also* collective bargaining.

bargaining agent any party (employers' association, trade union, etc.) undertaking negotiations on behalf of others in collective bargaining.

bargaining creep used to indicate slow progress in collective bargaining, with minimal concessions but no substantive agreement.

bargaining rights the rights of unions or workers to engage in collective bargaining.

bargaining unit group of workers engaged in collective bargaining, usually represented by a bargaining agent.

bargain theory theory that wage rates are generated naturally through the forces of supply and demand for labour.

barometric price leader a product or group of products whose prices reflect economic conditions and set a benchmark on which competitors base their prices.

barren money money which does not earn any income.

barrier any factor, economic or regulatory, which inhibits a company or individual from taking an action.

barriers to change factors that impede change in companies or markets.

barriers to entry factors which hinder companies wishing to enter new markets, usually to the advantage of companies already in that market.

barrister in the UK, qualified advocate who can plead in the higher courts.

BARS *see* behaviourally anchored rating scales.

barter direct exchange of goods or services without recourse to money.

base inventory level planned base inventory including aggregate inventory plus safety stocks.

base pay pay for a standard day, before overtime or bonuses.

base period standard period of time used for calculating economic measurements and index numbers.

base rate 1 rate of pay for a standard hour of work, before overtime or bonuses (*see* base pay); **2** in banking, the primary rate of interest on credit granted; **3** in the UK, the interest rate set by the Bank of England.

base stock method inventory method requiring that a basic level of stock be maintained at all times.

base time time required for the normal performance of a job or project.

basic product components or material required for the manufacture of other products.

basic rate *see* base rate.

basic wage *see* base pay.

basing point pricing where all sellers attempt to charge the same price for a particular product (illegal in many jurisdictions).

basis in taxation, base costs used when calculating capital gains or losses.

basis point one-hundredth of one per cent.

basket currency notional trading currency which is comprised of a number of real currencies, used in foreign exchange markets.

basket purchase single purchase of a group of goods or services for a consolidated price.

Bata system participative system of management developed by the Bata Corporation in the 1920s.

batch a group or lot, term normally associated with production planning and control.

batch processing computer processing where a computer undertakes a number of tasks sequentially.

batch production manufacture of products in lots too small to require continuous production; typically, batch production means the production line must be set up or reconfigured before each batch.

batch scheduling timetable techniques used in batch production.

BATNA *see* best alternative to a negotiated agreement.

baud measure of the speed at which computers can transmit or receive data.

Bayesian methodology statistical analysis technique used in forecasting, treats the best estimate of a given circumstance as a firm probability.

beachhead demand demands made in collective bargaining in hopes of gaining concessions in future bargaining sessions.

bear one who sells shares in the belief that their price will shortly fall.

bearer any person in possession of a negotiable instrument.

bearer bond *see* bond, bearer.

bearer certificate certificate which can be negotiated by the bearer, without endorsement.

bear market stock market where prices are falling.

bear position where a dealer sells stocks short, hoping that the market will fall; *see* bear.

beat down in bargaining for goods and services, to compel the selling party to lower the asking price.

Bedoucracy organizational structure found in Arab companies, based on older social structures.

beginning balance account balance at the start of a fiscal period.

beginning inventory stock held at the beginning of an accounting period.

behaviour activities or conduct of an individual in a given situation, can be prompted by both that person's internal make-up and character and by external stimuli.

behavioural decision model model describing the influence of behavioural factors in decision making.

behavioural economics branch of economics which employs behavioural science techniques to explain economic behaviour.

behaviourally anchored rating scales (BARS) form of performance appraisal which matches observed behaviour to one of a set of pre-defined behaviours posted on a rating scale.

behavioural observation scales form of critical incident technique which rates behaviour during an incident on a set of preset scales.

behavioural scores credit rating system based on the way a particular account is conducted and the level of risk it represents.

behavioural segmentation segmentation technique which focuses on the exhibited behaviours of consumers.

behavioural theory of the firm theory developed by March and Cyert which analyses organizations in terms of the behaviours of members and conflicts between such behaviours.

behaviour, consumer *see* consumer behaviour.

behaviour-focused format performance appraisal technique based on systems of rating the behaviour of those being assessed.

behaviourism branch of social psychology which studies human behaviour.

behaviourists, organizational branch of behaviourism which focuses on human behaviour inside organizations; *see also* organization behaviour.

behaviour, managerial *see* managerial behaviour.

below par at a discount.

below the line non-recurring expenditure or gain which does not normally affect operating budgets.

below the line promotion sales promotions other than media advertising; *see* above the line promotion).

benchmark set of standards or reference points used for comparison and for measuring the performance of other similar systems, products, companies or individuals.

benchmarking comparing the performance of a company against that of an identified benchmark company.

beneficiary the named person who will benefit from a trust, insurance policy or other similar contract; *see also* named insured.

benefit 1 generally, the advantage accruing to a company or person as a result of an action; **2** refers also to non-monetary rewards given as part of a salary package, as in 'pay and benefits'.

benefits *see* benefit.

benefit segmentation segmentation technique which sorts consumers according to the benefits they desire or need.

benefits in kind non-monetary benefits offered in lieu of wages.

Bertrand competition situation where oligopolies compete against each other on the basis of price.

best alternative to a negotiated agreement (BATNA) in collective bargaining, situation where taking industrial action would result in more benefit to one party or to the other than settling.

best practice practices and procedures generally agreed to be efficient and effective and held up as a model for others to copy.

beta stock class of stocks traded on the London stock market, about 500 frequently traded stocks outside the top 100.

beta-testing in industrial marketing, testing of products in test sites which simulate field conditions.

Beveridge curve the relationship between total unemployment and total job vacancies.

bid offer of a specific sum of money for a good or service.

bid and asked buyer's bid and seller's price for a specific stock or security offered for sale; *see also* quote, quotation.

bidding the act of offering a bid.

bidding up raising the price in competitive bidding situations in hope of outbidding competitors.

Big Bang colloquial term for the deregulation of UK financial and securities markets in October 1986.

big bath colloquial, the writing off of any large sum previously counted as an asset.

big business **1** any very large firm; **2** also refers more generally to the economic dominance of large corporations.

Big Six firms the major international accounting firms.

big ticket items exceptionally large and expensive merchandise.

bilateral agreement agreement involving two parties.

bilateral assistance foreign aid provided directly from one country to another.

bilateral contract contract where each party promises some action for the benefit of the other.

bilateral dependency in collective bargaining, phenomenon whereby unions and management are in fact dependent on each other, even when they are in dispute.

bilateralism the practice of bilateral trade.

bilateral monopoly occurs where there is only one buyer and one seller in a given market.

bilateral trade special reciprocal trading arrangements between two countries.

bill **1** another name for bank note; **2** also, short form for bill of sale; **3** also, short form for bill of exchange.

bill discounted bill of exchange from which interest is deducted in advance.

billed escrow regular escrow payment, adjusted for arrears or prepaid amounts.

billed principal total of normal principal amount plus any arrears.

billing **1** sending or presenting bills to customers for the price of services or goods already received; **2** in advertising, the gross fees charged to clients by an advertising agency.

bill of credit written instruction to a bank to provide money to the bearer on the credit of the writer.

bill of exchange written order by one party to another, requesting the second party to pay a named sum of money to a third party (the bearer of the bill) at a named time in the future.

bill of lading documentation accompanying a consignment of goods, identifying the goods, acknowledging their receipt and giving proof of title.

bill of materials document listing the materials and their quantities required for a specific manufacturing process.

bill of sale written document transferring title of goods to another party, in exchange for an agreed price; more simply, a statement of charges due, *see* invoice.

bill of sight permit allowing customs officers to open and examine imported goods.

bills payable total of credit, invoices and other notes owed by a business to its creditors.

bills receivable total of credit, invoices and other notes owed to a business by its customers and other debtors.

BIMBO *see* buy-in-management-buy-out.

binary notation two digits, 0 and 1, which are used in combinations representing all other numbers and characters in computer operations.

bin card form of record used in stock control.

binding arbitration arbitration where both parties agree in advance, or are compelled, to abide by the outcome of the arbitration process.

biodata short for biographical data; personal information concerning employees or job applicants.

biomass energy derived directly from natural sources, such as wood, oil and coal.

biotechnology the use of biological organisms and systems in technological or machine processes.

bird in the hand theory preference on the part of investors for dividends rather than capital appreciation.

bit 1 short form of binary digit, refers to the digits used in binary notation; 2 smallest unit of information in computer storage.

black book written description of a private securities placement; not the same as a prospectus.

black box the hidden mental processes that govern human decision making; its workings can be guessed at but not observed.

black economy economic activities outside official control, usually implying the evasion of tax.

Black Friday refers to major financial disasters occurring on a Friday, particularly the Wall Street crash of October 1929.

black-leg colloquial term for an employee who continues to work during a strike.

black list list of undesirable employees, often circulated between firms.

black market market where goods and, especially, foreign currency are bought and sold illegally.

black market rate exchange rate at which currency is sold illegally on the black market.

Black Monday 2 August 1993, the day when the falling value of the French franc effectively brought the European Exchange Rate Mechanism to an end.

black money money derived from illegal sources.

Black Wednesday 16 September 1992, the day the UK was forced to take its currency out of the European Exchange Rate Mechanism.

Black–Scholes model standard mathematical technique used in options pricing.

blank cheque cheque that has been signed but where the amount and/or the name of the payee have not yet been added.

blank-cheque buying the placing of an open order with a supplier, *see* open order.

blanket agreement agreement resulting from collective bargaining, covering an entire industry nationwide.

blanket coverage very large-scale advertising or direct mail aimed at the general population.

blanket injunction court order issued before or during a strike, banning certain activities.

blanket order standing order with a supplier for products or services up to a certain quantity.

blanket policy insurance policy covering several different properties, items or people as one insured item.

blind entry book-keeping entry which gives only the amounts credited and debited.

blind selling where customers purchase merchandise which they have not yet seen.

blind test test assessing consumer attitudes to products with the identity of the products not being revealed.

block **1** large quantity of data which is treated as a single unit in data processing; **2** large holding of stocks or securities.

blockade the physical prevention of commerce between nations, usually in time of war.

block check detailed audit of the accounts of a single division or department of a company.

blocked accounts bank accounts and financial holdings which are frozen on government order, usually because they are held by persons believed to enemies of the state.

blocked currency currency which may not legally be taken outside its country of origin.

blue chip safe investment, usually consisting of stocks in prominent and stable companies.

blue collar another term for manual work; a blue collar worker is a manual labourer.

blue skies research theoretical research aimed at discovering new scientific principles rather than at practical innovation.

board standing committee responsible for governing an organization; *see also* board of directors.

board lot stock exchange unit of trading, usually 100 shares.

board of directors senior executives and others appointed by shareholders to oversee the management of a company; *see* director; non-executive director.

board of trade executive committee which oversees local or national trade; *see also* chamber of commerce.

boardroom **1** chamber where the board of directors meets; **2** colloquial term for the centre of decision-making power.

board structure organization and composition of the board of directors.

body language non-verbal communication expressed through body movements and posture.

Boehm's Spiral Model development model used in new product development strategy.

bona fide legitimate, or in good faith.

bond 1 general term for an interest-bearing certificate issued as an acknowledgement of a debt to be repaid (the yield) after a stated time period (the maturity); 2 also, a guarantee to perform a certain service, usually with financial penalties for failure.

bond, adjustment income bond sometimes issued by firms after reorganization.

bond, assumed bond issued by one corporation, the liability for which is then assumed by another corporation.

bond, baby US, bond with a low face value.

bond, bearer bond with no named beneficiary which is simply payable to the holder.

bond, blanket broad-coverage bond issued by financial institutions to cover losses from theft or other criminal activity.

bond, callable bond which may be redeemed before maturity.

bond, civil US, bond issued by a government agency.

bond, classified bond which is designated as one of a series, to differentiate it from other bonds issued by the same debtor but which may have different maturity dates.

bond, clean bond that has not yet been endorsed.

bond, collateral bond where the issuer has also offered collateral for repayment.

bond, consolidated bond that replaces two or more previously issued bonds.

bond, continued bond that need not be redeemed at maturity and which can continue to accrue interest after that point.

bond, convertible bond which can be exchanged for other securities, such as stocks.

bond, coupon bond with interest coupons attached, which are removed and presented to the issuer when payment is due.

bond, cushion bond that sells at an above par price and usually has a higher yield on maturity.

bond, debenture bond for which the issuer has not provided any security for repayment.

bond discount reduction in price when a bond is sold at below face value.

bonded goods goods held by customs in a bonded warehouse.

bonded warehouse customs facility where imported goods are held pending re-export.

bond, endorsed bond that has been signed and is now ready to be sold.

bond, extended bond that has matured but where the creditor has agreed to accept repayment at a later date.

bond, fidelity a form of insurance against any loss caused by employee theft or dishonesty.

bond, free bond that can be disposed of immediately.

bond, gilt-edged bond that is very attractive to investors, usually because of the reputation of the issuing company.

bond, government bond issued by central government.

bond, guaranteed bond where a third party has guaranteed payment of principal and/or interest.

bond, improvement bond issued by local governments to finance particular infrastructure or other improvements.

bond, indemnity bond that protects the holder against losses suffered as a consequence of the actions, illegal or otherwise, of the issuer.

bonding the process by which a person or their employer pays in a bond as security for their correct and honest behaviour in the performance of their work; *see* bond, fidelity.

bonding company company whose business is providing sureties and indemnity bonds for others.

bond, intermediate callable bond with no fixed date of maturity.

bond, irredeemable bond which cannot be called or redeemed before maturity.

bond, junk bond offering higher than average rates of interest.

bond, maintenance bond guaranteeing against defective work.

bond markets, international *see* international bond markets.

bond, mortgage bond where the issuing company gives a mortgage on certain properties as security.

bond, non-callable bond that cannot be called, *see* bond, callable.

bond, optional *see* bond, callable.

bond, participating bond where the holder receives both interest and some of the profits of the issuing company.

bond, passive bond that does not provide any interest.

bond, performance bond which indemnifies one party against loss caused by the failure of the second party to perform to agreed specification; *see* bond, indemnity.

bond, preference any income or adjustment bond.

bond, premium 1 bond that sells for more than face value; **2** also, in Europe, a bond where holders receive income on the basis of a lottery.

bond, prior-lieu bond that has precedence over other bonds from the same issuer.

bond, public bond issued by a public agency or organization; *see also* bond, government.

bond rating credit rating which assesses the likelihood of an issuer being able to redeem a bond issue.

bond, redeemable bond which the issuer may buy back.

bond, redemption bond issued to supersede a previously issued bond.

bond, registered bond payable only to the registered owner of the bond.

bond, savings long-term bonds issued by governments.

bond, secured bond where collateral, usually in the form of assets, is offered as a guarantee of repayment.

bond, treasury long-term bond issued by the US government.

bond, zero-coupon bond sold at a discount and then redeemed at face value.

bonus payment to workers over and above their base pay.

bonus earnings earnings over and above the normal rate.

bonus scheme agreement for the payment of bonuses, usually by relating bonuses to the achievement of performance targets.

bonus share shares issued free by companies to existing shareholders.

book debt total of debts currently owing.

book inventory theoretical level of stocks or inventory based on records of existing stocks plus incoming goods less outgoing goods; not based on physical inventory, so will not reveal errors or shrinkage.

bookkeeper accounting staff member who is responsible for bookkeeping.

bookkeeping the keeping of ledgers which record business transactions.

book rate of return *see* return on capital employed.

book value the value of an asset as it is shown in accounts, usually consisting of original cost less depreciation; *see also* intrinsic value.

boom rapid economic expansion usually accompanied by full employment and rising prices.

bootleg illegal or counterfeit goods.

bootlegging **1** illegal trade of goods across borders; **2** trade in counterfeit goods.

booting the process of loading a computer software program.

bootstrap *see* booting.

bordereau form required for reinsurance transactions.

borrow to receive goods or services as a loan which must be repaid.

borrower a party who borrows from another.

borrowing allocation the maximum amount that an organization may borrow or owe at any one time.

Boston Box portfolio management technique which plots cash use against cash generation.

bottleneck point where communications or process flows are delayed, thus delaying the rest of the system.

bottom dropped out colloquial phrase meaning a very sharp and rapid fall in prices.

bottom line statement of company profitability.

bottom-up decision making system whereby lower levels of an organization have strong input into the decision-making process.

bottom-up management management style with a focus on bottom-up decision making and devolved control.

bounceback colloquial term for a rapid recovery or sharp rise in prices immediately after a fall.

boundary-spanning role **1** role in which workers must relate to two different organizations; **2** also, service personnel who are in frequent contact with customers.

bounded rationality in decision making, those things or issues which can be understood by use of logic or reason.

bourse Europe, a stock exchange or commodity market.

Box–Jenkins model technique used in forecasting which feeds back data from earlier forecasts, so improving the reliability of the present forecast.

boycott organized refusal to purchase a product or service, often for political reasons.

BPR *see* business process re-engineering.

Brady bonds bonds issued and traded in the secondary debt market, issued as part of major programme of Third World debt rescheduling in the 1980s.

brain drain the emigration of skilled labour and professionals to other countries.

brainstorming the generation of ideas or concepts through discussion among small groups of people.

branch a subsidiary part of an organization, usually at a remove from the organizational core.

branch office sales or other office on separate premises away from head office.

branch organization seldom-used term for an overseas subsidiary.

branch warehouse separate warehousing facility located at a distance from the main plant.

brand an easily identifiable product or service, usually associated with a name and a physical image which have the legal status of trade marks, made and/or sold by a single company.

brand awareness the extent to which potential customers of a brand are aware of its existence.

branded a product which has been associated with a brand image, including a name and mark, thereby becoming a brand.

branded goods products that have been branded.

branded manufacturers manufacturers of branded products and services.

brand equity the value to a company of its proprietary brands, generally realizable only on sale.

brand extension marketing strategy where the image associated with one brand is then applied to other products.

brand image the perception of the brand by the consumer, including brand name, mark, reputation and other qualities associated with the brand.

branding the process of developing a brand for a product.

brand leader brand that is recognized as the best quality in the market and/or has the largest market share.

brand loyalty the extent to which consumers of a brand will continue to use that brand rather than switch to alternatives.

brand mark the visual symbols associated with a brand.

brand manager executive responsible for marketing for a particular brand or group of brands; *see also* product manager.

brand name the word or phrase that identifies a brand and is part of the brand image.

brand recognition the extent to which potential customers will recognize a brand after having seen it previously.

brand strategy marketing strategy which focuses on a single brand or group of brands.

brand-switching model model used by marketing managers to assess the likelihood of consumers switching from one brand to another.

breach of contract the failure on the part of one party to fulfil the conditions of a contract.

breakage damage to merchandise, usually caused while being shipped.

break-even when total revenues equal total costs.

break-even analysis the determination of when break-even will occur.

break-even chart physical representation of break-even assessment, showing break-even points.

break-even point the point in time when break-even occurs; before this time the company or product is making a loss, while after this time it is making a profit.

break-even pricing pricing system based on the determination of break-even points for a product, brand or service.

breaking bulk the dividing up of very large lots of goods into smaller consignments.

breaking a strike *see* strikebreaking.

break-up value value of a company and its assets upon liquidation.

bribe illegal payment in exchange for benefits, such as preferential treatment or confidential information.

bribery the act of offering a bribe.

broad market market in which a large volume of securities are being traded.

broken lot a lot with an odd or unusual number of units.

broken time *see* split shift.

broker individual or company acting as an agent, handling orders to buy and sell.

brokerage commission paid to a broker by the principal for conducting purchases or sales on the latter's behalf.

brokerage house US, a company engaged in broking.

broking generic term for buying and selling on behalf of others; *see also* stockbroker.

broker's loan loan made to a stockbroker using stocks as collateral.

broker's market market where brokers are actively trading but investors are remaining broadly inactive.

broker's ticket written account of all buy and sell orders executed by a particular broker.

brown goods in retailing, goods including televisions, radios and stereo equipment.

Brownian motion mathematical representation of a diffusion process.

browser *see* web browser.

bubble company firm with little or no assets, which solicits investment and then collapses, taking the investors' money with it.

bubble economy economy which grows very rapidly but without stability, with a consequent danger of equally rapid decline or collapse.

bucket shop 1 dealer in cheap or cut-price goods, especially airline tickets; **2** in securities, a dubious or dishonest trader.

buddy system system where a new employee is assigned to an experienced worker for orientation and training.

budget itemized statement of expected costs, expenses and usually revenues over a defined period of time.

budget allocation total of expenditure or income in a budget.

budgetary control the process whereby budgets are used to control expenditure and, through analysis of budget variance, establish when projects are going out of control.

budget centre department or project which has its own budget.

budget deficit occurs when expenditure exceeds revenues.

budgeting the techniques and practices of setting budgets.

budget surplus occurs when revenues exceed expenditure.

budget variance difference between budgeted and actual costs or expenditure.

buffer 1 general term for storage of goods or information in one location to offset temporary shortages elsewhere; **2** in computers, buffers store information between transmitting and receiving devices; **3** more generally, a cushion or safeguard against shocks.

buffer stock quantity of merchandise or materials, usually small, kept in store in case an unexpected shortage arises.

buffer stock price stabilization the maintenance by UNCTAD of buffer stocks in certain key commodities, used to ensure that prices of these commodities do not fluctuate unduly.

bug design fault in a system or software program which causes it to fail or produce unexpected results.

building society UK financial institution specializing in providing mortgages.

build schedule in project management, a record of progress including any modifications kept as the project progresses.

built environment environment which has been designed and constructed by people, as opposed to the natural environment.

built-in obsolescence feature of a product which means that it will need to be replaced after a (usually short) time, due to wear and tear or technological redundancy.

bulk breaking *see* breaking bulk.

bulk discount lower price offered for purchase of larger than normal quantity of goods.

bulk freight usually raw materials, carried in large quantities without packaging or containers.

bull one who buys shares in the belief that their price will shortly rise.

bulletin board noticeboard where information and messages are posted, either mounted on a wall or accessed through a computer network.

bull market stock market where prices are rising.

bull position where a dealer holds stock, hoping the market will rise; *see* bull.

bullion gold or silver, which can be coined and used as currency.

bumping the demotion of a senior employee who then 'bumps' a more junior employee out of his/her job.

Bundesbank the central bank of the Federal Republic of Germany.

bundle of benefits the benefits which consumers associate with a particular brand or product.

bundling the grouping together of a number of goods or services in a single package with a single price.

bureaucracy level of administration within an organization, often used pejoratively.

bureaucracy, machine *see* machine bureaucracy.

bureaucracy, professional *see* professional bureaucracy.

bureaucracy, public sector *see* public sector bureaucracy.

bureaucratization the creation and organization of a bureaucracy.

business general term for the making, buying and selling of goods and services; 'doing business' is to engage in any of these activities.

business agent **1** *see* agent; **2** also in the USA, term for a local trade union official responsible for contracts and union business.

business associations associations of businesses in the same industrial sector or geographical region, formed to further the mutual interests of members.

business consultant *see* consultant.

business credit credit offered to buyers by sellers to enable the purchase of goods or services; *see also* credit.

business culture the culture inherent in a business organization; the way a business does things.

business cycle in economics, alternating periods of depression and growth; *see also* boom; slump.

business cycle, periodicity of the average length of a business cycle.

business development the establishment and expansion of new business.

business elites highly skilled and experienced senior executives who work in international companies around the world, usually in top positions for very high salaries.

business ethics the application of ethical standards to business.

business expenses costs incurred in the course of doing business, often tax-deductible.

business game simulation of business activity used as a training aid.

business history the study of business and companies in the past with a view to gaining new insights about present business.

business indicator factors which affect business performance, usually summarized in statistical form.

business information information about a business, its performance and its environment.

business interruption insurance insurance policy which compensates the firm should it for some reason be unable to conduct its normal business.

business logistics *see* logistics.

business manager *see* manager.

business name name or title adopted by a business, and by which it is legally known.

business networks networks of businesses which trade on favourable terms, engage in collaboration or exchange information.

business park *see* industrial estate.

business partnership *see* partnership.

business plan document setting out the means by which the business aims to achieve its goals; typically includes an analysis of market prospects and separate plans for research and development, finance, manufacturing and marketing as well as other specialist business areas.

business planning the process of drafting a business plan; often carried out on a continuous or rolling basis.

business portfolio 1 the number and type of products or services the firm produces; **2** alternatively, a listing of its assets.

business process redesign *see* business process re-engineering.

business process re-engineering (BPR) use of engineering techniques to redesign business processes so that they use resources more efficiently and focus on output instead of process.

business school institute of higher education specializing in education programmes for managers.

business systems general term for ways of organizing business activity.

business units sub-unit within a company engaged in distinct business activity; *see also* strategic business unit.

business-to-business marketing marketing activities aimed at other businesses rather than at individual consumers.

bust colloquial term for a severe economic depression.

butterfly spread in futures trading, the simultaneous purchase or sale of three futures contracts; *see also* spread.

buy to purchase a good or service; also used as a noun to describe the purchase itself.

buy-back agreement sales contract in which the seller agrees to buy back the property or good at a future date, usually for a much lower price.

buyclass in studies of buying behaviour, the type of purchase currently being contemplated, whether it be a new purchase, repeat purchase, etc.

buyer 1 anyone who buys a good, as opposed to the seller of that good; **2** more specifically, a manager responsible for purchasing and/or procurement.

buyers' market market where there is an oversupply of goods and where prices are falling.

buyer–supplier relationship general term for communications and business activity between buyers and suppliers in industrial marketing.

buy in entering a partnership or project in exchange for a contribution of capital; more colloquially, to accept or endorse a proposition.

buying the act of purchasing a good.

buying behaviour marketing term for the process by which a buyer decides whether to buy a product and chooses between competing products or services.

buying by specification buying according to a previously defined set of requirements rather than simply choosing from the options available on the shelf.

buying committee in retailing, a managerial group which decides which items will be purchased from wholesalers or manufacturers.

buying in the acquisition of goods, services or know-how not already available within the organization, as in 'buying in expertise'.

buying off the peg buying ready-made goods, rather than ordering goods made to specification; used especially in clothing retailing.

buying on balance occurs when a stockbroker's current buy orders exceed current sell orders.

buying policy index economic indicator reflecting current levels of industrial buying and purchasing.

buying power the amount of money or credit which can be spent on goods or services.

buy-in-management-buy-out (BIMBO) management buy-out in which management and external parties join forces to raise capital for the purchase.

buy-off a payment made in exchange for the other party's relinquishing all rights to property or goods.

buy out to acquire rights or ownership over a property or company through payment to the present owner; the purchaser is said to have 'bought out' the owner.

buzz group small group of people engaged in brainstorming.

buzzword fashionable slang term describing 'new' management concepts.

by-bidder one who makes fictitious bids at an auction.

byproduct in manufacturing, a secondary product which is produced either at the same time as the primary product or later out of waste material.

byte unit of computer memory, consisting of eight bits.

C

CAD 1 *see* Capital Adequacy Directive; **2** *see* computer-aided design.

CAD/CAM *see* computer-aided design and manufacture.

CAI *see* computer-aided instruction.

calendar year twelve-month period from 1 January to 31 December.

calibration very fine adjustments to machinery.

call generally, a demand for payment; can be applied to loans, callable bonds or other security.

callable bond *see* bond, callable.

callable finance *see* call loan.

call analysis measure of the effectiveness of sales visits to customers.

call-back second or subsequent visit by a salesperson or market researcher to a contact who has already been visited once.

call-back pay special wage paid to workers who are on standby or have completed a shift and are called back to work at short notice; *see also* call-in pay.

called-up capital later instalments on the price of shares which were not fully paid for when purchased; these later instalments can then be demanded by the issuer of the shares at a future date.

calling cycle average period of time between salesperson's or maintenance engineer's calls on customers.

call-in pay pay guaranteed to a worker who is called in to work at short notice.

call loan loan which is payable on demand by the lender.

call money money lent by banks which must be repaid on demand.

call option buyer's option to purchase a block of securities, which can be exercised at any point within a specified time limit.

call over practice in some stock exchanges whereby blocks of stocks are auctioned at particular times.

call premium for some callable bonds, the issuer may be required to make a payment to the holder when the bond is called in.

call provision contract provision whereby issuers may exercise their right to repurchase a share prior to maturity.

call rate the number of sales visits made by a salesperson in a specific time period; used as a measure of effectiveness.

call report report by salesperson to superiors after a sales visit.

call sale sale of a commodity at a given price but where the purchaser has the right to determine the date of delivery.

call up *see* call.

CAM *see* computer-aided manufacturing.

cambism the sale of foreign currencies.

CAMEL rating US system of scoring banks, used by bank examiners.

cancellation the termination or annulment of any agreement or contract.

cancellation clause provision in an agreement giving one or both parties the right to cancel.

canvas or canvass to interview a large number of people to gather their views or information on a specific subject.

CAP 1 *see* Common Agricultural Policy; **2** *see* computer-aided production.

capabilities the skills and abilities of a company's employees.

capability gap difference between the capabilities an organization needs, and those it actually has available.

capacity 1 the volume of goods or services which can be produced, transported or sold through a particular facility, usually expressed in terms of number of units of throughput in a given time; **2** also, the ability to pay a debt when due.

capacity cost the costs of operating a production line at its full designed capacity; in effect, the same as fixed costs.

capital 1 money or goods employed in a business to produce goods and services, including money invested, plant and facilities, and other assets; **2** in economics, one of the three factors of production, along with land and labour.

capital account 1 in balance of payments, refers to items not in the country's current account; **2** in accounting, an account which summarizes the equity held in a business by its owners.

Capital Adequacy Directive (CAD) European Commission directive setting capital adequacy requirements for European banks.

capital adjustment adjustment to the value of capital made during the process of inflation accounting.

capital appropriation capital set aside for future projects.

capital assets *see* fixed assets.

capital asset pricing model (CAPM) portfolio management tool which distinguishes between risks which can be diversified away, and those that cannot; *see also* weighted average cost of capital.

capital budgets budget setting aside funds for capital purchases.

capital consumption amount of capital which is actually consumed in the process of production.

capital consumption allowance funds set aside to compensate for capital consumption, for example, to allow for depreciation.

capital, cost of the cost required by a firm to service its debt and equity capital in the form of interest and other charges.

capital cut-off point point beyond which a company can no longer acquire capital economically.

capital employed 1 total of fixed and current assets; **2** total equity holdings in the business.

capital equipment plant and equipment required for the production process.

capital expenditure expenditure of fixed assets.

capital flight large-scale withdrawals of capital from a national economy, usually prompted by fear of political or economic instability.

capital formation the conversion of savings into capital or capital goods.

capital export neutrality situation where the incentives for investors to make capital investments at home and abroad are exactly equal.

capital gain profit made from the disposal of a capital asset over and above its original purchase price.

capital gains tax tax levied on capital gains.

capital goods equipment used for production rather than consumption, such as plant and machinery; *see* fixed assets.

capital intensive project requiring large amounts of capital investment.

capital investment money invested in capital assets or fixed assets, which will not be returned in the short term.

capitalism economic system where the means of production are owned by the investors of capital, rather than the state or the workers, the bulk of ownership thus being concentrated in the private sector; normally synonymous with free market.

capitalist one who invests capital in exchange for a share in the ownership of a business.

capitalize 1 to issue shares in a business; **2** in accounting and finance, to convert into capital.

capitalization total value of all issued shares and securities; alternatively, the sum of all investment in the firm.

capital liability bond or other instrument created to raise capital.

capital market market (usually invisible) where capital can be acquired and invested.

capital market regulation laws and codes of conduct by which all those involved in capital markets are expect to abide.

capital outlay capital spent on the acquisition of capital goods or fixed assets.

capital–output ratio in economics, ratio expressing the relationship between investment and production in a national economy.

capital rating appraisal of the net worth of a firm based on the value of its fixed assets.

capital requirement total capital required to create and operate a business.

capital stock total number of shares or stocks which a corporation is allowed to sell; not all of these may have been issued.

capital structure ratio of loan and equity capital to total capital; *see also* gearing.

capital surplus 1 excess of assets over liabilities; **2** share price in excess of par value.

CAPM *see* capital asset pricing model.

captive audience any group which is exposed automatically or involuntarily to communications messages.

captive insurer insurance company owned by another company and writing insurance policies for the parent company.

captive market market where customers have few or no alternative products or services from which to choose.

career an individual's pattern of education and employment over the course of their working life; typically includes changes in job or promotion to higher levels, but need not necessarily do so.

career development **1** process whereby a worker gradually progresses to more senior positions, with more responsibility and better pay; **2** training and education programmes aimed at preparing people for career advancement.

career management management and direction of the careers of individuals, both by employers and by the individuals themselves.

career path the sequence of jobs and posts which an individual holds (or plans to hold) in the course of a career.

career planning the process of planning and mapping out a career path that most closely matches the individual's own wants and needs.

career plateau a point in an individual's career where no further promotion or advancement can be expected.

career stages distinct phases or steps in a career, usually marked by promotions or changes in job.

career structure *see* career planning.

cargo goods being transported from one place to another.

carriage *see* freight.

carrier **1** business or other organization engaged in transporting goods; **2** more specifically, the firm responsible for transporting a particular consignment of goods.

carry **1** to transport goods; **2** in accounting, to enter an item in a ledger.

carry back tax reduction which compensates for an earlier excess payment.

carry forward *see* carry over.

carrying charge **1** interest on outstanding debt when payment is made by instalment; **2** in transportation, charge made for transporting or carrying goods.

carrying cost cost of holding goods in inventory.

carry over to transfer figures from one balance sheet to another in an account, also known as carry forward.

cartel group of businesses which collaborate to fix prices or determine markets so as to avoid competition (illegal in most jurisdictions).

cascade network type of critical path analysis which indicates the relationships between activities and their scale and duration.

cascade technique method of communication whereby each person briefs those on the organizational level immediately below them.

CASE *see* computer-aided software engineering.

case-based reasoning systems in artificial intelligence, system which involves matching present conditions to a battery of case histories, choosing the one which is most appropriate, and then adapting the techniques of that case to the present.

case method teaching or training method based on case studies.

case study study of an organization or individual in a particular situation, usually based on actual business situations, with a view to learning what factors were responsible for success for failure.

cash 1 currency or legal tender; **2** money in hand, in the form of currency, cheques or other negotiable instruments.

cash accounting system where revenues and expenditures are accounted for only when they are actually received and paid.

cash and carry wholesaler who does not deliver to customers and does not provide credit; purchases must be paid for at once and transported away by the buyer.

cash assets assets listed on the balance sheet in the form of cash in hand or in the bank.

cash audit audit of all cash transactions over a given period of time.

cash basis defines purchases which must be made for cash and where credit will not be allowed.

cash before delivery purchase where payment must be made before the goods are delivered.

cash book ledger in which receipts and payments are recorded.

cash budget budget which gives a schedule of expected cash receipts and payments.

cash buying outright purchase for cash, in exchange for immediate delivery.

cash cow term for a product or business activity which generates high levels of profit or revenue.

cash discount reduction in price provided payment is made in cash, on delivery or within a short period of time.

cash dividend dividends paid in cash, as opposed to shares.

cash flow general term for the income generated by a business activity; positive cash flow occurs when cash flow exceeds expenses, while negative cash flow occurs when cash flow is less than expenses.

cash flow accounting accounting procedures which report on the cash inflows and outflows of a business.

cash flow beta model regression coefficient of a firm's cash flows before interest and taxes on an aggregate price level.

cash flow exchange transaction between two parties in a forward contract.

cash flow management management techniques relating to the monitoring, control and use of cash flow.

cash forecast estimated cash flow for a given future period.

cashier employee directly responsible for taking and/or paying out cash to customers.

cash investments investment made using cash, as opposed to other, less liquid forms of capital.

cash nexus the importance to both employees and employer of cash as a method of payment.

cash on delivery purchase where payment must be made at the same time as the goods are delivered.

cash plan profit-sharing scheme where bonuses are paid in cash.

cash position ratio of cash to net assets.

cash principle accounting principle whereby revenue is recognized when the money is received, and expenses are recognized when the money is paid out.

cash ratio ratio of cash assets to current liabilities.

cash register machine used in retail outlets to hold cash received and register transactions; *see also* till.

cash refund refund, paid in cash, for a returned product.

cash reserve 1 cash or assets which can quickly be converted into cash; **2** also refers to the reserves which banks must hold to meet the requirements of depositors.

cash sale selling of goods or items for immediate payment rather than credit.

cash surrender value sum paid by insurance companies on the cancellation or surrender of a policy.

cash value value of an asset if it were to be sold immediately for cash.

casual labour workers employed when work is available, rather than on regular contracts.

casualty 1 person who has suffered death or injury; **2** in marine insurance, a vessel which has suffered damage or been lost.

catalogue showroom/store retail outlet where customers select goods from a printed catalogue, rather than from goods actually on display.

catalyst managerial role identified by Peter Drucker, in which the manager serves to act as a source of inspiration and a motivator to get things done.

catchment area geographical area which naturally focuses on a given point; used by companies to define geographical areas for both recruiting and marketing.

category killer brand which achieves such complete market dominance as to become synonymous with the product category in general.

catering general term for service industries in the food and beverage sectors.

cause and effect analysis analysis which attempts to describe cause and effect relationships between factors.

caveat emptor principle of 'let the buyer beware', meaning effectively that the customer is responsible for checking the price and quality of goods before making a purchase.

caveat subscriptor principle of 'let the signer beware', meaning that anyone who signs a legal document is held bound by that document regardless of whether he or she is aware of the contents.

caveat venditor principle of 'let the seller beware', meaning that the seller is responsible for any deviations from the contract of sale.

CBIS *see* computer-based information systems.

CCTV *see* closed circuit television.

CD-ROM *see* compact disc, read-only memory.

cell-level planning manufacturing planning based on individual manufacturing cells.

cellular systems manufacturing and production system based on the use of manufacturing cells.

central bank a banker's bank, or a bank which holds the national bank reserves and is responsible for controlling credit to other banks; usually serves as banker to the national government.

central buying buying strategy which involves all purchasing being carried out by a central office rather than by subsidiaries.

centralization concentration of power, resources, etc. in the centre of an organization.

centrally planned economy economic system dominated by governmental control rather than the free market.

central planning economic planning functions carried out by central government rather than being left to market mechanisms.

central processing unit (CPU) device within a computer where the primary calculations take place and where most computer functions are controlled.

central stock reserves reserves of stock held in a warehouse at a central location, rather than in regional or local sites.

CEO *see* chief executive officer.

certification 1 process of checking and examination which leads to the granting of a certificate; **2** assurance by an organization or professional body that the holder of the certificate has the professional qualifications he or she claims to have.

certificate document attesting to a fact.

certificate of deposit receipt for funds deposited in a bank.

certificate of insurance legal document that serves as evidence of the existence of an insurance policy.

certificate of origin document provided with exported goods, certifying in which country the goods have been manufactured.

certified accountant 1 accountant who has been certified as having a required level of proficiency; **2** in the UK, a member of the Professional Chartered Association of Certified Accountants.

certified cheque cheque where the drawer's bank has certified that he or she has sufficient funds to cover the cheque.

certified public accountant US accountant who has received a certificate authorizing the practice of his or her profession because he or she meets the state's legal standards.

ceteris paribus all other things being equal.

chaebol large South Korean corporation or conglomerate.

chain of command formal structure of authority and communication; orders and instructions are passed down the chain of command.

chain store 1 retail company with a large number of nearly identical retail outlets; *see* multiple; **2** alternatively, any store owned by such a company.

chain-store paradox in game theory, paradox which emerges when a game is repeated a finite number of times, suggesting that monopolists will not act to prevent new entrants into a market.

chairman one who presides over a meeting; more permanently, the head of a committee or department.

chairman of the board highest ranking executive of a corporation.

chamber of commerce voluntary organization of local business people, formed for the purpose of promoting trade.

change 1 in business terms, any departure from established or customary procedures and conditions; 2 when a purchaser hands over a sum of money greater than the purchase price of a good, the residue returned by the seller is known as 'change'.

change agent third party, outside the organization, who helps to guide and implement organizational change.

change, corporate any alteration to a corporation's structure, processes or personnel.

change, dominant strategic model current model regarded as the most appropriate method of implementing strategic change.

change implementation models models describing the best way of implementing change.

change, intervention model model of strategic change using a change agent who is tasked with intervening in the areas requiring change and implementing change in the most effective fashion.

change order formal agreement authorizing a change in the provisions of a contract.

change organizations organizations undergoing a period of transformation, either internally or externally.

change process process by which change is managed within an organization, usually planned as part of a larger strategy.

change, resistance to passive or active opposition to change on the part of individuals or organizations.

change strategies plans and strategies for the implementation of change in organizations.

channel of distribution the route by which goods travel from the manufacturer to retail outlets where they are offered for sale; *see also* sales chain.

channel intermediaries firms and organizations in the channel of distribution, who assist in the flow of goods from manufacturer to consumer.

channel management subset of marketing management, the practices and techniques of managing the flow of goods through the channel of distribution.

chaos theory physics theory describing the phenomena whereby very small changes can have large-scale, seemingly unrelated effects.

charge 1 a cost or expense; a fee or price demanded for a good or service; 2 also, to purchase on credit is sometimes referred to as 'charging' goods to a charge account.

charge account an account which offers retail customers credit for the purchase of goods and services.

charge hand lowest rank of supervisory worker; *see also* foreman.

charge off *see* write-off.

charges forward similar to cash on delivery, where the purchaser pays for ordered goods when they are delivered.

charity non-profit organization, the aims of which are social and philan-thropic rather than commercial.

charter **1** the hiring of a vehicle, ship, aircraft, etc.; **2** also, a document grant-ed by government recognizing the existence of a corporation or other organization and setting out the articles of association.

chartered accountant in the UK, an accountant who is a member of the Institute of Chartered Accountants; similar organizations exist in Ireland, Canada and Australia.

charting techniques general term for techniques used to map or diagram project work flows, schedules and so on.

chartism system for predicting future share price movement based on historical price movement.

chartist analyst who practices chartism.

chattel paper papers providing written evidence of a lease.

cheap inexpensive or low cost.

check **1** examination or verification, to ensure the truth, accuracy or cor-rect conduct of a statement or procedure; **2** also, US equivalent to cheque.

checking account US equivalent to current account.

check-list predetermined list of points to be examined or verified when making a check.

check-out point of sale in a store or supermarket, where goods selected by the customer are presented and paid for.

cheque draft order on a bank account, requesting the bank to pay money from that account to the person or organization specified as the payee.

cheque account bank account on which cheques may be drawn; *see also* current account.

cherry picking the selection by a purchaser of only the best quality goods on offer, leaving the others aside.

chief executive officer (CEO) highest ranking executive officer of a compa-ny, second only to the chairman of the board; also known as managing director (UK) or president (US).

chief financial officer highest-ranking finance executive, responsible for the financial affairs of a company.

chief operating officer highest-ranking operations executive, ultimately responsible for all production and distribution activities.

Chinese walls notional barriers within firms preventing the lateral flow of sensitive or confidential information.

chip *see* microchip.

churning **1** the rapid buying and selling of securities which generates broker commissions and causes share price uncertainty; **2** rapid workforce turnover.

Christopher's model model of logistics suggesting how the logistics process adds value to products.

CIM *see* computer-integrated manufacturing.

circuit breaker in securities trading, measures which aim to prevent sudden and rapid market falls; usually taking the form of market closure after the market has declined by a specified number of points.

circular flow of income in economics, the concept of the passage of income from one hand to another as goods and services are purchased, from production to consumption and back again.

circulating capital good any capital good that is consumed in a single use.

circulation **1** the total of money in the economy; **2** the total readership of a publication.

civil rights those rights considered by law to belong to each person in a society.

civil service administrators and managers employed by governments to oversee government affairs.

claim demand for payment or compensation, particularly for losses covered by an insurance policy.

class a group of items, products, information points, or people according to a particular characteristic; employees, for example, might be classed by age, length of service, or particular sets of skills.

class action legal action conducted by a large group of people, who have nothing in common other than the complaint that caused them to bring the action.

classical economics early economic theory beginning in the late eighteenth century, which sought to explain economic behaviour in terms of the flows of land, labour and capital.

classical management theory early schools of management thinking, most notably scientific management.

classification **1** means of grouping or ranking goods, information or people according to particular sets of characteristics; **2** to arrange in classes.

classified balance sheet balance sheet which classifies assets and liabilities, typically by factors such as source and usage.

claw-back **1** in the UK, term for government expenditure on a particular programme which is retrieved through tax increases; **2** generally, the recovery of money which might otherwise have been lost.

clean bill of lading bill of lading specifying that all goods shipped are in good condition.

clean-surplus valuation method whereby income determination and asset valuation mutually influence each other.

clear free from encumbrance or debt, as in 'free and clear'.

clearance **1** leave to undertake an action, usually granted by regulators; **2** the act of clearing; *see* clearing and settlement; **3** in retailing, a price reduction in order to clear out stocks held in inventory.

clearing account an account which holds money temporarily before transferring it to other accounts.

clearing and settlement the process whereby banks deliver cheques, notes, drafts and other instruments paid into them each day to a clearing house for settling; the clearing house totals the amounts owing to each bank and settles these with a single cheque.

clearing bank banks that deal with a clearing house for clearing and settlement; known in the USA as member banks.

clearing house establishment which undertakes clearing and settlement of inter-bank transactions.

clearing house controls financial controls present in bank clearing houses.

clearing union an international clearing house used by central banks.

clerical work low-level administrative work.

clerical worker employee engaged in clerical work, including secretaries, clerks, bookkeepers, etc.

client alternative term for customer; usually implies purchasers of professional services or industrial goods.

clocking in/out recording by workers of the times at which they start and finish work.

cloning executives process whereby management education programmes turn out trained managers who have more or less identical skills and perceptions.

close 1 termination; **2** the conclusion of a sale or bargain; **3** the conclusion of an accounting period.

closed circuit television (CCTV) television signals transmitted by cable rather than broadcast.

closed company company controlled by a very small number of shareholders.

closed-loop feedback continuous process where the output of a system is fed back into the system without external interference; the new input is used to correct the performance of the system.

closed-loop control engineering term for a system where output quality directly affects control procedures through a process of closed-loop feedback.

closed sale *see* completed transaction.

closed shop workplace where all workers must belong to a trade union.

closed stock merchandise which is sold in sets or lots.

closed structure organization characterized by inflexibility and tight control from the top.

close money stock market term for very narrow margins between asking and bid prices.

closing date 1 last date on which an advertisement can be accepted for publication; **2** last date on which a transaction can be made before the market closes.

closing entries final entries made in an account at the end of an accounting period.

closing rate method *see* current rate method.

closing price quoted price of a security at the close of the exchange, at the end of the trading day.

cluster analysis mathematical technique, used particularly by market researchers, to sort information into groups or clusters with similar features.

clustering tendency identified by Michael Porter for firms in the same industry to group together in close geographical proximity.

cluster sampling the definition of a market research sample where all members of the sample have broadly similar features.

coaching training and motivating of new employees or managers by older and more senior staff (*see* mentor) or by external consultants.

coalition association of persons or organizations that come together to seek a common purpose.

coalition bargaining collective bargaining where two or more unions join forces.

Coase Theorem Ronald Coase's theory of markets, stating that where there are a small number of players in a market, only allocation can ensure that property is distributed among them in an efficient manner.

codetermination system where employees elect representatives who may then vote on management decisions.

codification a way of organizing and incorporating knowledge into a system.

coemption the purchase of all existing stocks of a product.

cognition knowledge or perception by a person of a thing, circumstance or the environment around them.

cognitive biases misperceptions stemming from personal views or attitudes; tendency to take into account only that information which agrees with one's own preconceptions.

cognitive communities concentrations of firms within similar industries with similar attitudes and approaches to the market.

cognitive dissonance term describing the variance between a person's attitudes and values and their actual behaviour.

cognitive errors miscalculation; faulty reasoning.

cognitive mapping graphic representation of different forms of human reasoning.

cognitive research research into the nature of forms of human reasoning.

cognitive simulation *see* artificial intelligence.

coincidence simultaneous presence of two or more things, or simultaneous action of two or more parties, without causal connection.

coinsurance insurance held jointly by several parties.

cold calling unannounced sales visit to potential customer who has not previously been contacted.

collaboration working towards a mutual goal through cooperation; as opposed to competition.

collaborative agreements agreements between two or more firms to establish cooperation on a particular project or in a particular market.

collaborative models strategy implementation model where top management act as coordinators and bring all parts of the organization together.

collar maximum and minimum interest rates on a floating rate loan.

collateral security given by a borrower to a creditor as surety that a loan will be paid.

collateral bond *see* bond, collateral.

collateral loan loan where the borrower offers title to personal property as collateral.

collectible asset which can be converted into cash; *see also* liquid.

collection the recovery of a loan or other obligation.

collection cycle the period between the granting of a loan and its repayment.

collections systems in credit management, systems providing a record of contacts with customers.

collective action action undertaken jointly by a number of people for a common cause.

collective agreement agreement reached at the end of a process of collective bargaining.

collective bargaining negotiations between an employer and employees, the latter being represented by a trade union or bargaining unit, for the purpose of determining wages and conditions of employment.

collective bonuses bonuses paid to a group of workers and then divided equally or proportionately between them.

collective negotiation *see* collective bargaining.

collectivism joint ownership by workers and their families for the benefit of all.

collusion secret agreement or conspiracy.

collusive effect of research theory developed by Chris Argyris, that research programmes are unwittingly influenced by the beliefs and practices that dominate human activity, with a corresponding bias in their results.

combination policy insurance policy offering coverage against more than one kind of hazard.

command authority or the exercise of authority; *see* leadership.

commerce *see* trade.

commercial account *see* current account.

commercial agent *see* agent.

commercial arbitration adjudication of disputes between businesses, or between businesses and customers, before a private tribunal.

commercial bank bank whose primary business is receiving deposits and making short-term loans for companies and individuals, rather than investment or merchant banking.

commercial credit credit extended by one business to another.

commercialization the adaptation of non-profit or non-commercial organizations to commercial procedures and ways of thinking.

commercial law laws and regulations governing business activity within a national jurisdiction.

commercial paper cheques or promissory notes which are negotiable instruments; short-term debts sold in financial markets by large corporations.

commercial property property used for business purposes.

commission form of payment to sales staff or brokers, usually a percentage of the value of sales made.

commission agent agent paid on a commission basis.

commission house company which acts on a commission basis for others, buying and selling but without taking title to goods or securities.

commitment advance agreement to a contract; prior agreement by a lender to provide a loan at a later date; strong support by employees to their company and its goals.

commitment theory theory of cognition which shows how people can find themselves committed to a course of action without intending to do so.

committed fixed costs non-varying costs to which management are irrevocably committed and which cannot be altered or avoided; as opposed to managed costs.

committee sub-group of a larger organization formed to oversee a particular project or function.

commodity an item or good being traded, used most commonly of agricultural produce and raw materials; can be traded as either actuals or futures.

commodity agreement agreement between nations to control the price or output of a commodity.

commodity exchange markets where commodity actuals and futures are traded.

commodity loan government loan made to a commodity producer.

commodity theory of money theory that the value of money is determined by the value of the commodities which money can purchase.

Common Agricultural Policy (CAP) agricultural programme of the European Union, designed to support domestic agriculture.

common carrier transport organization that carries any good or person for a fee.

common cost generally incurred cost that cannot be clearly allocated to a particular activity.

Common Customs Tariff common external tariff in force around the member states of the European Union.

common external tariff customs duty or tariff charged in common by the member states of a common trading area and customs union on goods imported from non-member states; the European Union's Common Customs Tariff is an example

common market created when a number of countries agree to create both a customs union and a common external tariff.

common stock US term for securities that give the holder an ownership interest in the company, including voting rights and a say in the appointment of directors.

communication the passing of messages, verbal, written or electronic, from one party to one or more others, used to transmit news, information, sales offers, orders and requests, intelligence, etc.

communications and information technology *see* information and communications technology.

communications mix the combination of media and messages employed by a company to get its message across to the target audience.

communications technology technology that enables or enhances communication, including satellite broadcasting, the Internet and many other media as well as devices such as modems, faxes and so on; *see also* information and communications technology.

communication strategy firms' strategies for communicating effectively with customers, employees and other interest groups.

communism economic system based on communal ownership of the means of production, characterized by state control and central planning.

community action joint action by the residents of a particular community to protect their own rights or environment.

community rate of return value that a project will bring to the community and economy in the broad sense, rather than to the individual company.

commute 1 to travel to or from work; **2** to reduce or write-off debts or taxes which are still unpaid.

compact disk, read-only memory (CD-ROM) computer external storage medium, like a floppy disk but with a far higher memory capacity.

company an organization which exists for the purposes of conducting business for a profit; in most jurisdictions, companies must be legally registered and have limited liability (that is, their owners cannot be sued for their debts).

company agreement agreement reached by a company's management and its workforce as a result of collective bargaining.

company bargaining collective bargaining process leading to a company agreement.

company director member of the board of directors appointed by the shareholders to manage the company; in the US, also known as vice-president.

company groups in Japan, linked groups of related companies; *see also keiretsu.*

company law the laws and regulations governing the registration and operation of companies.

company mission *see* mission.

company objectives the aims and goals of a company, either short-term or long-term; *see also* goal; mission.

company registration the legal requirement in most jurisdictions that companies should be registered with a government authority; typically, registration includes the company name, the names of its directors, and the articles of association.

company secretary in the UK, director with responsibility for ensuring that the company conforms to all the legal requirements set out by British law.

company tax taxation payable by companies on profits.

company town community where most residents work for a single employer; that employer may also provide some social services and amenities for residents.

company-wide quality control (CWQC) single quality control system which spans all of a company's operations, not just a few departments.

comparative advantage advantage in terms of natural resources, labour, knowledge, etc. enjoyed by an area or country, which gives its businesses an advantage over competitors in rival areas.

comparative estimates estimating technique based on analysis of previous similar projects.

comparative management academic discipline which studies and compares management practices in different countries and cultures.

comparison shopping marketing information technique, where people are sent to the retail outlets of competitors to gather information about goods carried and prices.

compensating errors errors made by both parties which have the effect of cancelling each other.

compensation 1 US, pay and fringe benefits package offered to an employee; **2** in law, sum offered to another party as reparations for damage or loss.

competence ability to perform an activity; *see also* skill.

competence building training with the specific purpose of strengthening existing competences and/or developing new ones.

competence bundle theoretical concept of a firm as a combination of technical, cultural and managerial competences.

competency-based pay *see* skill-based pay.

competition 1 rivalry between firms, occurring when two or more firms are attempting to sell to the same customers in the same market; **2** can also be extended to include competition for scarce resources, labour, finance, etc.

competitive advantage advantage which one competing firm enjoys over its rivals, such as superior products or distribution.

competitive bid price offered for a good, usually which attempts to undercut other bids.

competitive environment the market or background in which competition takes place; the external circumstances affecting competition.

competitiveness the ability of a company to compete in a given environment.

competitive posture general term for the sum of a company's competitive strategies and activities; the image which a firm portrays to its competitors.

competitive price price achieved through bargaining, or where the seller attempts to offer a price lower than that offered by competitors.

competitive strategy strategies by which a company seeks to enhance its competitive position, increasing sales and/or market share.

competitive tendering bidding for contracts let by government agencies, usually featuring a number of private sector contractors offering sealed bids.

competitor benchmarking benchmarking directly against competitor firms rather than non-competing firms; *see* benchmarking.

competitor research systems market intelligence systems directed specifically at gathering research on competitor firms and their operations.

complementary products items which have no utility on their own but are combined with another product; for example, tyres are a complementary product to cars.

completed transaction transaction where all money and goods have changed hands; a closed sale.

composite demand term covering a situation where a product may be in demand by different groups who each need it for different reasons.

compound interest interest which accrues to a loan or credit at regular time intervals; if not paid, it is added to the sum of the principal and becomes part of the sum on which further interest is calculated.

compound period time period for which compound interest is calculated.

comprehensive budgeting budgeting process that covers all aspects of the company.

comprehensive planning planning which incorporates all departments and activities into a single plan.

comprehensive policy insurance policy providing protection against a variety of hazards.

compromise programming form of decision-making programming based on the notion of deviance or distance from an ideal solution.

comptroller *see* controller.

compulsory arbitration process whereby disputes between organizations or people are referred to a third-party arbitration body, which then imposes a legally binding settlement.

compulsory license court ruling granting a company the right to use a patent, effectively overruling the rights of the patent holder.

compulsory retirement policy whereby employees are compelled to retire on reaching a certain age level.

computer electronic data processing system, capable of processing very large quantities of data at high speed, functioning either on its own or in a network with other computers; requires the application of software to carry out specific tasks.

computer-aided design (CAD) partially automated design tools.

computer-aided design and manufacture (CAD/CAM) computer software combining features of computer-aided design and computer-aided manufacturing.

computer-aided instruction (CAI) instruction programmes where some or all teaching materials are delivered through a computer terminal.

computer-aided manufacturing (CAM) manufacturing processes which are in part controlled automatically by a computer program.

computer-aided production (CAP) *see* computer-aided manufacturing.

computer-aided software engineering (CASE) computer programs which, in effect, serve as tools for writing other computer programs.

computer-based information systems (CBIS) management and other information systems based on computer databases, with interface programs allowing the data to be interrogated according to the user's needs.

computer conferencing *see* tele-conferencing.

computer-integrated manufacturing (CIM) the complete integration of all manufacturing processes under the control of a single computer program.

computerized planning planning functions which are to some degree automated and controlled by a computer.

computer language basic format in which computer software is written, making it intelligible to the computer.

computer memory facility for storing and retrieving data in or through a computer; memory can be integral to or external to the computer; *see also* floppy disk; hard disk; compact disk, read-only memory.

computer numerical control the linking of numerical control machines to a computer system for automatic control; the computer inputs the necessary numerical codes used to control the machines, rather than having these done by hand.

computer program application allowing a user to carry out a specific task on a computer; generally, there are separate programs for word processing, data analysis, communications functions and so on; *see also* software.

computer programmer person who writes computer programs.

computer reservations systems (CRS) in hospitality and transport industries, computer networks which allow reservations to be made automatically from remote points.

computer terminal equipment, usually a monitor and a keyboard and/or mouse, where a user can input and retrieve data from a computer at some distance from the computer itself.

computer vision systems software and peripherals which allow a computer to scan and record visual data and/or interpret visual commands.

concentration **1** gathering of a large number of firms of a particular type in a single geographical area; **2** focus or drawing together of many resources on a single project.

concentration ratio shows the proportion of business in a single industry that is handled by the largest firms in that sector.

concept **1** idea or notion; **2** something which exists in the mind but not physically.

concept generation the development of new ideas, often through brain-storming, which can then be tested and translated into reality.

concession **1** reduction or relaxation of price or other terms of an agreement; **2** the right to carry out business on premises owned by another.

concessionaire holder of a concession.

conciliation process whereby two parties in a dispute try to overcome their differences, sometimes with the aid of a third party.

concurrent engineering approach to product development which uses parallel linked processes rather than a straight-line approach.

condition **1** the state of goods (i.e. in good condition means they are undamaged); **2** singular of 'conditions'.

conditional sales contract sales agreement where goods are not delivered until all conditions in the contract have been met.

conditional value value of a good conditional on a specific event occurring.

conditions **1** terms of agreement; 'on the condition that', meaning that a promise will be fulfilled only if certain other actions are carried out first; **2** also, circumstances or environment.

conditions of employment similar to terms of employment, defining issues such as hours of work, working conditions, health and safety and other factors in the working environment.

conference meeting or discussion devoted to a single issue.

confidence, consumer the extent to which consumers trust that a brand or product will deliver the expected benefits.

confidence level *see* standard error.

confidentiality secrecy; information given in confidence must not be disclosed to a third party.

configuration 1 the physical layout of the machinery required to carry out a certain process; **2** also refers to the particular combination of hardware and software in a computer system.

configuring systems artificial intelligence systems used in production planning, which generate a list of components and materials required to produce a product.

confirmation verification of an instruction or order to purchase.

confirming house export house which confirms orders placed by overseas buyers, issuing payment to the exporter as soon as the goods are shipped.

conflict direct clash of interests between two or more people or organizations.

conflict management the process of overcoming or ending conflict by reconciling differences and finding common ground between parties.

conformer someone who deliberately adopts the common values of a group.

Confucianism Chinese philosophical and ethical system, argued by many to have an influence on the structure and management of East Asian businesses today.

conglomerate large company with interests in many sectors, often created through the merger of a number of smaller firms.

consensus management management style in which senior managers strive to achieve broad agreement throughout the organization on particular decisions.

consequential loss loss which is the result of physical damage, also known as direct loss.

conservation the prudent management or use of stocks of materials to ensure that they last as long as possible.

consideration payment or fee.

consignment the handing over of goods to a sales agent, but retaining ownership of them until they are sold; such goods are said to be 'on consignment'.

consignment account accounts kept by an agent to record true ownership of goods held on consignment.

consignment note list of goods supplied to an agent on consignment.

consignment trade business activity where goods are offered for sale while held on consignment.

consolidated accounts the overall accounts of a group, incorporating the accounts of all subsidiary companies; sometimes also used to refer to a consolidated financial statement.

consolidated financial statement summary of the financial position of a company, combining the results of all other accounts and financial statements in a financial period.

consolidation combining of several departments or organizations into one, so as to reduce overheads.

consortium association of companies in order to undertake a business project.

conspicuous consumption spending by an individual for the main purpose of enhancing that person's image; buying goods and services in order to show off to one's neighbours.

constituent company *see* subsidiary.

constructive conflict Mary Parker Follett's theory that industrial disputes over a relatively minor issue can uncover other, more important problems.

consultant outside specialist brought into a company to advise on or help solve a particular problem.

consultation taking the advice and views of others before making a decision; *see also* joint consultation.

consultative management management style where managers consult widely with colleagues and subordinates to get their views before making a decision.

consume to employ a good or service in such a manner that it is used up.

consumer one who consumes or uses goods or services; usually, but not always, the same as a customer.

consumer acceptance stage in consumer buying behaviour when consumers have tried a product and found it satisfactory.

consumer action retaliation by consumers against retailers or manufacturers who have failed to satisfy consumer needs, particularly where issues of health, safety or the environment are involved.

consumer advocacy the defence of the rights, health and safety of consumers by an agency or person appointed as consumer advocates.

consumer attributes those aspects of consumer status and behaviour which can be identified, and which can be used to class consumers in the segmentation process.

consumer behaviour activities and, more generally, patterns of activity shown by consumers when making purchases, including such factors as frequency of purchase, average spend, product preferences and so on.

consumer boycott the boycotting by consumers of a certain product, or the products of a particular company.

consumer choice said to exist when consumers can choose freely between different competing brands and products.

consumer conversion the process of persuading potential customers to become actual customers; sometimes also refers to persuading consumers to switch from one brand or product to another.

consumer credit credit facilities offered by retailers to consumers.

consumer disposable product designed for immediate consumption or which can be used only once; as opposed to consumer durable.

consumer durable product designed for repeated use and which should not need to be replaced for some time; as opposed to consumer disposable.

consumer expendable *see* consumer disposable.

consumer electronics electronic goods such as televisions, radios, stereo equipment, personal computers and so on.

consumer goods goods purchased by the consumer through retail outlets for use and disposal, as opposed to capital goods or industrial goods; sometimes also refers to goods purchased for use in the household.

consumerism movement demanding greater rights for consumers and increased consumer sovereignty; *see also* consumer advocacy.

consumer needs primary motivators for consumer behaviour; consumers set out to fulfil needs, and purchase goods and services which they believe will do so.

consumer non-durable *see* consumer disposable.

consumer panel group of consumers used as a research sample by market researchers to test consumer behaviour and opinion.

consumer preference indication of which products or product features consumers value most, and which they are willing to buy.

consumer price index measure of the average retail price of consumer goods in the economy.

consumer research market research which deals particularly with consumer behaviour and preferences.

consumer society society where the values of consumers are particularly strong, and where their needs for acquisition and consumption dominate economic behaviour to a large extent.

consumer sovereignty concept that it is the needs of the consumer that ultimately determine what goods and services are produced and where they are delivered.

consumer theory academic theory devoted to understanding consumer behaviour and buying patterns.

consumption 1 the act of consuming; **2** more generally, the total spending in an economy on goods for consumption.

contact someone who has been visited by or responded to a questionnaire from a salesperson or market researcher.

container vessel for carrying cargoes by sea, road or rail.

content validity measure of the extent to which the content of a training programme is valid in real life situations.

contextual rationality rationality reached through an analysis of current context

contingency allowance in costing, an allowance for unforeseen circumstances which could increase costs.

contingency planning plans for dealing with accidents or unpredictable occurrences should they happen at a future date.

contingent liability liability which exists as a result of the actions of others.

contingent strategic success paradigm theory developed by H. Igor Ansoff to explain why a firm can be simultaneously successful in one area and unsuccessful in another.

contingent valuation methods in environmental economics, analysis of people's willingness to pay for environmental benefits or goods.

continuity principle in financial accounting, the assumption that the firm is likely to continue in business during the foreseeable future.

continuous assessment the constant monitoring of the progress of a project; continuous checking by instructors or trainers during a training course.

continuous credit credit facility which allows borrowing at any time up to a certain level; *see also* revolving loan.

continuous flow manufacturing (CFM) integrated production system organized so as to ensure constant throughput with minimal stock levels (*see also* just-in-time manufacturing; flow line production).

continuous improvement **1** constant updating and upgrading of procedures and processes, usually involving feedback from further along the production process; **2** a philosophy of constantly striving towards perfection.

continuous learning philosophy which emphasizes the constant acquisition of knowledge and skills by managers and employees, either in the workplace or through training programmes.

continuous production *see* flow line production.

continuous replenishment logistical function which ensures that stocks are constantly replenished to desired levels.

continuous shiftwork work schedule which enables a production line to operate around the clock.

continuous stocktaking stock control system based on continuous revolving checks on stock levels.

contract any agreement between two or more parties; can be verbal or written, but usually only the latter are legally enforceable.

contractarian theories theories of firm development which emphasize the firm as a nexus of contracts and relationships.

contracting in buying in services rather than hiring people directly to perform them.

contracting out subcontracting jobs previously carried out within the firm to external contractors.

contract law laws covering the nature and enforcement of contracts.

contract of employment legal document setting out the terms and conditions of employment between an employee and an employer.

contract of service special type of contract of employment, usually for a fixed period of time.

contributed capital money raised through share issues.

contributed value measure of value added as the total of revenues for a product less the costs of raw materials required to produce that product; *see also* value added.

contribution **1** payment into an insurance policy or pension plan; *see also* premium; **2** alternatively, the profits a product or brand returns to the owning firm.

contribution costing *see* variable cost.

contribution margin excess of revenue over variable costs.

contribution pricing pricing strategy which concentrates on covering variable costs.

contributory negligence situation where a person is held to be responsible for an accident, particularly one which affects themselves.

control direction or command.

control, corporate *see* corporate control.

control, panoptic *see* panoptic control.

control systems systems for ensuring control over processes and procedures; in effect, a control of controls.

controllable costs costs that can be changed or controlled by managers; *see also* variable cost.

controller senior financial executive responsible for auditing and accounting; in the US, known as comptroller.

convenience food food which has been precooked before sale, and requires little or no further preparation.

convenience good frequently purchased consumer disposables.

convenience store small retail outlets specializing in convenience goods, usually located in high population areas and open for long hours.

convenor senior shop steward.

convergence drawing together or onto parallel tracks; becoming similar.

convergent marketing marketing strategy whereby a large number of goods are sold through the same channels and using the same marketing mix.

conversion 1 changing from one thing to another; 2 replacing one type of equipment or plant with another; 3 the process of turning a potential customer into an actual customer; 4 colloquially, sometimes refers to moving goods from one jurisdiction to another (i.e. smuggling).

conversion cost 1 cost of adding value; 2 costs of the manufacturing process (total of labour and overheads); 3 any cost associated with a process of conversion.

convertibility the extent to which a currency can be exchanged for other currencies or gold.

convertible loan stock *see* convertibles.

convertibles debentures and preferred stocks which can later be exchanged for common stock.

convertible term policy term assurance policy which can later be changed into an endowment policy.

conveyancing transporting; in commercial law, the passage of deeds of ownership from one party to another.

cooling-off period 1 postponement of a strike or other industrial dispute to give the parties time to negotiate further, can be imposed by government in some jurisdictions; 2 generally, any imposed delay which allows the parties to a dispute time to reconsider.

cooperation two or more parties working together for a common aim (*see also* collaboration).

cooperative association, usually of consumers, engaged in business and sharing the profits among themselves; association for joint ownership and management of a business.

cooperative advertising advertising campaigns where manufacturers and retailers or distributors share costs and development work.

coordination management function that unifies and directs all the other parts of the organization, ensuring that all are moving in the right direction at the right time.

co-ownership where employees have part ownership of a firm, and often also have a say in management.

copy written text which forms part of an advertisement.

copyright exclusive right to reproduce articles, books, photographs, films or other representative material, usually held by the author or publisher of a work.

core benefit proposition principal or most important benefit in a bundle of benefits.

core business most important or central business activity of a company, usually focused on the firm's primary market; secondary or support activities are known as ancillary functions.

core competences primary or most important competences or skills possessed by a person, or required to do a certain job.

core workers permanent full-time employees, usually employed in the core business.

core time in flexible working hours, the times when all employees must be at their jobs; *see also* bandwidth.

corporate accountability extent to which large corporations are accountable for their actions to customers, government or the general public.

corporate change *see* change, corporate.

corporate control controls and limits on corporate behaviour set by governments and/or society.

corporate culture beliefs, values and customs which characterize how a company functions and the attitudes of its personnel to the market, the organization and themselves.

corporate decline long-term decline in corporate profits and performance.

corporate goals *see* corporate objectives.

corporate governance the mechanisms by which a corporation or company is run, including ethical and legal frameworks.

corporate identity the total package of images, including marks and logos employed on corporation property, products, etc., that conveys the corporate image to the mind of the consumer.

corporate image the perception of the company in the minds of its customers and employees, and the public at large; often reinforced by the development of a strong corporate identity.

corporate intelligence a company's overall environmental scanning and intelligence gathering functions.

corporate nationality defined by the country in which a company is registered or domiciled.

corporate objectives the overall objective which a company sets for itself, usually defined in terms of expected future market position or financial results; sets the tone for the company and defines its philosophy.

corporate pension fund pension fund established exclusively for the employees of a single company.

corporate performance measure of a company's success, financial or otherwise, over a given period of time.

corporate planning overall planning function which takes a company towards its objectives, setting goals in terms of market development, new product development and so on.

corporate profits tax *see* corporation tax.

corporate raider individual who makes rapid purchases of large blocks of shares in order to buy a controlling interest or to take over a company.

corporate state term used by some theorists to describe a country where corporations are more powerful than government, and where corporate values dominate.

corporate strategic change the complex processes required to realign a company from one set of strategic goals or objectives to another; often accompanied by cultural change.

corporate strategic planning *see* strategic planning.

corporate strategy means by which a company plans to reach its corporate objectives, including how it will serve its markets and compete successfully with its rivals.

corporate taxation *see* corporation tax.

corporate turnaround *see* turnaround.

corporation **1** association of people who are recognized by law as a legal entity, and which can buy, control and sell property, carry out business and conduct legal actions; **2** more generally, any association of persons into one organization.

corporation tax tax on corporate earnings or profits.

corporatism in business history, the development of professional management and the separation of ownership from control; the replacement of owner-managed firms by corporations.

corrective advertising advertisement which corrects errors or misleading information in an earlier advertisement.

corrective maintenance maintenance which takes place after a system or machine has failed or malfunctioned.

correlation **1** the relationship between two things; **2** in statistics, measure of the distance between two variables.

correspondent banking system where banks hold deposits for other banks; sometimes this is done by specialist correspondent banks.

corruption in business, illegal practices usually leading to financial gain, often linked to bribery.

cost money which must be expended to acquire or produce a product or service, or to undertake an activity; sometimes used synonymously with price.

cost absorption accounting procedure which allots portions of indirect costs to a particular product or cost centre.

cost accounting accounting processes which classify, record, allocate and report cost data as an aid to cost management.

cost advantage ability to produce or distribute goods more cheaply than competitors.

cost analysis the breakdown of costs to determine their exact composition and source.

cost and freight agreement to transport goods whereby the seller pays freight charges for the goods to their destination.

cost-benefit analysis analysis which compares the costs associated with a planned project and the benefits which that project can reasonably be expected to yield.

cost centre any department or process to which costs are allocated directly and where records of costs are kept.

cost control the process of monitoring and controlling costs, and of keeping them as close as possible to budgeted costs.

cost differentials measures of the difference between alternative costs.

cost-driven pricing pricing system which is based on the total cost to produce a good or service, rather than on the value attached to it by customers.

cost drivers factors which create costs or lead to costs being incurred.

cost effectiveness the extent to which a cost is covered by corresponding profits received from elsewhere; *see also* cost-benefit analysis.

cost efficiency condition of being cost efficient.

cost efficient costs which, when incurred, result in the maximum possible benefit.

costing the process of identifying and allocating costs.

costing system formal managerial procedures for costing, cost control and cost management.

cost management management techniques associated with costing and cost control.

cost of capital *see* capital, cost of.

cost-of-carry in forwards and futures markets, the cost of holding commodities until they are finally transferred to the buyer.

cost of finance rate of return which could be earned by investors by holding other financial assets at similar levels of risk.

cost of investment costs associated with making and holding a particular investment.

cost of living allowance additional pay offered to employees who must live away from home while working.

cost of living index index showing increases in the average cost of basic consumer goods.

cost-oriented pricing *see* cost-driven pricing.

cost-plus pricing pricing of goods by adding a fixed percentage to the total costs of production.

cost-push inflation inflation caused by increases in production costs; as opposed to demand inflation.

cost pools an agglomeration of costs from various sources, usually then assigned to one or more cost centres.

cost reduction any measure taken to reduce costs to lower levels, usually with the effect of improving profitability.

cost study *see* cost analysis.

cost theory theories of the relationship between costs and quantity.

cost tracing procedure procedure for determining where and how costs are incurred.

cost variance deviation between an actual cost and the original budgeted cost or standard cost.

cost–volume–price *see* break-even.

cost–volume–profit (CVP) analysis of the relationships between costs, gross revenue and net profit, used to identify sources of profit and which products or services are contributing most to overall profits.

cottage industry industry characterized by many very small-scale producers, often in dispersed locations.

counselling helping people to overcome problems, either professional or personal, through guidance, advice and support.

countercultures culture within a culture, which holds values opposed to those of the dominant culture.

counter-implementation strategies activities carried out by members of an organization who wish to prevent or resist a particular strategy.

counterparties the two parties involved in a forward contract.

counter-purchasing purchasing of goods in a foreign country on condition that goods of equal value are purchased in the home country and exported to the foreign country.

counter-trading *see* counter-purchasing.

countervailing duties tariffs on imported goods, imposed especially to counteract export subsidies in the country of origin.

country clusters groups of countries with similar cultures or values.

country of origin country in which goods or commodities are produced and from which they are being exported.

country risk analysis techniques for measuring the risk levels associated with investments in a particular country, taking into account current and likely future political and economic conditions.

coup d'état forcible seizure of control of a country or organization, and the deposition of the current leaders.

coupon interest payable on a bond or other fixed interest security; that portion of a bond which is redeemed in exchange for interest payments.

coupon advertising **1** advertising in newspapers or magazines where the reader can cut out a coupon (literally, part of the advertisement) and return it to the advertiser to order goods or services or get further information; **2** alternatively, a coupon may be used to purchase goods from participating retailers.

coupon clipping detaching coupons from a bond to present them for the payment of interest.

coupon-paying bonds fixed interest bonds with attached coupons.

Cournot competition situation where oligopolies compete on quantity.

covered term used of dealings where measures have been taken to avoid or restrict loss, used particularly in forwards and futures markets.

CPU *see* central processing unit.

craft production small-scale production in small workshops, usually on a customized product basis.

craftsman skilled worker, usually one who has completed an apprenticeship or technical education.

craftsmanship term for quality, connoting high quality or fine work.

craft union trade union whose members are skilled craftsmen, usually limited to a particular craft or skill.

crash cost additional cost required to execute a project more quickly than normal.

creative accounting accounting techniques which seek to maximize a company's use of its financial resources, rather than merely recording financial data.

creative conflict *see* constructive conflict.

creativity the facility of creating or inventing new things, a particularly important part of the design function.

creativity management management techniques which seek to stimulate and enhance creativity within an organization.

credit 1 the delivery of goods or services in exchange for payment at a later date; **2** borrowing up to a certain limit; **3** positive balance in a bank account; **4** the right-hand side of a ledger.

credit agency organization which researches and supplies information on the creditworthiness of individuals or companies.

credit bureau *see* credit agency.

credit card plastic card which is used to make purchases of consumer goods and services on credit; the card is issued by the company granting the credit and, unlike other forms of credit, can be used to make purchases from most retailers and service providers in developed countries.

credit, consumer *see* consumer credit.

credit control procedures used by banks and other credit-granting institutions for managing credit facilities, including checking the creditworthiness of prospective customers and ensuring customers stay within credit limits.

credit-granting institution financial institution which grants credit to organizations and individuals.

credit insurance insurance policy confirming that a seller of goods on credit will receive payment even if the customer defaults.

credit interchange exchange of information between firms about credit granted to a particular customer.

credit limit the maximum amount of credit which a credit-granting institution will allow to a customer.

credit line *see* line of credit.

credit manager manager responsible for granting credit, determining credit ratings, and credit control.

credit markets markets for credit, with banks and other financial institutions as 'sellers' and companies and individuals as 'buyers'.

credit note written document issued by sellers to customers when faulty goods are returned or when the wrong price has been charged, showing that the customer is now in credit for a certain sum of money.

creditor one who is owed money; as opposed to debtor.

credit rating estimate of the creditworthiness of a customer, which in turn affects the credit limit allowed to that customer.

credit rationing 1 restriction on the amount of credit available at a given time, to the point where the demand for credit exceeds supply; **2** more generally, restrictions on available credit.

credit risk measure of the likelihood that a customer will default.

credit sale sale of goods on credit; *see* credit.

credit scoring ranking of individual factors that go to make up a credit rating.

credit squeeze measures by central government to limit credit and lending so as to reduce consumer spending and therefore inflation.

credit union cooperative financial organization, accepting deposits from and making loans to members only.

credit vetting the checking of the background of a potential customer to establish creditworthiness and credit rating.

creditworthiness general term reflecting a customer's financial status and whether he or she is a good credit risk; used as the basis for determining credit rating.

crime illegal and wrongful actions.

crisis management management skills required for managing unexpected events; also management style characterized by reacting to events as they occur, rather than planning ahead.

criterion principle or standard by which judgements are made.

critical incident technique training technique which focuses on a particular incident, where participants describe their own experiences and analyse behaviour.

critical path analysis technique which combines planning and scheduling, listing all the individual activities involved in a process and how long they will take; important for highlighting those activities which are particularly crucial to success.

critical success factors factors which are most important or even essential to the success of a project.

cross-border acquisitions acquisitions of businesses in a country outside the acquiring company's home nation.

cross-border business *see* international trade.

cross-charging charges made by one department to another within the same company; *see also* transfer pricing.

cross-cultural communications communications between parties from different cultural backgrounds, requiring translation and interpretation of language, symbols, etc.

cross-cultural factors factors affecting cross-cultural communication and trade, generally serving to render these activities more complex.

cross-cultural training training programmes for employees and managers on working in other cultures and dealing with people from different cultural backgrounds.

cross-fertilization in advertising, process whereby effective advertising concepts developed in one regional market are transferred to other regional markets.

cross-investment situation where companies based in two different countries each invest in assets in the other country.

cross-subsidization the use of profits from one business activity to offset losses resulting from another.

CRS *see* computer reservations systems.

cryptosystems encrypted or coded computer systems, which cannot be read or used except by someone in possession of a key to the encryption.

cultural attitudes attitudes to particular subjects which are common to a culture.

cultural convergence process whereby cultures take on the attributes of each other as a result of increased trade or other forms of interchange.

culturalist theory theory of organization behaviour which focuses on organizations as cultures, with their own codes, symbols and so on.

cultural values values commonly held by members of a particular culture.

culture in general, the values, customs, beliefs, behaviours and norms of a particular group of people.

culture, cross-national a culture which spans national boundaries and is common to the residents of more than one nation.

culture, macro large cultures defined by only a few attributes, i.e. European culture, Asian culture.

culture, micro small cultures defined by a large number of attributes, usually subsets of macro cultures.

culture, organizational *see* organization culture.

culture shock the impact of sudden and rapid cultural change on the members of that culture.

cumulative preference share preference share where, if a dividend is omitted in one year, shareholders have first right to any dividends paid in the following year.

cumulative timing work measurement in which all the elements of a job are timed consecutively in a single measurement; as opposed to flyback timing.

currency money in the form of banknotes and coinage.

currency speculator someone who buys foreign currencies in the hopes of reselling them at a profit, thanks to fluctuating exchange rates.

currency swap financial derivative, where different currencies are exchanged for a specified period.

current account bank account from which customers can write cheques and make immediate withdrawals without penalty; in balance of payments, that portion of a balance of payments statement listing current imports and exports.

current assets cash, stocks, accounts receivable and other assets which could be consumed or disposed of in the short term; as opposed to fixed assets.

current cost the present replacement cost of an asset.

current cost accounting accounting techniques which value assets at their current cost, rather than their replacement cost; *see also* replacement cost accounting.

current knowledge knowledge that is readily available to all parties in negotiations.

current liability debts or liabilities which must be paid now or in the near future.

current purchasing power amount of goods or services which a given amount of currency will purchase.

current rate method accounting technique which values assets held in foreign countries and/or foreign currencies at the current rate of exchange.

current ratio ratio of current assets to current liabilities, dividing the latter into the former.

current spot price price at a given moment for goods for sale on a spot market; the price for which goods can be purchased and taken away at a given instant.

current transaction transaction appearing in the current account of the balance of payments.

current value accounting accounting method which values assets in terms of current prices rather than original acquisition costs.

current yield yield on investment; the figure is arrived at by expressing the current dividend as a percentage of the current market price of the securities.

curriculum vitae (CV) statement of biographical details by a job applicant, including personal background, education and professional experience/details of previous career.

customer anyone making a purchase; in marketing, the term is used more generally to include present and potential customers (usually, but not always, synonymous with consumer).

customer care marketing techniques for improving customer services and customer relations, including after-sales service.

customer communication any form of communication with customers which provides information about products and service, including methods such as advertising or point-of-sale promotions.

customer delight marketing term for when customers find that products or services provide even better value than expected when making the purchase; *see also* customer satisfaction.

customer demand demand or requirement by customers for a particular product, service or feature.

customerization the process of configuring goods or services to make them more acceptable to customers.

customization altering product features or making new products to a specification supplied by a customer.

customer loyalty tendency by customers to continue to purchase a company's brands or products and not switch to competing offers.

customer markets used to denote markets into which a firm sells its products and services, as opposed to labour markets and capital markets.

customer preferences those products, services and features most valued by customers.

customer retention marketing activities aimed to ensure customers continue to buy a product or brand and do not switch to rival alternatives.

customer satisfaction one of the aims of marketing, where customers find that a product or service meets their needs and represents value for money.

customer segmentation *see* market segmentation.

customer service service provided to customers either in pure services businesses or as an adjunct to the purchase of a physical product.

customer–supplier relationships the views and attitudes of customers and suppliers to each other; good customer–supplier relationships are usually held to result in more sales.

customs 1 taxes on the import or export of goods; *see also* tariff; **2** the agencies responsible for imposing and collecting these taxes.

customs controls checks made at border crossings to ensure customs and tariffs are paid.

customs union agreement by two or more countries to remove customs barriers and trade restrictions between themselves.

cut-price cheap, reduced in price.

CV *see* curriculum vitae.

CVP *see* cost–volume–profit.

CWQC *see* company-wide quality control.

cybernetics the science of systems.

cyberspace term for the worldwide complex of telecommunications and computer networks; sometimes used to refer to the Internet.

cycle recurring series of events; *see also* business cycle.

cyclical demand variations in demand which can to some extent be forecast or predicted based on past experience.

cyclical forecast forecast of the timing of events in a particular cycle.

cyclical unemployment unemployment which rises and falls in correlation with the fluctuations of the business cycle.

cyclograph method work study method developed by Frank and Lillian Gilbreth for mapping worker movements.

D

daily contracted hours number of hours an employee is required to work each day, usually specified by contract.

data 1 basic factual information, often in numerical or statistical form; **2** information in a form in which it can be processed by a computer.

data analysis the examination of large quantities of data in order to discern patterns or reach conclusions, often carried out by a computer.

database collection of data, often very large amounts, which can be analysed by a computer and results produced for use in strategy forming, decision making, control, etc.

database management systems computerized systems for ordering, maintaining and interrogating databases.

data capture the acquisition, conversion and storage of information in the form of data, usually in databases.

data capture technology computer and other technologies which collect data and store it in databases.

data confidentiality legal requirement in many jurisdictions that data on persons or corporations must be kept confidential and may not be widely disseminated.

data degradation 1 loss of data stored in computer memory as a result of mechanical or operator failure; **2** alternatively, the process of data becoming out of date and obsolete.

data dictionary in a computerized system, a categorization of all data stored in a data repository.

data flow diagram in systems design, graphic depiction of how data is generated and flows through an organization.

data processing the processing of data by computers into formats which can be read and understood by users; *see also* data analysis.

data repository storage place for data, most commonly in computer memory.

data security controls placed on access to data, most commonly involving the use of passwords to gain access, either for the purposes of legally required data confidentiality or to protect valuable information from competitors.

data store *see* data repository.

data subject person or item on whom data has been acquired and is held.

data transformation processing of raw data into usable formats; *see* data processing.

data user person or organization holding and using data for whatever purpose.

day loan one-day loan granted to stockbrokers for the purchase of securities.

day order in securities trading, an order to buy or sell that, if not carried out, expires at the end of the trading day.

day work basic payment scheme related to time on the job, usually expressed in terms of an hourly rate.

deadline time limit; time by which a contract must be fulfilled or a sale must be concluded.

dead stock merchandise for which there is no apparent demand, and which cannot be sold.

dead time non-productive time, or time lost in a production process; in payment-by-results schemes, workers must usually be compensated for dead time.

deal transaction or purchase.

dealer **1** similar to trader, one who sells a particular good; **2** in securities trading, one who acts as a principal, buying and selling on their own account, rather than as an agent.

debase devalue, or lower the value of a good or currency.

debenture loan which is sold as an investment, at a stipulated interest and to be redeemed on a given date, irrespective of whether the issuing company makes a profit.

debenture bond *see* bond, debenture.

debenture capital capital obtained from the sale of debentures.

debit **1** any amount which is owed to another party; **2** left-hand side of a ledger.

debit card **1** plastic card which allows bank customers to withdraw money from automated teller machines; **2** an alternative to cash when making purchases, with the use of the card automatically transferring money from the customer's bank account to that of the seller.

debt **1** money owed; **2** any obligation or liability.

debt capital money borrowed to finance business operations and on which a fixed rate of interest is paid.

debt collection the retrieval of debts owed, particularly those which are overdue.

debt control policies and strategies of central banks to control government debt.

debt–equity ratio debt capital as a proportion of total capital issued.

debt finance money obtained through loans.

debtor any person or organization that owes money to another.

debtor nation nation that has borrowed money from other nations or institutions such as the World Bank.

debtors to sales ratio total sales divided by number of debtors.

debt markets *see* credit markets.

debt rationing policy by banks of restricting the level of debt which clients may incur; *see also* credit rationing.

debt ratios ratios showing the level of indebtedness of an organization, such as debt to equity, debt to assets, etc.

debt–service ratio ratio of money paid to service a national debt, to gross national product or income.

debt to net worth ratio current liabilities divided by net value.

debug *see* debugging.

debugging process of finding and eliminating bugs in a computer or other piece of equipment.

debureaucratization the breaking down of hierarchies in organizations, including the devolution of responsibility to lower levels and the redefinition of employee and managerial roles.

decelerating bonus bonus where the rate of bonus pay decreases for each additional hour worked.

deceleration gradually slowing down or lessening of the rate of growth.

decentralization reducing the power of the central functions of a firm, and devolving responsibility to departments and subsidiaries.

decentralized control manufacturing system where control is devolved as far as possible to individual workers or teams.

decision resolution or judgement; making up one's mind to a course of action.

decision aids general term for a variety of simulations and models, many computer-based, which can be used in decision making.

decision maker person with primary or ultimate responsibility for taking decisions which affect others.

decision making the analysis of alternatives and the choice between them; the act of taking a decision.

decision-making unit group or team responsible for decision making, usually where the decision-making process is very complex.

decision matrix graphic depiction showing the range of possible decisions in a given situation.

decision science the application of scientific techniques to decision making and problem solving.

decision support system computer-based information system which provides information and analysis to support decision making.

decision theory group of mathematical models designed to help eliminate forecasting errors and allow decision makers to conduct better analyses and (hopefully) more accurate decisions.

decision to participate behavioural theory, that people will participate in an organization so long as the benefits to them are greater than their own contribution.

decision tree analysis type of flowchart used in decision making, which sets out alternatives and options in different situations.

declaration legal statement setting out the ownership of property and goods.

declaration date date when a share-issuing company announces payment of a dividend, and the amount.

declared value stated value of merchandise accepted for transport, used for insurance and customs purposes.

decline 1 falling off of business performance in terms of sales, profits or revenue; 2 economic state where growth rates are falling and unemployment is rising.

decline stage stage in the product life cycle, where saturation has been reached and overall sales are falling; generally ends with abandonment.

decommission to take out of service.

decommissioning cost costs involved in decommissioning, usually for a large item of plant.

deconglomeration splitting up of a conglomerate organization so that more control is devolved to its constituent parts.

deconstruction analysis the application of the theories of deconstruction to management and organizations.

decouple 1 to treat separately things which were formerly treated together; 2 to detach one part of an organization from another; 3 to treat price inflation and wage inflation separately when making cost of living adjustments to wages.

decreasing costs costs that decline proportionately as output increases.

decruitment programme offered to senior and middle managers in the final years before retirement, offering them lower positions and salaries.

deductible 1 anything which can be deducted; 2 allowances which can be deducted from taxable income.

deduction anything which is deducted; *see also* deductible.

deed legal document which conveys ownership of property.

deed of arrangement document assigning property to a trustee on behalf of the owner.

defalcation where trustees or persons responsible for money placed in their care are unable to account for that money; *see also* embezzlement.

defamation speech or writings that attack the character or reputation of another.

default failure to meet an obligation, particularly a loan or contract.

default premium higher yield derived from bonds which carry the risk of default.

defence fund reserve funds kept by some trade unions to meet expenses and provide financial assistance to members during a strike.

defend and hold strategic option which aims to consolidate and maintain current market position.

defensive flexibility strategic option which concentrates on making the organization flexible so that it can respond quickly to sudden change.

defensive investment investment, the primary aim of which is to reduce risk rather than to maximize returns; as opposed to speculation.

deferral revenue collected before it is recognized as being earned.

deferred annuity policy whereby the payment of the annuity is deferred until a certain specified time (for example, when the beneficiary reaches a certain age).

deferred charges expenditures written off over a period of time.

deferred compensation the putting off of income due (wages, dividends and so on) until some time in the future.

deferred credit credit that is put back until some future date.

deferred expense *see* prepaid expense.

deferred liability liability that does not have to be met until some time in the future.

deferred shares shares entitled to a dividend but where that dividend is not paid until a certain stated date, or where the dividend is payable only after dividends have been paid out on ordinary shares.

deferred stocks *see* deferred shares.

deferred tax tax on income which has been reported but will not become taxable until a later date.

deferred wage rise wage increases in subsequent years which are set out in a contract of employment.

deficient-demand unemployment unemployment caused when the demand for labour declines more quickly than real wages.

deficit excess of expenditure over revenue; amount by which liabilities exceed assets.

deficit financing borrowing by governments to meet budgetary requirements in years when expenditure exceeds revenue.

deficit spending the expenditure of public funds raised through deficit financing.

deflation downturn in economic activity, characterized by stable or falling prices and less money in circulation.

deflationary gap amount by which the demand for employment falls short of supply, leading to rising unemployment.

deforestation the consumption of forestry resources without renewing these through replanting; the conversion of forest land into agricultural land.

defray to pay.

defunct no longer in existence.

degree course training or education programme that leads to the granting of a university degree.

delayering programme of organizational rationalization which focuses on reducing the number of middle managers.

delegate 1 to give authority to another; **2** also, a person authorized to act as representative for others.

delegated authority authority given by one party to another to engage in negotiations, trade, and so on.

delegation the process of delegating.

delinquency failure to pay a debt on the due date, *see also* default.

delisting 1 removal of any person or organization from an accredited list; **2** withdrawal of listed status from a security by stock exchange regulators.

delivered cost total cost of goods and transportation to the customer.

delivery handing over of purchased goods to the buyer, usually on the latter's premises; handing over of share certificates representing purchased shares to the buyer's broker.

delivery date 1 agreed date by which the seller will deliver goods to the buyer; **2** in futures, the first day of the month in which delivery will be made.

delivery duty paid terms of an export where the exporter agrees to pay all taxes and tariffs.

delivery period time between the placing of an order and the delivery of the goods ordered.

Delphi method research technique where a panel of experts from different disciplines give their views on likely future developments in their own and other fields.

deluxe high-priced, high-prestige goods or services.

delta stocks class of stocks traded on the London stock market, about 600 infrequently traded stocks.

demand a combination of want and purchasing power, where customers express a desire for a certain product or service and have the means to pay for it.

demand analysis market research technique for measuring the nature and quantity of demand for a product or service.

demand creation stimulation of demand for a product or service, particularly one based on a new technology, where no demand existed before.

demand deposit account containing funds which a depositor can withdraw without prior notice, *see also* current account.

demand elasticity extent to which demand for or sales of a product changes in response to price changes; *see also* elasticity.

demand, income elasticity of *see* income elasticity of demand.

demand, inelastic *see* inelastic demand.

demand inflation inflation caused by increasing demand which pushes up prices; as opposed to cost-push inflation.

demand loan loan with no fixed maturity date but where the loan can be called in at any time by the lending bank.

demand management in economics, the stimulation or reduction of demand in order to achieve a desired level of employment and economic performance.

demand note any financial instrument where the holder of a note can demand payment at any time.

demand price the price a customer offers to pay, or is willing to pay, for a good or service.

demand pull *see* demand inflation.

demand theory theoretical principles relating to the demand for goods.

demarcation boundary line between geographical areas, departmental functions and so on.

demarketing marketing activities which aim to discourage customers from buying a good or service.

democracy organization or society in which government represents the views and wishes of those being governed.

democratic management management style founded on democracy, encouraging employee participation and consultation.

demographics characteristics such as age, income, gender and marital status which define an area's population and are used in market segmentation.

demonetization withdrawing a currency from circulation so that it is no longer legal tender.

demotion downgrading of an employee to a more junior, less well-paid job.

demurrage additional costs which must be paid by shipowners if a ship remains berthed after the time allowed for loading or unloading.

denationalization transfer of state-owned firms to the private sector; *see also* privatization.

denominating debt in international trade, designating the currency in which a particular debt will be paid.

denomination face value of currency.

de novo **problem** optimization problem encountered in system design, where original inequalities have been changed to equalities but an additional constraint on total budget has been added.

density dependence model theoretical explanation of the density of organizational populations at any given moment.

department any major administrative unit within an organization, usually based on a function such as production, marketing, and so on.

departmentalization the structure of an organization in terms of its departments and divisions.

departmentation the process of setting up and establish departments within in an organization.

department store large retail outlet selling a very wide variety of consumer goods.

dependant thing or person which relies on another for support or even existence.

dependency condition of being dependent or reliant on another thing or person.

dependency ratio ratio between the number of employed and retired people in a national economy.

depletion the physical diminishing of a fixed asset, or the accounting charges which reflect this diminishment.

depletion allowance tax deduction allowed as a result of depletion.

deposit 1 money entrusted to a bank or other financial institution for safe-keeping; **2** also, a partial initial payment; *see* downpayment.

deposit account bank account where depositors are normally required to give notice before withdrawing funds; also known as savings account.

depositary institution, such as a bank, with whom a deposit is made.

deposit bank bank whose primary business is the taking of deposits.

deposit creation multiplier in banking, the money available for lending created directly by new money placed on deposit.

deposit funds *see* escrow.

deposit insurance insurance which protects bank account holders against the business failure of their bank.

deposition written testimony which can be used as evidence in court.

depositor one who deposits money in an account with a depositary.

depot storehouse or warehouse; hub of a transport operation where vehicles are parked and maintained when not in use.

depreciated cost cost less depreciation.

depreciation gradual decline in the value of business assets over their operating life, through wear and tear or obsolescence.

depreciation charges money which can be written off in accounts to reflect the actual effects of depreciation, thus reducing the book value of assets.

depressed area region where economic performance is lower, and unemployment higher, than the national average.

depression severe economic recession characterized by high unemployment, low purchasing power and high rates of business failure.

deprival value cost incurred should the company lose the use of an asset.

depth interview unstructured interview technique used in market research, in which the respondent is encouraged to give information and opinions on a wide range of subjects.

deregulation removal of legal and other restrictions on trade in a particular market, with the aim of creating a free market in that sector.

derivatives financial instruments for managing interest rate and exchange rate exposure.

derived demand *see* indirect demand.

descriptive billing billing system which details the goods purchased, rather than supplying copies of original invoices.

descriptive research research which sets out to describe the present state of the subject under investigation.

design plan, blueprint or specification for a good, service, or procedure.

design engineering use of engineering techniques in design; alternatively, the design of engineering systems.

design factor market research term, indicates the reliability of a sample used for surveys.

design for assembly (DFA) design technique which attempts to simplify products, especially by reducing the number of parts required.

design for manufacture (DFM) design system where the need to move to early manufacture is a key goal.

design management the employment and application by managers of design techniques to products and processes.

design parameters the outline of a particular design, within which individual functional requirements are planned and added.

desire 1 *see* customer demand; 2 want.

desk fixed point where managerial or clerical work is carried out; *see also* workstation.

desk audit *see* work audit.

de-skilling reduction in the skill levels required to perform a job, usually accompanied by a reduction in pay.

desk research research derived from previously published or collected information; as opposed to fieldwork.

desktop publishing (DTP) computer software which enables typesetting and document layout to be handled as a single process.

determinant attributes product characteristics which influence consumer behaviour and awareness.

determinism theory that human action is not entirely free and is in part determined by other forces.

deterrence discouragement or hindrance.

devaluation reduction in the official value of a currency relative to other currencies.

developed countries countries with advanced industrial or post-industrial economies.

developing countries countries whose economies have not yet reached full industrialization.

development 1 improvement or enhancement; **2** aid offered to developing countries.

development loan loan made for the development of unimproved property or infrastructure building.

development management 1 branch of management associated with developing new products, processes, etc.; **2** alternatively, management of development projects in the Third World.

deviance behaviour which departs from the norm, often associated with criminal behaviour.

deviation departure from a previously set standard; measure of the number of items in a set which depart from the average, or the extent to which they depart.

DFA *see* design for assembly.

DFM *see* design for manufacture.

diagnosis descriptive analysis of a situation or problem.

diagnostic ability ability to conduct diagnosis; ability to perceive and analyse situations and relationships.

diagnostic model model for corporate change which stresses understanding and changing corporate systems and networks.

diagnostic program computer program that analyses other programs, looking for faults or bugs.

diagnostic routine *see* diagnostic program.

diagnostic system expert systems for diagnosis of equipment problems and, usually, the correction of such problems.

diagonal communication communication flows across an organization between departments or people.

diagonal expansion expansion into new product areas involving products that can be produced using existing facilities.

dialectical theory the concept that any solution to a problem will create a situation where fresh problems will evolve.

diary schedule of meetings and appointments kept by a manager or assistant.

diary method marketing research technique determining frequency of purchases, where sample households keep a daily log of purchases which are then analysed by the researchers.

dichotomous question question which can only be answered by one of two possible answers (such as 'yes' or 'no').

dies non holiday, or day on which business is not normally conducted.

differential specific difference between factors or objects; difference between levels of pay for different types or grades of employee.

differential advantage marketing advantages enjoyed by a firm over its competitors; *see also* competitive advantage.

differential cost cost difference between the present price and the price that may be offered in the future.

differential costing *see* marginal costing.

differential piece work bonus pay system where bonuses increase at a rate less than the rate of increase in performance or output.

differential sample research sample biased towards a particular target group, as opposed to random sampling.

differentiated marketing **1** offering the same product to several different market segments with a different marketing strategy for each; **2** alternatively, marketing different products to different segments at the same time.

differentiated product product with features that distinguish it from competitor products in the minds of customers.

differentiated service service with features that distinguish it from competing services in the minds of customers.

differentiation the process of developing particular attributes which set a product, service, brand or organization apart from its competitors, while at the same time presenting a positive image to customers.

diff swap form of hedging contract used to lay off interest rates.

diffusion **1** spreading out; **2** widespread distribution through an organization or society.

diffusion index statistical technique for measuring the extent of diffusion.

diffusion theory **1** in economics, theory that wealth eventually spreads to all parts of the population; **2** also, that tax income raised by governments eventually finds its way back into the pockets of the people.

digested securities securities held as long-term investments.

digital refers to the processing or storage of data using binary notation.

dilution weakening or reducing impact; the reduction in the power of individuals' shareholdings by the conversion of securities or the issue of new share capital.

diminishing marginal utility point beyond which additional consumption produces ever-diminishing rates of marginal utility.

diminishing returns point beyond which additional labour or capital inputs produce ever-diminishing rates of increase in output.

direct advertising printed advertising in the form of leaflets and brochures which is posted or given by hand to potential customers.

direct agent *see* agent, direct.

direct cost any cost which can be directly attributed to the production of a good or service; as opposed to indirect costs.

direct costing *see* standard costing system.

direct debit system whereby an account holder instructs the bank to debit his or her account and pay the money directly to another party.

direct deposit (of payroll) system where employees' wages are deposited directly into their bank accounts, usually electronically.

direct expense *see* direct cost.

direct finance raising capital by means other than issuing shares.

direct financial compensation wages and other forms of remuneration paid to employees; as opposed to fringe benefits.

direct foreign investment investments by companies in subsidiaries or joint ventures in other countries.

direct index performance appraisal technique which measures criteria such as personal productivity, absenteeism and so on, plotting these against an index of performance.

direct investment *see* direct foreign investment.

directional policy matrix graphic depiction of strategic options used in corporate planning.

directive 1 order; **2** communication setting out rules and regulations.

direct labour workforce directly involved in production and marketing, as opposed to indirect labour.

direct labour hours (DLH) total hours spent on direct labour.

direct liability any obligation owed by a debtor to another party; as opposed to indirect liability.

direct mail sending advertising material through the post directly to customers or prospective customers; *see also* direct advertising.

direct marketing marketing involving direct contact between the marketer or salesperson and the customer, which aims to build relationships that will lead to sales.

direct numerical control computer numerical control where a single computer controls more than one machine or operation.

director 1 member of a board of directors; **2** chief executive of a foundation or institution.

direct overhead expenses incurred while producing and selling a product or service; *see also* direct cost.

direct profit sum remaining after direct costs are deducted from sales revenue.

direct response promotion sales promotions that aim to elicit a response from customers, in order to collect information or make direct sales.

direct sales sales by the manufacturer direct to the customer, without use of intermediaries.

direct selling term for a manufacturer selling goods and services directly to customers, either by telephone or through a sales force calling directly on customers.

direct tax income tax or wealth tax.

dirty float situation where monetary authorities intervene to control the extent of exchange rate fluctuations, though not actually freezing exchange rates.

disability congenital condition or accident with permanent effects which impairs a person's ability to work.

disability income money paid to a person with disabilities to compensate them for their loss of earning power.

disablement incapacitating injury or damage suffered as a result of an accident.

disaster **1** sudden accident of great magnitude, usually with very severe consequences for those caught up in the event; **2** for business, any incident which threatens the lives of employees or widespread damage to operations.

disaster management management techniques and skills required to deal with disasters or large-scale accidents.

disbursement payment of cash or money to another party.

discharge **1** to settle a contract or fulfil obligations, or to be released from a contract; **2** to terminate an employee's contract; *see also* dismissal; fire.

discharge of contract occurs when all conditions of a contract have been fulfilled.

disciplinary layoff temporary suspension of an employee without pay as a disciplinary measure.

disciplinary takeover takeover which occurs in response to poor company performance, and which may be supported by many shareholders.

discipline rules and regulations, and their enforcement.

disclaimer notice that the disclaiming party refuses to accept liability in certain specified conditions.

disclosure **1** requirement that financial and other information about a company should be made public (the extent and timing of the publication varies between jurisdictions and types of company); **2** also, the exchange of financial and other information between parties contemplating a joint venture or merger.

disclosures: information which is required to be presented in financial statements.

discontent factors factors leading to discontent or dissatisfaction in the workplace.

discontinuity interruption or break in a series.

discotetic state the confusion and uncertainty which develops in companies which are subject to continuous change and reorganization to no apparent purpose or result.

discount **1** reduction in price to below normal levels; **2** in foreign exchange, a currency which is valued at a lower level than another is said to be at a discount to the latter; **3** in securities trading, to buy or sell a security after the value of dividends or other interest has been discounted from the par value.

discounted cash flow accounting and budgeting technique in which expected future cash flow is discounted so as to reflect the change in value of money over time, in order to establish net present value.

discounted payback *see* payback.

discounted present value comparison of discounted cash flow with the overall level of investment required in a project.

discounted rate of return comparison of discounted cash flow with the initial cost of investment in a project.

discount house 1 retail outlet selling goods at a discount; **2** in the UK, a financial institution which buys promissory notes at a discount and then holds them until they mature or sells them on.

discounting 1 generally, to lower or reduce a price for whatever reason; *see* discount; **2** also, to set aside or leave out of consideration.

discount market the buying and selling of discounted securities by discount houses.

discount period period of time between the date of issue and the date of maturity of a security.

discount rate 1 amount or level of discount; **2** in some countries, the rate of interest charged by the central bank to other banks; *see* bank rate.

discount store *see* discount house.

discovery period 1 period before a contract comes into force, during which either side may gather information to satisfy themselves that the facts have been represented correctly; **2** time allowed for the discovery process to take place.

discretion freedom allowed to individual managers and employees to use their own judgement and make decisions.

discretionary account account where a customer gives permission to a broker or agent to buy and sell freely using that account, remaining only within the limits of that account.

discretionary costs fixed costs incurred as a result of high-level management decisions, usually incurred as a result of the appropriations of acquisitions.

discretionary reserves *see* reserves, discretionary.

discriminant function analysis research technique used in surveys which enables all of an individual's responses to be treated as a set rather than as individual points of data.

discrimination 1 ability to tell one item from another; favouring of one thing or person over another; **2** prejudicial and often illegal employment practices favouring people of one gender or ethnic background over another.

discrimination test market research technique for testing customers' abilities to discriminate between products.

discriminatory pricing sale of a product in two or more places and/or to two or more customer segments at different prices; in addition, these prices reflect the nature of the market, not the costs involved in distributing or selling the goods.

diseconomies of scale proportional increase in costs as businesses reach a certain size, counteracting economies of scale.

disempowerment 1 withdrawal or removal of empowerment; **2** placing people in a situation where they no longer have a say in what is happening to them.

disequilibrium period of flux and change, particularly used of markets where prices have yet to find the market level.

disequilibrium theory economic theory that business cycles are the result of in-built economic factors leading to disequilibrium.

disinflation economic downturn, usually the result of a deliberate government policy to contain or reduce prices.

disinvestment reduction in investment.

disk or magnetic disk, a common form for bulk storage of data in computers, alternative spelling disc; *see also* hard disk; floppy disk.

diskette *see* floppy disk.

dismissal the termination of a contract of employment, usually as a disciplinary measure.

dispatch to ship or forward goods to the customer, or to send materials between factories.

dispatcher person responsible for the dispatch of goods and materials.

dispersion statistical measure of the extent to which individual data points deviate from the average or mean; *see also* standard deviation.

displaced equipment *see* displaced plant.

displaced plant plant made obsolete or taken out of commission earlier than expected.

displacement 1 goods or people which are removed from their accustomed place; **2** the act of superseding products, plant, jobs and so on which are out of date; **3** standard measure of the capacity of a ship.

display advertisement advertisement placed in a newspaper, magazine or other printed medium, designed to attract the maximum level of attention.

disposable *see* consumer disposable.

disposable income income after tax, that which a person has available to spend.

disposal the sale or retirement of an asset.

dispute *see* industrial dispute.

dispute resolution the ending of an industrial dispute, usually by finding a compromise to which both parties can agree.

disputes procedure dispute resolution procedures laid down and agreed to by employers and employees or their trade unions.

disqualification judgement that a person is no longer qualified to hold a certain position, having previously demonstrated malpractice or dishonesty.

dissatisfaction 1 marketing term for when customers are unhappy with a product or service, usually because it has not provided the benefits they expected when making the original purchase; **2** also, condition in the workplace where workers are not satisfied and are poorly motivated.

dissatisfiers factors identified by Frederick Herzberg which lead to dissatisfaction in the workplace.

dissaving seldom-used term for excess of spending over income.

dissemination the passing on of information and knowledge, typically involving the sharing of such with a wide circle or group of people.

disseminator managerial role identified by Mintzberg, where the manager is responsible for disseminating information to subordinates and colleagues.

dissociative groups in marketing research, a type of reference group composed of individuals of many different types and behaviours.

dissolution termination of an agreement by mutual consent; ending of a partnership or other business association; break-up of a corporation and ending of its business activities.

distance learning training and education programmes where instructors and learner are not in personal contact, but conduct lessons using videos, computer links, and so on.

distancing term for the subcontracting of work formerly done within the company to external contractors.

distinctive competences the important competences on which a firm relies to do business and achieve competitive advantage.

distress damage or reduction in value; distressed goods are those which can no longer be sold at the usual price and are therefore offered at a substantial discount.

distributed computing technology general term for computer networks that allow system components and functions to be distributed geographically.

distributed data processing data processing over a network, using data held or retrieved from several physical locations.

distributed decision making decision making which has been devolved or farmed out to several people or parts of the organization; usually accompanies decentralization.

distributed system computer system including several computers connected by a network and sharing tasks; more generally referred to as a network.

distribution process of physically moving goods from the manufacturer to the end consumer, often using intermediaries such as agents and wholesalers; the division of profits among shareholders; *see also* dividend.

distribution centre depot or warehouse where goods are temporarily stored and transferred to vehicles for shipment.

distribution chain the organizations that transport, distribute and store goods as they pass from the manufacturer to the final customer, and the links between them; *see also* channel of distribution.

distribution channel *see* channel of distribution.

distribution cost cost of transportation and/or cost of selling goods to a particular market.

distribution cost analysis breakdown of direct and indirect costs incurred as part of distribution costs.

distribution mix combination of distribution channels used to reach a particular market or markets.

distribution planning planning and preparing programmes for efficient and effective distribution of goods from producer to market.

distribution requirements planning (DRP) distribution planning function which identifies requirements at the point of plan and then devises routes down which products will travel to those points.

distribution resource planning distribution planning function which sets out the resources required to achieve efficient distribution.

distributive leadership delegation or sharing of leadership roles; *see also* democratic management.

distributive trades generic term including both retailing and wholesaling businesses.

distributor middleman in the channel of distribution, typically a wholesaler or agent.

disturbance disruption or unexpected alteration in a flow or pattern; used in economics and also to describe some industrial disputes.

divergence going in different directions; used to describe situations where strategies, policies or behaviours seem to be opposed to one another.

diversification developing activities in several business areas, to avoid overdependence on one market or type of investment; often seen as a means of laying off risk in a primary market or investment type.

diversity the presence of different kinds of goods, people from different backgrounds, etc. in a single place or milieu; as opposed to uniformity.

divest to remove a vested interest; to sell or dispose of an investment or asset.

divest and exit strategy strategic option to sell an asset or close down a product line in order to exit a market where business is no longer profitable.

divestment the act of divesting a business of unwanted assets.

dividend 1 payment, a portion of a firm's profit, that the firm pays to its shareholders; the portion of this profit received by each shareholder; **2** more generally, a proportion of a return on investment; *see also* yield.

dividend cover *see* earnings–dividend ratio

dividend payout ratio ratio of dividends per share to earnings per share.

dividend policy company policy with relation to the calculation and payment of dividends.

dividend rate the total annual dividend per share.

dividends in arrears dividends owed but not paid; usually refers to dividends that have been deferred by certain classes of preferred shareholders.

dividends per share *see* dividend yield.

dividend yield actual dividend received per share, usually on a quarterly basis.

division of labour the breaking down of operations into individual tasks, and the assigning of a specialized job to carry out each task.

divisionalization creation of self-managing units within an organization, and the devolvement of much responsibility on to the heads of these.

DIY *see* do-it-yourself.

DLH *see* direct labour hours.

document written statement, on paper or in an electronic medium, setting forth certain facts or views, containing data, information or knowledge.

documentation documents required by law and custom to accompany a transaction, including deeds of title, manifests, contracts and so on.

document management technology general term for computer-based programs for the generation, dissemination and storage of documents.

dock 1 facility for loading and unloading ships; **2** also colloquially, a deduction from basic wages.

dog colloquial term for a business activity which is losing money and urgently requires to be either revamped or closed down.

do-it-yourself (DIY) retail sector specializing in providing tools and materials for private home improvement projects.

dollar area refers to countries whose currency is pegged to the US dollar.

domain knowledge knowledge of a particular domain or field which is encoded into an expert system.

domestic assets assets held within the home country.

domestic exports sale and shipment of goods to another region within the country of origin, outside the firm's local market.

domicile country in which a corporation establishes its head office; the corporation is then subject to local tax rates and must abide by local business law.

dominant coalition executives responsible for decision making at the highest level.

donor market in not-for-profit marketing, the market where fundraisers attempt to raise funds for investment in goods and services to clients; *see also* fundraising.

door-to-door selling method whereby the salesperson goes from house-to-house and attempts to sell to customers in their own homes.

dormant account *see* inactive account.

dormant partner partner who is not active in managing the business and whose identity is not widely known.

DOS acronym for disk operating system; basic operating system used by computers to manage disks, including storage and retrieval operations.

double-bind logic logical principle that one should act as if messages are consistent, unambiguous and not open to discussion.

double counting in bookkeeping, the practice of counting every sum twice; *see* double-entry bookkeeping.

double employment holding of two jobs by one person.

double entry method of entering items in ledgers as part of the process of double-entry bookkeeping.

double-entry bookkeeping standard bookkeeping practice in which transactions are entered as a debt in one account and a credit in another; thus the totals of debt and credit match exactly.

double indemnity life insurance policy provision whereby double the normal benefit is paid out if the insured dies in an accident.

double insurance insurance which insures against the same risk twice.

double-loop learning theory developed by Chris Argyris, whereby feedback not only alters processes but questions the basis of underlying assumptions.

double pricing the setting of a second price on a product, undercutting the original, as a special offer.

double taxation occurs when the same income or profits are taxed twice, usually because they are taxable in two different countries.

double time wages paid at twice the usual rate, usually as compensation for working overtime.

downgrading demotion or reduction in job grade, usually accompanied by a decrease in pay.

downpayment first instalment on the purchase price, made at the time of purchase.

downsizing reduction in the size of a workforce.

downstairs merger merger whereby a parent corporation becomes a subsidiary.

downstream business activity at a lower level of the organization, or further down the production/distribution process.

downstream integration *see* forward integration.

downtime period of enforced idleness, when plant and workers are not able to produce.

downtime log record kept of the length of time that a given piece of equipment is out of production or off line.

down tools colloquial term for a work stoppage as part of an industrial dispute.

downward communication communication flows which run from the upper levels of an organization to the lower.

Dragon economies developing countries of East Asia, whose economies are (or were) characterized by rapid industrialization and very high growth rates.

drawback repayment of import tariffs when goods are re-exported.

drawee any party named on a bill, cheque or note as being the recipient of funds drawn from an account.

drawer any signatory to a bill, cheque or note drawing funds from an account to pay another.

drawing the removal of money from an account, usually to make a payment to another.

drawing account account used to make cash payments to cover expenses or as advances on salary.

drive motivation or pressure.

driver factor helping to create or direct a trend.

drive to maturity period period of economic growth following take-off and preceding maturity.

dropout person undertaking a training course who leaves before the course is finished.

drop shipment goods which are shipped directly from the manufacturer to the retailer.

drop shipper wholesaler who arranges delivery direct from manufacturer to retailer, without taking possession of the product.

DRP *see* distribution requirements planning.

drug testing practice in some companies of randomly testing employees for illegal drug use.

DTP *see* desktop publishing.

dual capacity the ability to carry out two functions simultaneously; in stock markets, a dual capacity firm is one which can function as both stock-broker and stock jobber.

dual-career couples married or cohabiting couples where both partners are engaged in separate businesses or professions.

dual distribution selling a product through two or more separate channels of distribution.

dual-income household household or family group where two or more members are engaged in paid work.

dual supervision situation where control and management functions are divided between two managers; employees may be required to report to both.

due owing or required.

due care reasonable attention or conduct required to avoid mishaps.

due date date on which repayment of a loan or credit is required.

due diligence the auditing or inspection of a company's financial and other records before purchasing that company, in some cases, entering into a merger or joint venture.

due process the processes of legal action and of bringing a case before a court.

dues membership fees paid by employees to their trade union.

dummy activity technique in critical path planning and network analysis for events related to but not directly connected to the network.

dummy invoice substitute or temporary replacement invoice.

dump bin in retailing, a special display unit containing reduced-price or special offer goods.

dumping offering large blocks of product on a market at low prices, usually with the aim of undercutting competition; used particularly by exporters in an effort to undercut home market goods.

dun invoice or request for payment of a debt.

Dunscore scoring system developed by Dun and Bradstreet to measure the position of industries over time.

duopoly market sector dominated by two producers selling on equal terms.

duopsony market sector in which there are only two buyers.

durability measure of how long a good or product can be expected to last, given normal use.

durable *see* consumer durable.

duress force; often refers to the forced seizure of goods for repayment of debt.

Dutch auction auction where prices are gradually lowered from the starting price until a sale is made.

'Dutch disease' in commodities trading, the situation where a sudden boom in exports of one commodity may have a negative impact on other sectors of the economy.

duties the responsibilities of a manager or employer towards the firm and his or her colleagues, superiors and subordinates.

duty tax, particularly on imports.

duty drawback tariff concessions or repayment on goods imported for the sole purpose of re-export.

duty free description of goods exempt from customs duty.

dyadic interaction any interchange which involves only two people or organizations.

dynamic economy an economy which is growing and expanding quickly.

dynamic programming **1** decision-making techniques which are used in situations where a number of decisions are required in rapid succession; **2** the breaking of one problem into a number of related smaller ones.

dynamic theory of profit theory developed by Frank Hyneman Knight, describing how entrepreneurs are rewarded for their assumption of risk.

dynamism **1** energy; **2** motivation to change and grow.

dysfunction abnormal function; *see also* malfunction.

dysfunctional behaviour behaviour which is abnormal or outside accepted limits.

E

each way refers to the double commission earned by a broker when acting for both buyer and seller.

EAF *see* environmental analysis framework.

early retirement retirement prior to reaching the mandatory retirement age.

early retirement benefits benefits received on early retirement, usually consisting of a reduced pension but sometimes with a corresponding lump sum.

earned income income derived from sales, fees, wages or annuities.

earnest money money paid out at the time of the signing of a contract as a sign of good faith, and to be kept by the other party if the payer fails to uphold obligations.

earning power the potential wage earnings of an individual over the course of his or her working life.

earnings 1 wages or salary; 2 company profits available for distribution of dividends.

earnings–dividend ratio ratio of dividends declared to total profits declared, sometimes also referred to as dividend cover.

earnings drift or wage drift, the marginal increase in wage rates above the rate of inflation.

earnings per share (EPS) total sum available for dividends divided by number of ordinary shares in circulation; *see also* yield.

earnings potential potential ability of a project or operation to generate cash flow and profits.

earnings-related benefit benefit which is directly linked to the level of the beneficiary's former earnings.

earnings report statement of earnings or losses.

earnings yield ratio of post-tax earnings per share to market price of the share; *see also* price-earnings ratio.

earn-out in acquisitions, agreement whereby the shareholders of the firm being acquired receive compensation at a later date, contingent on the acquiring firm's reaching certain financial targets.

e-cash *see* electronic cash.

ecofactory manufacturing plant or factory based on the use of environmentally friendly technologies and/or processes.

ecological theory application of concepts derived from ecology or biology to organizational structure or populations.

ecology scientific theory of interaction of organisms in an environment, sometimes applied to human interaction as well.

e-commerce *see* electronic commerce.

econometric forecasting economic forecasts based on data derived from econometrics.

econometric models economic models summarizing data derived from econometrics.

econometrics 1 application of mathematics to economics; **2** the measuring of economic data; **3** branch of economics which is concerned with the application of mathematical and statistical methods to establish relationships (if any) between economic variables.

economic 1 singular of economics, used of anything having to do with economic or business activity; **2** also, low cost or representing value for money.

economic activity general term for all manufacturing, trade and purchasing carried out by both private and public sectors; all factors involving labour or capital are usually included.

economic actors person or organization undertaking any form of economic activity.

economic agents *see* economic actors.

economic analysis measurement and analysis of economic activity over a given period.

Economic and Monetary Union (EMU) the European Union's programme of combined customs, economic and monetary union.

economic batch determination production planning process whereby the most economic or cost-effective batch size for a job is determined.

economic behaviour the behaviour exhibited by economic actors during economic activity.

economic climate summary of the overall conditions for economic activity, including general confidence, perceptions of risk, money supply, government policy and so on.

economic decline decreasing levels of economic activity.

economic democracy situation where workers own some or all of the capital of the company that employs them.

economic depreciation *see* depreciation.

economic depression *see* slump.

economic development *see* economic growth.

economic efficiency distribution of economic resources that improves the welfare of some while not reducing the welfare of any; *see also* Pareto optimality.

economic environment *see* economic climate.

economic exposure foreign exchange risk associated with doing business in other countries.

economic forecasting science of predicting future economic trends and developments.

economic goods items produced from scarce resources.

economic growth in a national economy, expansion of output and increasing income.

economic growth rate rate at which the national economy grows in a given year, usually expressed as a percentage increase over and above the previous year's totals.

economic indicator classification of economic information for use in economic analysis and forecasting; indicators typically express movement in terms of output, income and other economic activity.

economic integration the complete merging of the economies of two or more countries, including customs, economic and monetary union and the free flow of goods and people across borders.

economic life time period during which an asset or investment can expect to earn a profit.

economic lot size (ELS) for ordering or stock control, the lot size with the lowest associated storage and distribution costs per unit, or with the lowest·overall costs.

economic man now largely obsolete theory, that financial incentives and maximization of profit are the primary motivators for human behaviour.

economic management the management and control of the economy practised by government and related institutions such as central banks.

economic manufacturing quantity (EMQ) in production planning, the most economic or cost-effective size for a production run, with the lowest costs per unit; *see also* economic batch determination; minimum manufacturing quantity.

economic order quantity (EOQ) *see* economic lot size.

economic performance the summary of economic activity over a given time period.

economic policy policies laid down by governments for economic management, concerning such issues as free trade, controlling inflation, growth targets and so on; *see also* fiscal policy; monetary policy.

economic profit *see* pure profit.

economic recovery increasing levels of economic activity following a period of decline.

economic rents the amount earned above the minimum necessary to make an investment attractive to investors.

economics the study of economic and business activity, including the manufacture, distribution, purchase and consumption of goods and services.

economic systems the ways in which national economies are organized, usually as some variant of a free market or centrally planned economy.

economic theory theoretical conceptualizations of how economies function.

economic trends overall changes, upwards or downwards, in economic growth and activity, usually as evidenced by economic indicators.

economic union 1 act of harmonizing the economies of two or more countries; **2** the political framework for economic integration.

economic value value which attaches to an item as a reflection of its utility and scarcity; not always synonymous with either price or cost.

economic zones designated regions where governments wish to encourage investment and other economic activity.

economies of scale the phenomenon whereby increasing the overall level of output leads to decreasing production costs per unit.

economies of scope the increase in cost levels incurred as the company diversifies its product or service range.

economizing reducing costs, choosing the cheapest or most cost-effective alternative input or product; to use resources sparingly.

economy general term for the total of business and economic activity in a country; more specifically, the careful use of resources; *see also* economizing.

ecosystems contraction of 'ecological systems'; integrated natural systems and hierarchies of biological organisms, sometimes mimicked by organizations.

ECU *see* European Currency Unit.

EDI *see* electronic data interchange.

E-direct distribution direct distribution using electronic ordering systems.

EDP *see* electronic data processing.

education the process of learning; the development of new knowledge, skills and competences, usually through broad-based and formal programmes.

education and training general term for management development encompassing both broad-based education programmes and more focused training programmes.

education technology technological aids used to deliver education and training programmes, including computer programs and communications technology.

effective communication communication where the intended message of the sender is clearly understood by the receiver.

effective date 1 the date on which a contract or provision takes effect; 2 starting date.

effective debt total debt owed by a business or individual.

effective gross income total income which can be generated by a company or a project.

effective interest rate the actual rate of interest on a loan or debt once all considerations have been taken into account.

effectiveness fitness for purpose; the measure of whether a thing, person, product or programme fulfils its stated purpose and meets the needs of those affected by it.

efficiency the maximization of utility; the achievement of the best possible result from the lowest possible input.

efficiency expert specialist who analyses the efficiency of operations and advises on how they could be improved.

efficiency ratio *see* activity ratio.

efficient market hypothesis in finance theory, the concept that securities prices reflect all available information and change instantaneously to reflect new information; *see also* perfect market.

effort attempt or exertion towards a specific goal.

EFTA *see* European Free Trade Area.

EFTPOS *see* electronic funds transfer at point of sale.

EFTS *see* electronic funds transfer system.

ego 1 self-esteem; **2** aspect of consciousness which drives people to seek approval from others.

egoistic needs needs for satisfaction other than monetary reward; examples include self-respect, the respect of others, personal achievement and fulfilment of personal goals.

elastic demand situation where a very small change in the sale price of a product or service will have a strong effect on demand; as opposed to inelastic demand.

elasticity general term for the impact which price changes have on volume flows, usually in terms of the positive or negative impact on demand; *see* demand elasticity; in banking, the ability of a bank to meet demands for credit and cash.

elasticity of demand *see* demand elasticity.

elasticity theory theoretical conceptualizations of demand elasticity.

elastic supply situation where a very small change in the sale price of a product or service will have a strong effect on supply.

eclectic paradigm theory developed by J. H. Dunning to explain differing patterns in foreign direct investment.

election procedure for choosing representatives of a group by ballot of that group; used, for example, to elect members to a board of directors or to elect union representatives.

electronic assembly assembly of electronic products into finished goods.

electronic banking conducting banking transactions through computer networks, using facilities such as automated teller machines.

electronic cash money which has no physical existence but which circulates in electronic form on the Internet.

electronic commerce business which is transacted entirely using the Internet or other electronic media, with no physical contact between parties.

electronic communication communication by electronic means, such as fax, e-mail and so on.

electronic data interchange (EDI) computer networks encompassing manufacturers, suppliers and/or customers, allowing near-instantaneous communication between all parties.

electronic data processing (EDP) computerized data processing systems which allow the processing of very large amounts of data at very high speed.

electronic funds transfer at point of sale (EFTPOS) electronic purchasing system using a smart card which debits the purchaser's bank account at the point of sale; no cash or cheques change hands.

electronic funds transfer system (EFTS) general term for electronic systems that handle fund transfers between bank accounts.

electronic mail *see* e-mail.

electronic manufacturing strategy general term for a manufacturing strategy which uses computerized processes and communications to achieve short process times and higher quality.

electronic office office environment which is fully equipped with information and communications technology; *see also* virtual office.

electronic point of sale (EPOS) any point of sale capable of handling transactions and storing data electronically; data captured by EPOS transactions is an important source for market research.

electronic publishing publishing using electronic media such as CD-ROMs or on the Internet.

electronics 1 technology based on the movement of electrons; **2** miniaturized systems that form the basis for much of modern technology.

electronic shopping choosing and ordering goods using electronic media, usually the Internet.

eligible bills bills of exchange with early maturity dates, used as a means of raising short-term capital during a credit squeeze.

eligible investment any investment which is perceived by investors as being a good risk and providing a suitable level of income.

elites, international *see* business elites.

elitism the practice of promoting and encouraging excellence in a small percentage of the population.

ELS *see* economic lot size.

e-mail or electronic mail, the sending of messages and documents between computers using a modem which connects to either an internal network or the Internet.

embargo 1 restriction or prohibition; **2** government directive which restricts or prohibits trade with another country for political reasons; **3** in public relations, a prohibition on quoting a document or press release before a certain time.

embezzlement theft of property or money, where the owner had previously entrusted the same property or money to the embezzler.

emergency maintenance maintenance work which must be carried out due to an unexpected fault, or to prevent machine failure.

emergent strategy strategy which emerges gradually rather than being deliberately planned.

emerging businesses businesses which have been started and are now growing and establishing their market condition.

EMIP see equivalent mean investment period.

emissions gases or other substances which are byproducts of manufacturing processes and are released into the environment at large; gases and heat from internal combustion engines which enter the atmosphere; *see also* pollution.

emolument payment or financial reward for employment or services.

empire building acquisition by an individual over resources and/or subordinates that increase his or her power in the organization.

empiricism studies or analysis based on experience, observation or experiment.

employ to use, or use the services of.

employable 1 a person or capital good which can be employed for a particular purpose; **2** person who is able to work.

employee someone who works for and draws a wage from a company; technically, refers to all who work for the firm, but often used to describe the lower, non-managerial ranks.

employee association organization of workers, less formal and usually smaller than a trade union.

employee behaviour attitudes and actions of employees towards their work and their employer.

employee benefits rewards for work in addition to wages, including pensions, insurance and other benefits; also known as fringe benefits.

employee development general term for training and education to enhance employee skills and competences, and to assist in personal development.

employee deviance employee behaviour which falls outside expected or tolerated behaviour; can include criminal behaviour.

employee diversity extent to which a company's workforce represents people of different backgrounds, ethnic groups and so on.

employee ownership type of business where part or all of the capital is held by employees, who have a corresponding say in the management of the business.

employee relations personnel management function concerned with ensuring communication and motivation among employees, and with dealing with any potential disputes.

employee share option plan (ESOP) scheme by which a specific number of issued shares are allotted to employees of the firm, should they desire to purchase them.

employee stock ownership plan *see* employee share option plan.

employer anyone or any organization employing others for work.

employer association association of employers concerned primarily with employment and industrial relations.

employer organization *see* employer association.

employment being employed; more generally, the overall level of employment, reflecting the number of people employed proportional to the number available for employment.

employment agency organization whose purpose is to supply firms with potential employees.

employment costs total of direct remuneration to employees plus fringe benefits whose costs must be met by employees.

employment exchange office where job vacancies are advertised directly to the employed.

employment subsidy paid by government to employers to stimulate employment, in the form of either a stock subsidy or a flow subsidy; *see also* job subsidy.

employment training training programmes aimed at the long-term unemployed or those new to the workforce, helping them to become more suitable for employment.

emporium major trade centre.

empowerment the granting to employees and subordinates greater discretionary freedom to make decisions and take responsibility for their own work.

EMQ *see* economic manufacturing quantity.

EMTN *see* Euro-medium-term-note.

emulative product new product which mimics many of the features of existing products.

EMU *see* Economic and Monetary Union.

enactment carrying out or implementation; making something valid by decree.

encapsulation concept whereby objects are said to encapsulate the data they contain.

encounter group group training method used in some forms of psychological counselling.

encroachment infringement on another's property.

encumbrance **1** hindrance; **2** charges attaching to goods which much be paid for before delivery.

endogenous growth growth from within, internal growth.

endorsee person to whom an order which has been endorsed and is now payable.

endorsement amendment to a contract; signature on a document approving a change in a contract, or approving transfer of ownership to another party.

endorser person whose signature on a document serves as an endorsement.

endowment **1** payment of a fixed sum; **2** gift to a foundation or institution.

endowment assurance assurance policy paying out a set sum on a fixed date at the expiration of the policy.

end price support policy of the Common Agricultural Policy of the European Union, guaranteeing minimum prices of certain commodities.

energy power, usually from either electricity or direct from fossil fuels, required to work machinery.

energy economics the economics of energy generation and distribution.

Engel's Law the lower the income of a household, the greater the proportion of that income will be spent on food.

engineering **1** the control and use of power, and the design of systems for doing so; **2** the design, control and management of machines or systems.

engineering query note document used to resolve production difficulties when there are variances between manufacturing and design.

engineering risk definition of risk in terms of the probability of an adverse event.

engineers personnel skilled in engineering.

enterprise general term for a business or business activity; any activity where there is a level or risk but also the potential for reward.

enterprise agency local government agency supported by business, established to help businesses grow and to create jobs.

enterprise trust trust set up to promote local business and job creation; *see also* enterprise agency.

enterprise union in Japan, unions recruited from the employees of a single company only.

enterprise zone area where government attempts to encourage business by offering special concessions to encourage industrial and commercial activity; in the Far East, these are sometimes known as special economic zones.

entity concept in consolidated accounting, definition of an entity as all the assets and liabilities of a company and its subsidiaries.

entity principle in financial accounting, the definition of the entity being reported on; *see also* entity concept.

entity-relationship diagram graphic depiction of the relationship between various elements of a system, used in systems analysis and design.

entrainment phenomenon whereby firms' performance is guided and shaped by domestic market characteristics.

entrepôt 1 depot or storage centre; **2** centre for international trade.

entrepreneur person who initiates and manages creative business activities, either on his or her own account or inside a larger organization.

entrepreneurial behaviour managerial behaviour which is characterized by a willingness to take risks, the ability to recognize and take advantage of opportunities and a proactive approach to the environment.

entrepreneurial strategies strategic options which are characteristic of entrepreneurial behaviour.

entrepreneurship entrepreneurial actions and behaviour.

entropy equation theory developed by C. E. Shannon to explain links between energy and information.

entry 1 item or line in an account book or ledger; **2** in marketing, 'entry into new markets' means developing new markets either geographically or in terms of market sectors.

entry strategies marketing strategies for entry into new markets.

environment background or circumstances in which a firm operates, including local culture, economic conditions and so on; often used to mean the natural environment, or biosphere.

environmental analysis framework (EAF) analytical tool which helps to identify and categorize factors in the business environment.

environmental concerns fears or apprehensions by society at large by the damage being done by pollution and development to the environment or biospheres.

environmental economics the study by economists of the relationships between economic activity and the natural environment or biosphere.

environmental management management techniques which take into account the effects of a firm's operations on the natural environment, focusing on issues such as ecological sensitivity, green accounting and sustainability.

environmental reporting formal reporting by companies of the impacts of their operations on the natural environment.

environmental uncertainty the level of complexity and uncertainty to be found in a firm's operating environment.

environment analysis scanning and analysis of the current environment and conditions within which business is conducted.

environment audits list of environmental factors affecting the way a firm operates.

environment change changing environmental conditions which require that the firm adjust its strategic and competitive response, or even realign its goals.

environment concern *see* environmental concerns.

environment conditions the competitive, regulatory and social conditions in which a firm conducts its business.

environment design in design management, the techniques involved in designing the physical environment in which work is carried out, the workplace.

environment dynamics the nature and rate of change in a given environment.

environment, ecological the natural environment, or biosphere.

environment, economic *see* economic climate.

environment management *see* environmental management.

environment management systems management systems used in environmental management, which generate data used in environmental reporting.

environment scanning the process of researching a firm's operating environment to find new opportunities, technologies, markets, etc. that can be turned to technological advantage.

environment valuation contingent valuation techniques used to determine the value people place on the natural environment.

envy ratio ratio of number of shares available to individuals as opposed to the number of shares available to financial institutions in management buy outs.

EOQ *see* economic order quantity.

EPOS *see* electronic point of sale.

EPS 1 *see* earnings per share; **2** *see* extended problem solving.

equal employment opportunity policy of ensuring all job applicants have an equal chance of being hired, regardless of age, gender, ethnic background or other personal circumstances.

equality condition of being equal; where two or more things are equivalent in value.

equal opportunities policies and legislation which ensure that minority groups have opportunities for work and advancement equal to those of the dominant group.

equal pay or equal pay for equal work, the concept that all employees doing similar jobs should be paid similar rates, regardless of age, gender, ethnic background or other personal circumstances.

equation price price, arrived at through market forces, where demand equates with supply.

equilibrium state of balance.

equilibrium exchange rate exchange rate which allows a national economy to maintain an appropriate balance of trade, with the currency neither overvalued nor undervalued against those of its trading partners.

equilibrium price price arrived at through the balancing forces of supply and demand.

equilibrium quantity amount of goods in production arrived at through the balancing forces of supply and demand.

equipment machinery or tools required in production.

equipment-type flow process chart flow process chart which details items of plant or equipment used in the actual process.

equitable conversion conversion of real property into personal property.

equities, foreign *see* foreign equity investment.

equity 1 generally, the value of ownership of property; **2** more specifically, the total of shares in a company which are held by shareholders; **3** also, fairness or just treatment.

equity accounting accounting and reporting on equity investments held in other businesses.

equity and debt *see* debt capital; equity capital.

equity capital capital injected into a company by shareholders through the purchase of shares.

equity dilution occurs when new shares are issued; each previously existing share then has proportionately less importance in terms of ownership and control, as it represents a smaller fraction of outstanding share capital.

equity financing the selling of shares to raise capital.

equity securities any issued share in a company.

equity share *see* share.

equity share capital value of all issued shares.

equity turnover ratio of sales to shareholders' equity.

equivalent mean investment period (EMIP) period between the commencement of a project and arrival at the break-even point.

ERASMUS European Community Action Scheme for the Mobility of University Students; education and training programme sponsored by the European Union.

ergonomics study of the workplace environment and how it affects workers, physically and psychologically.

error 1 mistake or incorrect fact; **2** statistical term for the variance between recorded value and actual value.

ES *see* expert systems.

escalation clause clause in a contract agreeing to an increase in price if the seller's costs should also increase.

escalator clause 1 clause in an employment contract making provision for cost of living increases; **2** also as escalation clause.

escape clause clause in a contract allowing either or both parties to terminate the agreement on certain conditions.

escrow money promised by one party to another, which is held in trust by a third party until the receiver of the money has fulfilled certain conditions.

escrow agreement agreement by two parties, arranging to place funds in escrow with a third party.

ESOP *see* employee share option plan.

espionage acquiring confidential information held by another, surreptitiously and often illegally.

ESS *see* expert support systems.

establishment factory or other facility on a single site or in a defined area.

establishment expense *see* indirect cost.

estate management management of landed property or real estate.

esteem needs in Abraham Maslow's hierarchy of needs, the need for self-respect and respect from other people.

estimate supposition or reasonable guess, approximate judgement; used particularly to establish the likely costs of a proposed project.

estimate analysis in cost accounting, the estimating of future costs and profits.

estimated cost most likely cost of a future project; *see also* estimate.

estimated revenues approximate or most likely revenues which would be generated by a proposed project.

estimating markets estimating the total demand for a particular good in a given market.

estimation models software tools used to estimate product costs at the development stage.

ethics 1 moral or right behaviour; **2** socially correct and responsible action by a manager or company; *see also* business ethics.

ethnicity general term covering ethnic and/or racial origin and characteristics.

ethnocentrism theory that one's own ethnic group is more important than that of others.

EU *see* European Union.

Euro- prefix, short for European; indicates something common to all of Europe, particularly within the European Union.

Eurobonds bonds issued in countries outside Europe, which are intended for sale in Europe.

Euroclear international securities market clearing house, based in Brussels.

Eurocommerce trade within Europe, or more particularly within the European Union.

Euro-commercial paper commercial paper sold in European financial markets.

Eurocurrency *see* Euromoney.

Eurodollar dollars traded in European financial markets.

Eurodollar deposit market market for deposits in Eurodollars.

Euroequities stocks which are issued for sale in foreign markets.

Euroequity markets market in which Euroequities are traded.

Euromarkets 1 markets for the trading of foreign securities; **2** markets where a security's currency of denomination is not that of the country in which it is traded.

Euro-medium-term-note (EMTN) short- or medium-term bond sold in Euromarkets.

Euromoney money, particularly from non-European countries, which is traded in European financial markets; *see also* Eurodollars.

European Commission the civil service of the European Union; the president of the European Commission is the senior civil servant in the EU.

European Community European organization of states which preceded the European Union.

European Currency Unit (ECU) money of account used in the European Union.

European Free Trade Area (EFTA) formed in 1959 as a counter to the Common Market (now European Union); nearly all the original members now belong to the EU.

European Regional Development Fund European Union fund which grants funds to correct regional imbalances in the EU.

European Union (EU) community of European states created by the Treaty of Maastricht in 1992, formerly known as the European Community and the Common Market.

Euro-yen yen traded in European financial markets.

evaluated maintenance programme set of preventive maintenance routines for machinery and equipment.

evaluation 1 post-completion assessment of the efficiency and effectiveness of a particular project; assessment of the effectiveness of a training programme; *see also* validation; **2** assessment of the fitness of a person or item of equipment for a particular job or task.

event 1 something which happens or occurs; **2** in insurance, any incident of which the insurer must be notified.

evolution gradual or progressive change.

evolutionary economics application of the scientific study of biological evolution to economics.

evolutionary management management theory that shifts the focus of management away from rational forms of control to setting the parameters within which a business can evolve naturally.

evolutionary operation computer controlled process using feedback to make continual minor adjustments.

evolutionary optimal strategy strategy which aims to encourage the evolutionary development of organizations.

evolutionary theories of the firm theories of firm development which suggest that firms develop along evolutionary biological lines.

evolutionary theory, organizational application of the theories of biological and societal evolution to the structure and growth of organizations.

evolutionary thinking general term for theories of evolution, including biological evolution, societal evolution and so on.

excepted provident fund pension fund where the benefit may be payable on retirement either as a pension or as a lump sum.

exception principle 1 generally, any system that highlights or flags up exceptions; *see also* management by exception; **2** in management information systems, procedure for reporting on items that deviate from norms.

exception report report form used in management by exception.

excess 1 over and above specified or normal amount; **2** insurance, deductible amount from any claim that must be paid by the insured party.

excess capacity unused production capacity, or capacity over and above what is required for a particular process.

excess insurance insurance policy against excessive or extraordinary losses.

excess profits tax additional tax on extraordinary profits.

excess reserves reserve funds held by a bank in excess of the minimum legal requirement.

exchange 1 transaction or purchase; **2** place for doing business; *see also* foreign exchange; **3** in retailing, the right of customers to return defective or unsatisfactory goods in exchange for others.

exchange control controls which limit the convertibility of a currency, or otherwise restrict the extent to which a currency can be traded or exchanged for other currencies.

exchange loss losses suffered as a result of adverse changes in exchange rates.

exchange rate rate or value of one currency in comparison to another; the amount of one currency that another will buy.

exchange rate determination the determination of the relative price between two currencies.

exchange rate management managerial techniques used to measure and assess foreign exchange exposure and risk, and to devise solutions to reduce these risks.

exchange rate quotations stated rate of exchange between two currencies at a given point in time.

exchange rate volatility rate of fluctuation in exchange rates; volatile rates are ones which change rapidly and unpredictably.

exchange risk risk of a project or venture being adversely affected by exchange rate fluctuations.

exchange theory theoretical conceptualization of the processes by which people and organizations trade goods, services, money, etc.

excise duty taxes on goods and services within their country of origin.

excise tax *see* excise duty.

exclusion 1 leaving out or setting aside; **2** restriction or limitation.

exclusion allowance part of an annuity or other lump sum payment which can be deducted from income tax.

exclusive *see* exclusive distribution.

exclusive agent *see* agent, exclusive.

exclusive distribution agreement whereby a single distributor or retailer has sole right to stock a product or brand.

exclusive listing real estate term whereby one firm or agent has exclusive rights to advertise and sell a property.

exclusivity having exclusive rights.

ex-dividend meaning without dividend, refers to the price of securities without reference to any dividends due or paid.

execute to complete or carry out a previously agreed plan, contract or other arrangement.

execution skills skills required to implement a strategy or carry out a planned project.

executive 1 manager who has authority over others and decision-making powers; 2 refers to the overall management or administration of a firm.

executive centres training centres for the delivery of executive education.

executive committee formally constituted group of executives responsible for some aspect of management.

executive compensation total remuneration paid to an executive; usually refers only to direct salary and bonuses, not fringe benefits.

executive director company director who is also an executive employed by the firm; as opposed to a non-executive director.

executive information system management information system designed specifically for more senior managers and decision makers; *see also* management information system.

executive role the duties and responsibilities of an executive.

executive search process of recruiting, including identifying possible recruits, for executive jobs; *see also* headhunter.

executive succession planning to ensure that leaving or retiring executives are succeeded by new people with appropriate skills, in a manner which involves a smooth transition.

executive support system *see* executive information system.

executive training specialized training programmes designed for senior executives to prepare them for the task of holding high positions in large companies.

exemplary damages damages awarded by a court as settlement of a suit, with the intent not only of compensating the wronged party but of setting a level for damages in similar future cases.

exemption tax allowance; sum which can deducted from gross income prior to the calculation of taxable income.

exercise price input options and call options, the price (fixed at the time of the option) for which a security is sold.

ex gratia payment payment under the terms of which the payer does not accept any liability or responsibility.

exhaust price price at which a broker is forced to sell a security purchased on margin.

exhaustion of rights expiry date of copyright or trade mark.

existing use value future value of an asset such as property or plant, assuming it continues in its current use, rather than if it were put to some other use.

exit 1 to discontinue operations in a particular market and to effectively abandon that market to competitors; 2 to sell out of a particular shareholding.

exit interview interview conducted by personnel managers with employees who are leaving the organization.

expansion 1 growing a company or business; 2 increasing levels of activity in current business operations, or developing new markets or facilities.

expansion demand in marketing, demand stemming from new customers for an existing product or service.

expansion finance finance raised by small businesses with the specific purpose of helping them to expand.

expatriates 1 workers or managers employed outside their home country; **2** also sometimes refers to foreign companies.

expatriation going abroad to work, either for a current employer or to seek a new job.

expectancy chart charting technique used to predict performance in psychological testing.

expectancy theory motivation theory to the effect that an employee's performance on the job is determined by the probability and value of reward.

expected exit value cash return expected from an asset when it is finally sold.

expected return anticipated profit from an investment.

expected value the value of expected cash flow at or by a future date.

expected yield anticipated dividend to be paid by an investment.

expenditure 1 money spent on goods or assets; **2** money disbursed to meet costs, the sum of which is deducted from revenue to determine levels of profit or loss.

expenditure tax *see* indirect taxation.

expense synonymous with cost.

expense account 1 money paid to employees on a regular basis to cover expenses; **2** account established for the payment of expenses.

expense budget budget establishing the anticipated costs of a project.

expenses costs of doing business such as travel, accommodation, etc. which can be recovered from an employer or declared tax deductible.

experience 1 to experience an event personally; **2** the sum total of an individual's past experience; **3** the gaining of skills and knowledge through work and practice rather than education or training.

experience curve measure of the rate at which a person acquires experience; *see also* learning curve.

experiments investigation or test of a hypothesis in controlled conditions.

expert someone who possesses above ordinary levels of skill or experience in a particular field.

expertise the knowledge or skills of an expert.

expert knowledge-based systems *see* expert systems.

expert support systems (ESS) use of expert systems as decision support systems.

expert systems (ES) 1 system (usually operated by computer) which mimics the action of an expert person; **2** system into which high levels of knowledge or skill have been built.

expert witness expert called on to give evidence on a technical matter in a court of law.

expiration termination of an agreement after an agreed period of time.

expire terminate by running out of time.

explicit costs direct cost outlays on resources, labour, etc. required for production; *see also* direct cost.

exploratory forecasting forecasting technique which projects future developments in a single field without reference to other subject areas.

exploratory research preliminary research into the characteristics of a market which a company is considering entering for the first time.

exponential smoothing mathematical technique used in forecasting, which adjusts forecasts so as to account for the most recent events and trends.

export *see* exports.

export agent agent who acts for a company to arrange exports.

export finance house financial institution specializing in arranging credit for export business.

export house intermediary business in exporting which either acts as an agent or buys and sells goods on its own account.

exporting the process of selling goods to foreign customers.

export leasing leasing equipment or plant to an overseas customer.

exports goods shipped outside their country of origin.

export subsidy government subsidy paid to producers selling goods for export, where the market price is deemed low enough to provide the producers with sufficient profit.

exposure 1 general term for level of investment, particularly where risk is involved; **2** alternatively, measure of media coverage or public attention being paid to a person or event.

expropriation 1 compulsory nationalization; **2** seizure by government of business assets, with or without compensation.

extend to increase the time span of an agreement or contract beyond the period originally set; to grant or give, as in 'to extend credit'.

extended a business whose liabilities exceed assets; *see also* overextended.

extended problem solving (EPS) model of complex consumer decision-making processes.

extension 1 postponement; **2** the extending of the time period of an agreement or contract.

external audit audit of a firm's business activities conducted by an external party, usually an accounting firm.

external course *see* external programme.

external currency market market for a particular currency outside its own country, for example, the Eurodollar market.

external programme training programme provided off the premises of the organization, usually conducted by a professional training organization.

external factors factors which affect business operations and which stem from outside the business or operation.

external labour market labour market where a company recruits new employees.

external markets markets outside the company's own organization; as opposed to internal markets.

external storage device computer storage unit that is not part of the main computer but can be accessed by it.

external users 1 people outside an organization who have access to some or all of its systems; **2** creditors, investors and others with an interest in a company but not involved in its management.

extinguish **1** to terminate an obligation; **2** to settle a debt either by repayment or by writing off.

extraction cost costs involved in extracting natural resources and transporting them for processing.

extractive industry industry based on the extraction of natural resources, such as forestry or mining.

extraordinary item **1** in accounting, any unusual non-recurring expense; **2** alternatively, any item that does not belong to any established category.

extraordinary loss/gain loss or profit incurred as a result of some unexpected event.

extrinsic reward total reward or benefits received by an employee including pay, fringe benefits, working conditions and personal satisfaction.

F

fabless production production system whereby the producing company does not directly own fabrication or manufacturing facilities, but instead contracts these processes out to smaller firms.

fabrication 1 the making of physical products; **2** assembling parts into a finished product.

face amount *see* face value.

face-to-face skills skills required for effective verbal communication, particularly in small groups or dyadic interactions.

face value nominal value of a share, note or other financial instrument, for which that instrument can be redeemed; also known as par value.

facilitation and support approach strategy implementation approach which helps to implement strategy and overcome resistance to change by providing various types of support to people having difficulty managing change at their level.

facilitator agent or agency who makes a result possible, or helps to achieve a goal.

facilities management the management, usually by an external agency or contractor, of plant maintenance, computer systems or other support services.

facility credit granted by a lending institution; *see also* credit limit.

facsimile *see* fax.

factor 1 commission agent, who buys and sells goods on behalf of the owner; **2** also, significant attribute or fact which must be considered when analysing a situation or making a decision.

factorage fees or commissions paid to a factor.

factor analysis job evaluation technique which breaks jobs down into their constituent parts and assigns points to each, with salaries usually being based on the number of points each job is worth.

factor comparison *see* factor analysis.

factor derivation *see* market factor derivation.

factoring 1 operating as a factor; **2** the selling of debts or accounts before their due date to a third party agency which undertakes to collect the debts, usually for a percentage of the amount owing.

factoring company company which specializes in factoring, either as an agency for buying and selling, *see* factor; or as a buyer of debts, *see* factoring.

factor model *see* arbitrage pricing theory.

factor price ratios which express relative values of input and output, such as average price per ton of materials, or average cost per unit for distribution.

factor rating similar to factor analysis, a performance appraisal technique which identifies certain factors or qualities which are ideally required in a manager and then rates managers according to which factors they possess.

factory production facility where products or components are made or assembled.

factory agreement collective agreement between workers and management which covers all workers in a particular factory or site.

factory cost direct cost plus manufacturing indirect cost.

factory expense *see* factory overhead.

factory gate the point where goods leave a production facility, being delivered to a shipper, wholesaler, retailer or end customer.

factory overhead costs incurred in running a factory, excepting direct labour and materials costs.

factory price price of finished goods as they leave the factory, not including transportation or distribution costs.

factory profit selling price of a product less production costs.

failure the inability of a business or business activity to meet its financial obligations; when used of companies, usually synonymous with going out of business.

fair market value price determined by the market, which is considered appropriate by both buyers and sellers.

fair price price which is considered equitable, in that it is both affordable to the customer and renders a reasonable rate of profit to the seller.

fair trade trade which is regulated or self-policed by firms to some extent to ensure that prices are kept to equitable levels.

fair value value assigned to goods and assets.

fall-back pay base pay or minimum pay before bonuses are paid.

fall-back price *see* reserve price.

false advertising advertising that is misleading in some way, usually about either the features of a product or its price.

false market market dominated by false information, which affects prices and customer expectations.

familism business culture where, even if a company is not family-owned, the culture strongly resembles that of a family structure.

family brand brand used by a company (often the company's own name) across a variety of products.

family group in marketing research, a buying unit which consists of the combined tastes and spending power of a family or household.

family life cycle marketing research term indicating stages in tastes and purchasing power of a family over time, from marriage to retirement.

fast food food which is prepared and consumed quickly, either on the premises or elsewhere.

fast-moving consumer goods (FMCG) consumer goods, usually consumables, which are bought regularly and frequently.

fast track career plan for people deemed to have management potential, which provides them with training and rapid promotion to senior levels.

fat 1 excess or reserves; **2** money which can be earned easily.

fatigue physical or mental tiredness that can affect work performance.

favourable balance of trade balance of trade where the total value of exports exceeds that of imports.

favouritism preferential treatment shown to someone, such as an employee or a customer.

fax device which scans paper copies of text and images and transmits them electronically, printing them out on paper once more at the receiving end.

FCF *see* financing cash flow.

FDI *see* foreign direct investment.

feasibility likelihood that a particular project can be carried out successfully.

feasibility study assessment of whether a proposed project is possible, given available resources.

feather bedding pay for unnecessary work, or for work not completed.

feature attribute of a product (colour, shape, function, etc.) which provides benefit to customers.

federalism organizational system whereby divisions retain responsibility for their own affairs, reporting to head office only on matters which concern the entire organization.

Federal Reserve System central banking system of the USA.

federation loose association of organizations or states.

fee payment in exchange for services rendered, usually refers to professional services.

fee basis contract for professional service stating that a fixed fee will be paid for the service.

feedback 1 process whereby data or knowledge acquired at the end of a process is collected and input into earlier stages of the process; **2** using learning gained from past experience to improve future performance.

fictitious assets items with no realizable value but which must still appear on a balance sheet.

fiddle unscrupulous practice in work or accounting to either gain money or conceal losses, e.g. 'fiddling the books'.

fidelity insurance insurance against embezzlement or theft by employees or agents.

fiduciary person or organization who holds property or money in trust for others.

fiduciary accounting accounting for money or property held in trust.

fiduciary loan loan granted without security apart from the borrower's pledge.

field 1 in sales, the physical territory for which a salesperson is responsible; **2** synonym for sector or area of activity; **3** in computing, a part of a database that holds a particular class of data.

field inspection visit by senior manager to check on the performance of sales staff in the field.

field research research which studies research samples to collect new information, not previously published; as opposed to desk research.

field studies *see* field research.

field testing testing a new product in conditions which approximate those in which it is likely to be used.

FIFO *see* first in, first out.

fight or flight reaction psychologists' description of responses to stress, whereby people either seek to eliminate the source of the stress, or avoid it altogether.

file 1 collection of documents pertaining to a particular subject; **2** in computing, user-created storage unit which contains documents, spreadsheets, parts of a database, etc.

file interrogation program software which searches and summarizes the contents of existing computer files using batch processing.

file maintenance updating stored files (either computer files or paper documents) and deleting those which are now redundant.

file management *see* file maintenance.

file transfer the movement of files across the Internet from one computer to another.

filter criteria used in filtering in order to decide which information should be retained and which discarded.

filtering sorting of collected information in order to discard that which is deemed irrelevant.

final demand demand for payment issued after one or more previous demands.

final salary pension plan pension scheme whereby the level of pension paid is based on the employee's salary on retirement rather than the average salary over the whole time.

finance capital in the form of money; to raise finance is to acquire debt capital and/or equity capital from one or more sources; *see also* finance theory.

finance company company that specializes in lending money directly, or in arranging loans.

finance house *see* finance company.

finance theory branch of economics devoted to the study of finance, including credit, money, banking, valuation and so on.

financial accounting accounting function which collects, analyses and presents financial data, primarily in the form of balance sheets and profit and loss accounts, for both internal use and for reporting to shareholders and regulators.

financial analysis the analysis of a firm's financial position from recorded data.

financial controls techniques for controlling the inflows and outflows of money, for ensuring that expenditures and revenues match plans and for alerting management when significant variances occur.

financial derivatives *see* derivatives.

financial forecast forecast of future financial positions based on available existing data.

financial futures futures contracts for the lending or borrowing of foreign currency; *see* futures.

financial instrument any note or document that transfers money from one party to another, including loans, promissory notes, futures contracts, bonds and shares.

financial intermediaries agents or companies in financial markets who specialize in bringing borrowers and lenders together.

financial leverage *see* gearing; leverage.

financial management management of a company's financial resources.

financial markets markets where financial instruments are bought and sold, including money markets and capital markets.

financial planning planning the use and acquisition of financial resources.

financial position current levels of assets and liabilities, as shown on a balance sheet.

financial ratio *see* management ratio; also known as accounting ratio.

financial reporting 1 process by which companies report on their financial position, either for internal purposes or for public information; *see also* financial accounting; management accounting; **2** reporting on a company's financial situation to comply with the principles of accountability.

financial services general term for companies providing services related to finance, including banks and finance companies.

financial statement statement of financial status used in financial reporting.

financial statement analysis the interpretation and use of financial statements.

financial statistics statistical data which set out some part of a company's financial position.

financial year twelve-month period over which a company conducts most of its financial analysis and reporting activities; does not necessarily correspond with the calendar year.

financier person who supplies finance for other businesses, either acting as an agent or using his or her own money.

financing cash flow (FCF) cash flow which is the result of finance raised.

financing transactions money which flows overseas as a result of a balance-of-payments deficit.

finder's fee payment to an agent for locating prospective customers or partners, or for finding and recovering lost goods or money.

fine paper very low-risk securities.

finished goods manufactured and assembled products ready for use by consumers.

finite-difference method mathematical model used in option pricing.

fire to dismiss an employee summarily, usually as a disciplinary measure.

fire fighting reactive management style which focuses on concentrating short-term efforts on problems as they arise.

fire insurance insurance policy which covers losses sustained through fire or smoke damage.

firm 1 general term used for a business enterprise, often synonymous with company; **2** definite, as in 'firm offer'.

firmware software which is stored in read-only memory (ROM) which cannot be altered or rewritten.

first-day premium price of shares on the day of issue.

first-hand distribution distribution method using a few wholesalers taking very large consignments, which are then broken up and sold in smaller lots to other wholesalers.

first in, first out (FIFO) 1 in inventory, the principle whereby the items longest in inventory will be the first to be sold; **2** in finance, the practice of using the money longest on deposit for computing interest or dividends.

first level 1 lowest level or simplest factor; **2** lowest level of hierarchy in an organization.

first-party insurance insurance which covers only the policy holder and his or her own property.

fiscal monetary or financial.

fiscal charges costs incurred in the course of ordinary business.

fiscal drag time lag between the implementation of a government fiscal measure and its effect.

fiscal measures changes in taxation or spending by governments in line with fiscal policy.

fiscal period *see* financial year.

fiscal policy government policy on spending and revenue, including detailed fiscal measures for raising taxes and other revenue.

fiscal year *see* financial year.

fishbone technique problem-solving technique used in particular in total quality management.

fitness for use extent to which a product or service meets the customer's requirements, or will perform the function for which it was designed.

five forces model model developed by Michael Porter to describe the competitive forces that determine industry competition.

five-year plans strategic and development plans set on a five-year basis.

fixed annuity annuity paid at the same rate and frequency throughout the annuity period.

fixed assets land and capital equipment such as machinery which is designed for continued use rather than being converted into cash.

fixed budget budget based on a forecast which does not make provision for variations in actual conditions.

fixed charge expenses that are fixed at a certain amount and are not directly related to levels of business activity or volume of production.

fixed cost cost that remains constant no matter what the volume of production may be; also known as standing cost.

fixed duration contracts contracts which expire after a set period of time.

fixed exchange rate official exchange rate set by a government for its national currency; as opposed to floating exchange rate.

fixed expense *see* fixed cost.

fixed factors of production factors of production which cannot be easily altered.

fixed income income or pension paid at a non-varying rate, regardless of inflation or increases in cost of living.

fixed interest cover loan provided at a fixed rate of interest.

fixed interest securities securities which pay the bearer a fixed rate of interest.

fixed investments investments in assets which cannot be easily moved or disposed of.

fixed-price contract contract for goods or services for a set price, which cannot be altered or increased later in the term of the contract.

fixed-term contract contract for goods or services, or for employment, covering a specific period of time.

fixing a price establishing a price, either through negotiation or by arbitrary decision of the seller; not to be confused with price fixing.

fixture asset that is permanently attached to another asset or property.

flag of convenience registration of a ship in a country other than where its owners are domiciled, usually with the purpose of paying lower taxes and wages.

flagship store headquarters of a retail chain, often its largest and most prestigious store.

flash pack small leaflet advertising special offers.

flat price of a bond which takes into account any unpaid interest to date.

flat interest rate quote for the average rate of interest on a loan.

flat organization *see* flat structure.

flat pyramid *see* flat structure.

flat rate standard or uniform rate.

flat structure organization with few layers of hierarchy, usually marked by decentralization and autonomy on the part of junior managers.

fleet vehicles, ships or aircraft owned and/or managed by a company.

FLES *see* fuzzy logic expert system scheduler.

flexibility adaptability or versatility, usually used to describe the extent to which a person or organization can adapt to and manage change.

flexible access system optical fibre telecommunications system designed to carry large quantities of data in many forms.

flexible budget budget which covers several different activities and/or contains provisions for different outcomes.

flexible firm theory organizational theory that divides a firm into core and peripheral activities, with different labour requirements; *see also* shamrock organization.

flexible hours *see* flexible working hours.

flexible learning use of a variety of learning techniques to deliver learning programmes adapted to the specific needs of managers.

flexible manufacturing system automated production system used in manufacturing.

flexible rostering working agreement collective agreement that allows management to assign workers to different shifts or working hours as needed.

flexible time in flexible working hours, times of the day when employees may choose their own working hours; as opposed to core time.

flexible working hours work scheduling system whereby employees can choose their own start and finishing times, so long as they work a certain number of hours per day; *see also* core time; flexible time.

flexing in budgeting, the process of adjusting previously set budgets to reflect changes in production, sales or revenue.

flexiplace *see* teleworking.

flexitime *see* flexible working hours.

flexiwork *see* flexible working hours.

flier or flyer printed advertising leaflet.

flight of capital movement of capital out of a country, usually in anticipation of a market decline or political problems.

float 1 cash kept on hand for petty cash; **2** in critical path analysis, contingencies in the time allowed for particular functions.

floating a company turning a business into a public company by offering shares for sale.

floating asset *see* current assets.

floating debt short-term debt.

floating exchange rate exchange rate that fluctuates in accordance with market forces; as opposed to fixed exchange rate.

floating labour workers who change their jobs and or job locations from time to time.

floating rate *see* floating exchange rate.

floor trading area of a stock exchange or commodities exchange, or dealing room of a brokerage house.

floor broker member of a stock exchange who carries out buy and sell orders.

floor limit limit of credit, or highest value of a transaction which an agent or dealer can undertake without referring to higher authority.

floor price *see* reserve price.

floppy disk small and easily portable external storage device for computers; alternative spelling disc.

flotation the process of floating a company or issuing securities for sale on the market.

flow the order in which activities are carried out in order to complete a process.

flow chart chart showing the flow of activities in a system or process, showing the relationship between stages or activities and the time required for each.

flowcharting the analysis of activities required for the design of a flow chart.

flow diagram *see* flow chart.

flow line production organization of factory production based on division of labour, with products passing between operators who are each responsible for separate stages; *see also* assembly-line production.

flow process chart chart showing the order and timings of operations in a particular process; *see also* flow chart.

fluctuating price contract contract where it is agreed that the price may vary depending on changes in costs or other circumstances.

fluctuation short-term variations in a factor such as demand or price.

flux flow; also used to mean 'fluctuate'; *see* fluctuation.

flyback timing work measurement in which each element of a job is measured and timed separately; as opposed to cumulative timing.

'flying geese' model model of economic development which describes how the development of one nation has impacts on the development of neighbouring nations.

flying picket striking workers who travel to picket a place of work other than their own, for the purpose of assisting local pickets or disrupting an industry more broadly.

FMCG *see* fast-moving consumer goods.

focus interview interview which concentrates on a single subject or topic.

focus point theory in cognition, the tendency of people to focus on a single known point in a generally uncertain situation.

following skills interpersonal skills which help people to listen to and understand what others are saying.

forced choice approach market research, technique where people being questioned are asked whether a particular attribute is applicable to a particular brand, usually being required to give a yes/no answer.

forced sale compulsory sale or disposal of an asset, usually in order to comply with legal requirements.

force-field analysis graphic technique used in problem solving.

Fordism management philosophy focusing on high levels of mass production.

forecast prediction of likely possible developments in the future.

forecasting the analysis of data and information required to produce forecasts, often using a variety of mathematical and statistical techniques.

foreign currency money from another country, which normally must be exchanged for the local currency before it can be used in trading.

foreign direct investment (FDI) investment by a foreign company in production or other facilities, which are then either directly or jointly owned by the investing company.

foreign equity investment buying shares or equity in foreign companies.

foreign exchange the conversion of one currency into another; market where currencies are traded.

foreign exchange rate the value of one currency when exchanged or traded for another.

foreign exchange risk risks that a currency might devalue relative to another currency.

foreign investment investing in a country by foreign companies or organizations; *see also* foreign direct investment.

foreign language acquisition becoming literate in a second language, usually as a result of training before an overseas posting.

foreign market entry strategies strategic options available to a company seeking to enter a particular overseas market for the first time.

foreign markets markets in a country other than the one where the company is domiciled.

foreign nationals employees who are not citizens of the countries where they are working.

foreign service premium salary increase for employees who accept overseas postings.

foreign subsidiaries overseas subsidiary companies or operations.

foreign trade multiplier principle whereby variations in levels of foreign trade result in variations in national income.

foreman member of the first level of management, with responsibility for directly overseeing workers.

forgery creation of false or fraudulent documents, either by creating entirely false documents or by wrongly signing someone else's name (on a cheque, for example).

forked tariff list of variable charges within an upper and lower limit.

formalization 1 placing procedures or ways of doing business on a formal footing; 2 the making of rules.

formation expenses *see* preliminary expenses.

forward and futures contracts *see* forward contract; futures.

forward contract contract agreed in a futures or forward market, where a price is set but the goods, commodities or money do not change hands until a later date.

forward cover money set aside to cover a forward contract.

forward exchange fixed price bill of exchange, payable on a given future date.

forward exchange rates rates at which forward exchange bills are payable.

forwarding *see* carry over.

forward integration expansion by a manufacturer or wholesaler down the product chain to acquire a distribution or retail outlet; as opposed to backward integration.

forward interest rates interest rates projected at a given point in the future.

forward market market for trading securities, commodities and foreign currency, which are traded at fixed prices at set dates in the future; as opposed to spot market.

forward participation agreement method of hedging foreign exchange risk.

forward price agreed price for a forward contract.

forward rate agreed exchange rate for a forward contract.

forward range agreement (FRA) method of hedging foreign exchange risk.

fossil fuels coal or petroleum byproducts which are used to propel engines or power plants.

foundation non-profit, privately funded institution which conducts research or engages in social causes.

founding rate number of employees required when a company is first established.

four Ps the four fundamental elements of marketing, namely product, price, place (or channel of distribution) and promotion (or communication).

fourth market market in unlisted securities, with trading carried out directly between investors rather than on stock markets.

FRA *see* forward range agreement.

fractional currency currency of denominations smaller than a standard unit (for example, less than £1).

franchise license to make, distribute or sell a product or service in return for payment.

franchised dealer retailer selling goods under the terms of a franchise.

franchisee company or person holding a franchise, with the right to make, distribute or sell goods under licence from another party; depending on the terms of the franchise, the franchisee may be free to deal in other competing products, or may be restricted to dealing in the franchised products only.

franchiser company granting franchises to another.

franchise store retail outlet operated on a franchise basis; *see also* franchised dealer.

franchising the practice of granting franchises; often used as a strategic option for expanding quickly into new markets with comparatively little risk.

F ratio formula used in variance analysis for determining extent of variance between independent and dependent variables.

fraud 1 acting with intent to deceive; **2** deliberate misrepresentation of the facts for the purposes of financial gain.

free 1 without charge or cost, at zero price; **2** without obligations or encumbrances.

free agent *see* agent, free.

free alongside ship shipping terms whereby goods are delivered with costs paid to the side of the ship, but where the buyer must meet the cost of carrying the goods on board ship and all other costs thereafter.

free and open market *see* free market.

free balance control inventory control system which ensures stocks are kept up to the correct level, and also takes into account future stock requirements.

free carrier shipping terms whereby goods are delivered with all costs paid to a depot or warehouse of the customer's choice.

free choice approach market research technique where people being questioned are asked whether a particular attribute is applicable to any brand; as opposed to forced choice.

free collective bargaining collective bargaining between employer and employees which is carried out without restriction or interference by any third party.

freedom of association the right to associate or form organizations, groups, unions and so on.

free economy economy where business is conducted with a minimum of government control; *see also* laissez-faire.

free enterprise economic condition where private individuals and companies own the means of production and distribution and conduct business activities with a minimum of government control.

free exchange *see* free trade.

free float in network planning, the amount of additional time that can be consumed by an activity before it begins to interfere with or delay other activities.

free goods goods which are abundant and widely available, and for which no charge is commonly made.

free goods offer offer of products free of charge, usually as part of a promotion.

freehold unrestricted title or full ownership of property.

free market market in which neither supply nor demand are regulated and all parties are free to trade without hindrance.

free market economy *see* free economy.

free movement of capital unrestricted movement of capital between countries without exchange controls or any other form of government intervention.

free movement of labour arrangement between governments to allow unrestricted flows of labour across national boundaries.

free on board shipping terms whereby goods are delivered on board ship with all costs paid, with the buyer responsible for all costs thereafter.

free on rail shipping terms whereby goods are delivered to the railhead with all costs paid, with the buyer responsible for all costs thereafter.

free overside shipping terms whereby goods are delivered to their destination and offloaded from the ship with all costs paid, with the buyer responsible for all costs thereafter.

free port 1 port where no duties are charged on imported or exported goods; 2 port where facilities are open to all ships on equal terms.

free ride in securities trading, the practice of buying and immediately reselling, allowing the buyer to make a profit without actually putting up capital.

free rider non-union employee who qualifies for the same benefits as unionized employees, particularly where those benefits have been negotiated through collective bargaining.

free share distribution issuing of shares to existing shareholders free of payment.

free trade unrestricted trade between two countries, without customs or tariffs.

free trade area trading area created by two or more states to promote free trade between them; *see also* customs union.

freeze legal right of banks or governments to, in some circumstances, prevent assets from being bought and sold, or prevent withdrawals from bank accounts.

freight merchandise and goods being physically transported from one place to another.

freight forwarder *see* shipping and forwarding agent.

frequency analysis analysis of the rate of interaction in dyadic interactions.

frequency distribution technique used in statistics to agglomerate large quantities of data around the most common variables.

frequent flyer programmes customer retention programme used by many airlines to reward regular customers, usually by awarding points which can be used as part payment for future travel.

frictional overhead term used by Peter Drucker to describe non-productive and non-functional administrative staff and managers.

frictional unemployment short-term unemployment which arises as people move between jobs or through seasonal fluctuations in labour demand.

fringe bank institution that carries out some banking activities but does not have the status of a bank.

fringe benefits *see* employee benefits.

front-line worker service employees who work at the interface between the firm and its customers, either in person or on the telephone.

front money 1 money which must be paid in advance; **2** costs incurred in the course of setting up a project from scratch.

front office office and administrative functions which closely support the front-line staff and which must be on the same site as the service delivery operation.

front of house 1 area in catering and hospitality industries where customers interact with employees; **2** spaces on the premises of a business where the public has access.

frozen assets or money whose sale and movement has been prohibited; *see also* freeze.

frozen account bank account which has been frozen.

frozen asset asset which has been frozen, banning its sale or disposal.

frozen pension pension plan where the employee has left the firm and no more contributions are being paid in; *see also* paid-up pension.

FTSE-100 index of 100 leading shares on the International Stock Exchange, London.

full cost total of all direct and indirect costs involved in manufacturing.

full-cost pricing pricing based on calculation of full costs.

full coverage insurance policy which covers all losses, with nothing being deductible.

full employment economic condition where there is effectively zero unemployment, and where there is an excess of demand for labour over supply.

full service a complete service package, meeting all the customer's service requirements.

full service agency advertising agency that manages the entire advertising process for its clients, including planning and production of advertisements and their placement with the appropriate media.

full-time employee employee who works a standard working week, typically 35 or more hours.

fully vested holding all appropriate rights, without qualification.

function specific activity or operation, usually describing activities such as sales, marketing, production, purchasing and so on; sometimes synonymous with role.

functional authority authority vested in managers to make decisions regarding a particular function within their jurisdiction.

functional costing the allocation of costs to the various functions which incurred them.

functional equivalence instance where tools, processes, etc. achieve the same result, though possibly from different means.

functional flexibility the ability to perform more than one skill, or to switch functions.

functional form organizational hierarchy which divides organizations into departments by function.

functional manager manager specializing in or responsible for a particular function.

functional obsolescence defective design that renders a product obsolete after a certain period of time; *see also* built-in obsolescence; planned obsolescence.

functional organization scientific management term for an organization structured by functions, rather than by processes.

fund 1 amount of money; 2 money under management for investment purposes.

fundamental design method design technique, involving analysis of the design by the designer at predetermined points in the process.

funded debt general term for long-term loans, bonds and debentures.

fund flow analysis analysis of flows of money (revenue, expenditure, investment and so on) into and out of an organization.

funding funds or money required to support a project, collected through investment or loans.

fundraising in not-for-profit marketing, the raising of money for charitable or other purposes from donors or sponsors.

funds money or investment; a pool of money used for purchasing or investment.

funds statement 1 statement of investments; 2 statement of fund flow analysis.

fungible goods or securities where any one unit is identical to any other unit.

funnel interview interviewing technique where the subject is gradually guided towards the subject of the interview.

funny money 1 forged or non-negotiable currency; 2 money with little or no value.

further education post-secondary school education that does not lead to a degree, often vocational in nature.

future contracts *see* futures contract.

future dividends dividends due at some point in the future.

futures contracts for the purchase of commodities or foreign currency which will be delivered at a named date in the future rather than immediately.

futures contract contract for the purchase of futures, specifying the date of delivery and the price to be paid.

future sum total repayments on a loan, including the principal advanced and all accrued interest.

future worth value of an asset at a particular point in the future.

futurology the study of current trends in order to anticipate future developments.

fuzzy expert systems expert systems based on generalized methods of inference and fuzzy logic.

fuzzy logic logic based on imprecise or minimally specific values.

fuzzy logic expert system scheduler (FLES) job shop scheduling model based on fuzzy logic.

G

G3 countries Germany, Japan and the USA

G7 countries Germany, Japan, the USA, the UK, France, Italy and Canada.

GAAP *see* generally accepted accounting practice.

gainsharing work incentive scheme in which the bonuses paid to workers increase progressively as output increases or time is saved.

galloping inflation very rapid inflation which threatens to run out of control, thereby leading to economic disaster.

game theory case study technique in which contestants work through a simulated case, competing to see who can devise the best solution.

gaming the use of game theory and simulations in decision making and planning.

gamma stocks class of stocks traded on the London stock market, including about 2000 companies.

Gantt chart bar chart used in project planning and control to plot actual performance against target performance.

gap analysis 1 analysis which identifies gaps or missing areas of coverage in research projects; **2** also, analysis which investigates the 'gap' between planned and actual performance and investigates why this should occur.

garbage in, garbage out (GIGO) in research, meaning that the quality of the information that comes out of a research programme is dependent on the quality of the data that goes into it; has a similar meaning in computing.

garnishee 1 a debtor on whom an order of garnishment has been served; **2** also as garnishment.

garnishment court order directing part of a debtor's wages or other income to be paid directly to creditors.

gatekeeper person or device controlling flows of goods of information through a single channel.

gathering process process of collecting information and data for later analysis.

GATT *see* General Agreement on Tariffs and Trade.

gaussian curve symmetrical curve which shows the frequency distribution of phenomena across a large population.

gaze visual monitoring of employees in the workplace using electronic surveillance technology.

gazumping 1 accepting a higher offer from a bidder after another bid has already been made and accepted; **2** raising the price after a purchase has been agreed.

GDP *see* gross domestic product.

GDRs *see* global depository receipts.

geared incentive scheme work incentive scheme which increases bonuses in fixed stages rather than tying them directly to productivity levels.

gearing proportion of debt capital to equity capital, or of preference and outside loan capital to ordinary shares and reserves; in each case a company with a high proportion of the former is said to be highly geared, while one with a high proportion of the latter is said to have low gearing; also known as leverage.

gearing ratio ratio which expresses the level of gearing.

genba-shugi 'respectable shop floor', Japanese term for the phenomenon whereby many top managers start their careers as shop floor workers.

gender the sex of a person (i.e. male or female).

gender discrimination *see* sex discrimination.

gendered organizing process process whereby gender discrimination is built into an organization.

gender-organization-system (GOS) sociological approach to the role and opportunities for women in business organizations.

General Agreement on Tariffs and Trade (GATT) international agreement to harmonize and lower tariffs, which led to the establishment of the World Trade Organization (WTO).

general equilibrium theory in neo-classical economics, the generally accepted model of the organization of economic activity.

general fund money that has not been set aside for a particular purpose.

generalist managers managers who have a broad perspective rather than being specialists in particular functional disciplines.

generalized system of preferences (GSP) European Union system for establishing preferential trade deals with African, Caribbean and Pacific countries.

general ledger bank record of every transaction during the course of a business day.

generally accepted accounting practice (GAAP) set of accounting and financial standards developed in the UK, which establishes best practice for all accountants.

general management the overall or all-round management of a company, encompassing all its focuses and activities and with responsibility as well for strategy and leadership.

general manager manager responsible for the overall business of a company, rather than for one specific function.

general sales tax tax on goods and services at the point of sale.

generic benchmarking benchmarking against similar processes or functions in very different types of companies.

generic strategies strategic concepts which have application in a broad range of situations.

genetic algorithms search procedures used in artificial intelligence, based on natural selection and genetics.

genetic diversity the vast array of genetic material which can be found in natural environments.

geocentricism philosophy of management found in true transnational or multinational firms, which are comfortable operating in almost any country in the world.

geodemographic segmentation segmentation based on a combination of geographic areas and the demographics of that area's population.

geographical migration systems demographers term for large-scale immigration/emigration flows.

geographic segmentation segmentation based solely on the geographical areas in which people live or in which firms are established.

gestalt organized whole that is greater than the sum of its parts; view that a complete picture of someone's personality is needed in order to understand how they think about a particular issue.

gift certificate certificate bearing a certain monetary value, which can be used as a cash equivalent when purchasing goods from the retailer who issued the certificate.

gigantism term for the very large size of many transnational corporations.

GIGO *see* garbage in, garbage out.

gilt synonym for a gilt-edged security, share, etc.

gilt-edged describes securities, shares or other investments which have very low levels of associated risk, and which usually offer moderate yields; also known as blue chip.

Giro money transfer system operated through the post office in some parts of Europe.

giveaway the giving of goods or money free to consumers for promotional purposes, sometimes as part of a contest.

glamour issue issue of shares in a company in a 'fashionable' industry, such as biotechnology or software.

glass ceiling term suggesting that there is an invisible barrier preventing female managers from rising beyond a certain level in many organizations.

global banking banking operations which span the world, usually on a 24-hour system.

global brand brand which is sold in many parts of the world, often using the same or a similar logo and brand name and backed up by standardized advertising.

global business business activities which are conducted simultaneously in many different parts of the world.

global city city which is a centre of international business and trade, with large multi-ethnic populations, effectively partaking of a 'global' culture.

global corporation corporation with operations and interests in every major market around the world; *see also* multinational corporations.

global culture the theoretical endpoint of cultural convergence, when cultures become more or less homogeneous around the world.

global currency currency which is accepted around the world.

global decision support systems decision support systems capable of supporting global corporations.

global depository receipts (GDRs) source of finance capital available to firms in developing countries.

global economy term reflecting the increasing internationalization of capital flows and trade, the growth of global corporations, and increasing labour mobility.

global environmental change environmental change which affects the entire world to some extent.

global financial markets financial markets such as those of London, New York and Tokyo where trade is conducted with buyers and sellers around the world.

globalism 1 outlook which sees the world as a single entity; **2** management approach which sees the entire world as a potential market and/or operating area.

globalism, stateless *see* stateless globalism.

globalization general term for the worldwide convergence of markets, cultures, etc., made possible by global communications networks.

global localization strategy adopted by global corporations in which they localize operations and marketing in many different markets.

globally oriented manager manager who has a global outlook, and can conceive of strategy and operations in global terms.

global manufacturing manufacturing operations in different parts of the world, sometimes parts sourcing or individual manufacturing stages for the same product being carried out in different countries.

global marketing marketing programmes for a brand or product which are carried out simultaneously in major markets around the world.

global market market which exists in many different countries and cultures, which can be reached by the same or similar marketing programmes.

global models models of economic and business activity which represent the entire world economy.

global outlook attitude or world view which focuses on international and worldwide markets, issues, etc.

global production production strategy which sites facilities where conditions for raw materials, labour, distribution and so on are most advantageous, regardless of what country they happen to be in.

global reach the ability to send communications to or to market in any country in the world.

global strategic alliance alliance between multinational corporations allowing them to enhance global marketing, global production, global reach and so on.

global strategic planning strategic planning which encompasses all the corporation's activities worldwide.

global telecommunications telecommunications networks that span every country, allowing rapid communication between any one part of the globe and any other.

global trade the total flows of goods, services and invisibles between countries.

global village term coined by Marshall McLuhan for worldwide cultural convergence, propelled by the increasing power of global communications.

global webs networks which run around the world.

global workforce worldwide labour force.

globo-localism *see* global localization.

glut oversupply of money, goods, commodities, labour and so on.

GMAT *see* Graduate Management Admission Test.

gnome colloquial term for senior bankers and financial experts who deal in international financial markets; most notably the leading Swiss bankers ('the gnomes of Zurich').

GNP *see* gross national product.

goal objective or target.

goal congruence extent to which the goals of individuals and those of the organizations they belong to are in harmony.

goal programming methods of establishing and prioritizing goals in decision making.

goals *see* goal.

goal setting the definition of the goals or targets that a project or plan should achieve.

godown Chinese and Southeast Asian term for a warehouse or depot.

going concern business which is trading actively and profitably, and will continue to do so for the foreseeable future.

going public *see* floating a company.

going rate current market price.

goldbricking 1 colloquial term for deliberate inactivity during working hours; 2 not working while giving the appearance of working.

golden circle group of very similar brands which dominate a particular product category.

golden handshake lump sum paid to senior or valued employees on retirement or on leaving their jobs.

golden hello lump sum paid to employees on joining a company, used as an incentive when recruiting certain types of particularly skilled staff.

gold standard currency which is backed by gold bullion, that is, it can be exchanged for gold equivalent to the full face value of the currency.

gonin gumi Japanese term meaning a five-person work team.

good 1 a product or service; *see also* goods; 2 anything which has value and/or provides benefits; *see also* capital goods; free goods.

good faith bargaining condition where it is assumed that both parties are dealing honestly with each other and desire to reach a mutually satisfactory agreement.

good money money in which people have confidence, which has a perceived value and is deemed unlikely to be subject to devaluation.

goodness of fit extent to which a product or service meets the need for which it was designed; *see also* fitness for use.

goods products to which value is attached; in strict economic terms, 'goods' also includes services and money.

goods and services synonymous with 'goods', reflecting the fact that in commercial terms 'goods' often refers only to physical products.

goods flow *see* logistics.

goods on consignment goods which are accepted on a consignment basis; *see also* consignment.

goodwill intangible value of a business derived primarily from its reputation with customers and suppliers, which in turn represents competitive advantage; this value is often considered part of the total value of a business when it is sold.

GOS *see* gender-organization-system.

go slow form of industrial action which involves working slowly so as to hold up production and disrupt operations; *see also* work-to-rule.

gouge to overcharge, usually in situations where the customer has little choice but to accept the offered price.

government the administration of a country, among whose functions are fiscal and monetary policy and the regulation of business and trade.

government agency government department or other organization charged with enforcing or implementing government policy.

government borrowing requirement the amount of money a government must borrow in the course of a financial year to meet its spending commitments.

government–business relations the general climate of relations between government and private business, and more specific contacts between government and business, the latter usually being represented by industry and professional associations.

government control condition where a company or institution is owned and managed by the state.

government debt liabilities incurred by government; *see also* government deficit.

government deficit excess of income over expenditure incurred by government when meeting its various responsibilities.

government incentives direct payments, tax relief and other forms of incentive provided by government to businesses in support of particular policies, such as job creation, exports and so on.

government income revenues received by government from all sources, including taxation, income from state companies, and so on.

government intervention government policies which affect the workings of an otherwise free market; examples include affirmative action, subsidies and incentives, and measures to prevent monopolies and cartels.

government monopoly monopoly owned or controlled by government.

government ownership refers to a company or organization which is partly or wholly owned by government.

government policy national policy formulated by government with respect to business, trade, money supply or some other aspect of the economy.

government revenue total government income from taxes, charges, sales and so on, exclusive of money raised through borrowing.

government securities instruments through which governments borrow money.

Gozinto graph *see* assembly chart.

grade level of classification or hierarchy.

grade creep tendency in a grading structure for people, things, jobs and so on to be classified upwards; in the case of job grades, this is done for the purpose of allowing increases in pay.

grading the methods used in classifying things, people, jobs and so on into grades.

grading structure the overall hierarchy within which grades are determined, specifying the number of grades and the qualification for each.

gradualism gradual reduction in the rate of money supply to counteract inflation.

graduated securities stocks that move from one exchange to another, usually to a more prominent exchange.

graduated tax tax where the tax rate per unit increases as the number of units increases.

Graduate Management Admission Test (GMAT) standard test used to determine management aptitude in a number of areas, used by business schools as a pre-requisite to admission.

graduate programme any training programme for which a first university degree or equivalent is a pre-requisite for admission.

graduate training training provided to managers or employees who already have a first university degree or equivalent.

grandfather clause where a regulation prohibits or restricts certain activities, this clause provides exemptions for those already engaged in these activities.

grapevine unofficial communications network by which news, information and rumours spread rapidly through an organization.

graphical user interface (GUI) computer technology which allows commands to be given using a menu which appears on the screen, rather than by typing them in.

graphic presentation presentation of information using pictures and symbols as well as words, for example, different types of graph or chart.

graphic rating scales system used in performance appraisal, in which performance is measured against absolute scales rather than by objective judgement.

graphology technique for determining personality traits through an analysis of that person's handwriting; has no scientific basis, but is sometimes used in selection procedures.

graph theory branch of mathematics used in the study and modelling of networks.

grass-roots method research method involving the gathering of information from the field.

graveyard shift in shift work, the night shift.

green loosely, that which is rooted in or supportive of ecological/environmental issues; used of people or organizations when speaking of ecological/environmental lobby and pressure groups.

green accounting accounting practices which attempt to put a monetary value on ecological assets, and on the damage which is done to them through deforestation, pollution and so on.

greenfield 1 describes a site not previously built upon; **2** also used for any development or project, such as the building of a new factory, on land not previously built upon.

green issues environmental issues which are of concern to the general public, particularly to an organization's customers.

green manufacturing manufacturing using technologies which limit or eliminate pollution and/or have beneficial environmental impacts.

green marketing marketing strategies based on environmental issues, providing products and services that seek to satisfy people's basic concerns about the environment.

green revolution rapid increase in agricultural production, propelled by more scientific methods of farming.

green stakeholders stakeholders who give high priority to environmental issues, and make demands on companies accordingly.

Gresham's Law 'bad money drives out good money': people will spend money in which they do not have confidence, and save or hoard good money.

grey market 1 speculative market in which goods are bought and sold usually at rates far above the market price; **2** market in which business methods, though still legal, are questionable on ethical grounds.

grey trade in international marketing, situation where because of exchange rate fluctuations, a product may be cheaper in an export market than its home market.

grid theory management theory based on the interaction within organizations of three elements: people, production and managerial hierarchy; *see also* managerial grid.

grievance formal complaint by employees against management.

grievance procedure agreed procedure laid down by management and unions for the handling of grievances.

gross 1 total amount, before deductions; **2** also, a somewhat archaic term meaning twelve dozen.

gross business product portion of the gross national product which can be attributed to business and trade.

gross domestic product (GDP) total monetary value of all goods, services and invisibles produced in or exported into a country in a given year, excepting income from overseas investments and earnings; *see also* gross national product.

gross earnings total business income before any deductions.

gross income total personal income before deductions; *see also* taxable income.

gross investment total value of an investment before depreciation.

gross line total of insurance and reinsurance cover for a particular risk.

gross margin total sales revenue less total cost of goods sold.

gross margin performance sales revenue minus cost of sales adjusted for the cost of stock.

gross national debt total of debts owed by government.

gross national expenditure total expenditure on goods and services by all sectors of the economy; *see also* gross national product.

gross national income *see* gross national product.

gross national product (GNP) total monetary value of all goods, services and invisibles produced in or exported into a country in a given year, including income from overseas investments and earnings; *see also* gross domestic product.

gross price method accounting or sales recording method where all sales are recorded at their full price value; the value of any discounts is recorded in separate account.

gross profit total sales revenue less factory cost of the goods sold; *see also* gross margin.

gross profit method inventory method, calculated as being inventory less cost of goods sold, plus net purchases, leading to an estimate of final inventory.

gross profit ratio ratio of sales revenue to factory cost; *see* gross profit.

gross revenue total sales revenue before any deductions for costs.

gross sales total sales before any deductions for discounts, returns, etc..

group any collection of people, usually exhibiting some similar behaviours; *see also* team.

group accounts summary accounts produced through consolidated accounting.

group appraisal performance appraisal carried out by a group of superiors or peers.

group banking banking enterprise where several banks combine to create joint operations.

group decision making decision-making techniques based on analysis and consensus by a group of managers or experts.

group depreciation calculation of depreciation on assets combined in groups, rather than separately.

group development the process by which groups are formed and become effective working units.

group discount *see* bulk discount.

group dynamics the study of behaviour within groups and the interactions of individuals in groups.

group incentives scheme pay bonus system where payment is based on the total output of a team, rather than on individual output.

group interview selection interview where candidates are interviewed *en masse* rather than separately.

groupism philosophy in Japanese business and culture which puts the interests of the group over the individual.

group life assurance policy policy taken out by an employer on some or all of the firm's employees.

group problem solving problem solving techniques where a group of people attempt to analyse and solve a problem, sometimes using brainstorming techniques; *see also* group decision making.

group process the interactions within and between groups of people; *see also* group dynamics.

group selection selection techniques where candidates are assessed as a group, and where their interactions are viewed as part of the selection process.

group technology cells in manufacturing, production groups or teams based around a particular process or machine.

group theory organization behaviour theory covering the behaviour of groups and group members.

groupthink the process whereby groups arrive at decisions by consensus or compromise; generally used pejoratively.

group training methods training methods which use groups and interactions between group members to deliver learning, using techniques such as gaming and roleplaying.

group training scheme training schemes in which a number of firms share, sometimes on a cooperative basis.

groupware communications and decisions support software that enables groups of people, often in remote locations, to collaborate in work processes.

group work work organization method which increases autonomy by devolving responsibility for work on to work groups or teams.

grow to increase in size, value or scope.

grow and penetrate strategy strategy designed to increase the size and sales of a firm, primarily by entering new markets or increasing leverage in existing markets.

growth the process of increasing size or value.

growth share matrix matrix comparing market growth with market share, used to keep track of a company's position in a given market.

growth stage phase in a product's life cycle, when the product has been accepted in the market and sales are increasing.

growth stock shares deemed to have prospects for further growth in profits and share market price.

GSP *see* generalized system of preferences.

guanxi Chinese term roughly equivalent to relationship, in both business or social senses; a *guanxiwang* is a network of relationships.

guarantee 1 in retailing, a statement that the product meets certain quality specifications, usually with a promise of compensation should it fail to do so; **2** also, one to whom a guaranty is made; *see also* guaranty.

guaranteed annual wage specified minimum wage for an annual period, believed to ensure job and wage security.

guaranteed annuity option in endowment assurance schemes, option for an endowment sum to be converted into an annuity upon maturity.

guaranteed income policy, usually backed by government, of providing a basic income to all citizens, even if not employed.

guaranteed letter of credit *see* letter of credit.

guaranteed stock stocks where the payment of dividends is guaranteed, usually by another company acting as a third party.

guaranteed working week minimum number of hours per week for which employees will be paid, regardless of whether they actually work that number of hours.

guarantor party making a guaranty.

guaranty promise that one party will fulfil a contract or agreement made with a second party (the guarantee), for which a third party (the guarantor) stands surety, and will make recompense if the first party fails.

guest workers foreign workers who are permitted to enter a country to work for a period of time, but may not settle permanently or bring their dependents with them.

GUI *see* graphical user interface.

guide-chart profile job evaluation technique which assesses levels of knowledge, problem solving and accountability associated with a particular job.

guide price the desired price for a particular commodity; in the European Union's farm policy, price support measures are used to maintain this price.

guild term of medieval origin, referring to an association of traders or artisans usually involved in the same trade or profession.

guillotine in meetings, the time limit on a subject being discussed, at which point the meeting proceeds to the next item on the agenda.

guru leading management thinker who is widely regarded as possessing special insight into some of the problems and issues of management.

guru concept the idea that some management thinkers (gurus) may possess special insights which can be copied and implemented by other managers.

guru intervention the idea that a guru can intervene in the management of a business to solve existing problems which the firm's own management are incapable of solving.

H

hacker someone who illegally enters a computer system and steals data and/or sabotages the system.

hacking illegally breaking into computer systems or databases, either using the computer's own terminal or remotely over the Internet.

halo rating errors errors which occur in performance appraisal when appraisers focus on one favourable trait in a candidate, often to the exclusion of all other traits.

Halsey–Weir incentive schemes incentive schemes whereby bonuses are paid for exceeding production targets, but not necessarily in proportion to the increase in production.

hammer colloquial term: **1** to hammer the competition meaning to win decisively; **2** under the hammer, meaning up for sale.

hammering the process of expelling a member of a stock exchange who is no longer able to meet his or her debts.

hammering the market colloquial term for the effect on the market of a number of speculators taking a persistent bear position.

handling cost costs associated with handling goods in inventory or in the distribution channel.

handover **1** the transfer of goods from one party to another; **2** the transition period when one party leaves a job and hands over the duties to another entering that position.

handover pay special payment to shift workers who are responsible for handing on work to colleagues in the following shift.

hard copy paper copy of a document, as opposed to a version on film or in electronic storage.

hard-core unemployed people who are unable to find work and remain out of work for long periods; generally characterized by low levels of education and skill.

hard currency stable currency which can be traded and exchanged internationally.

hard disk large capacity computer storage disk, usually found fixed inside a PC.

hard loan loan that must be paid in hard currency.

hard money situation in which interest rates are high and loans are difficult; also as hard currency.

hard sales promotion sales promotion aimed at increasing the volume of sales, rather than profits.

hard sell aggressive, and sometimes unethical, sales techniques.

hardship and danger premiums special payments made to employees where they are required to work in hostile environmental conditions.

hard skills accounting, technical and engineering skills; as opposed to soft skills.

hard systems systems which can be engineered or configured.

hardware physical machinery of a computer including chips, hard disks and circuits; as opposed to software.

harmonization bringing systems into line with each other; synchronization.

Harrod–Domar model a standard neoclassical model of economic growth.

Harvard case method management teaching method developed at Harvard Business School, relying primarily on case studies.

harvest strategy strategic option focusing on maximizing profits from a stable and secure market.

harvesting taking profits from a secure market.

Hawthorne effect phenomenon whereby behaviour changes when people become aware that they are being observed.

Hawthorne experiments performance studies undertaken at Western Electric's Hawthorne plant, focusing on organization behaviour issues.

HCCs *see* high-context cultures.

headhunter recruitment consultant who specializes in headhunting.

headhunting the process of identifying suitable executives who might fill particular vacancies and then attempting to recruit them to fill those vacancies.

health insurance insurance policies which cover costs of treatment in the event of illness or accident.

health services general term for services, both private and public, which supply all aspects of healthcare.

heavy half theory in marketing, theory of rate of usage or consumption, showing that half of a firm's customers are responsible for purchasing 80 per cent of its goods.

heavy industry industrial sectors engaged in heavy engineering or requiring large and complex plants.

hedge fund money invested in such a way as to provide a hedge against other, risky investments.

hedging 1 actions taken to minimize or lay off risk; **2** investments made with the sole purpose offsetting potential losses from other investments.

hedonic method form of environmental valuation which focuses on the environment as a provider of amenities.

hegemony domination of an economic or political system by one or more actors in that system.

helping skills specific set of skills useful in assisting others to perform their jobs.

heroes people of outstanding ability who are looked up to by their colleagues and expected to provide leadership.

heuristic pertaining to investigation or discovery.

heuristic models models built on the results of practical experience.

hidden assets assets not directly recorded on a balance sheet.

hidden clause clause in a contract, not easily identifiable, that may be harmful to one party's interests.

hidden tax tax which cannot be easily identified, often included in other taxes or hidden in sales prices, transfer costs and so on.

hierarchy organization based on a series of grades or classes.

hierarchy of effects marketing theory of the effect of promotions and advertising on the target audience, with effects progressing from awareness to action; *see also* AIDA model.

hierarchy of needs behaviour theory relating to human fulfilment, whereby as one set of needs is fulfilled, another set then becomes the focus of the person's attention.

high-context cultures (HCCs) cultures in which verbal communication tends not to provide complete messages and in which some reading of context is also required to grasp meaning.

high day rate a higher than usual hourly or daily rate of pay, offered to exceptionally skilled workers.

high finance complex or large-scale financial management.

high flier employee or manager regarded as having exceptional potential and suitable for rapid promotion; *see also* fast track.

high frequency work sampling work sampling method which involves frequent sampling and a combination of records kept by the work study officer and the workers themselves.

high performance work systems (HPWS) production system relying on teams which each take responsibility for a stage of production.

high potential personnel employees regarded as having exceptional potential.

high street bank *see* commercial bank.

high-technology products products using very complex or advanced technologies, such as electronics or biotechnology.

high value added (HVA) production flow production processes which alter the original materials or components in such a way as to add exceptional levels of value added.

hire and fire practices company policies with relation to the recruitment and dismissal of employees.

hire purchase method of purchase where the buyer pays off the purchase price in regular instalments, possibly with interest; the buyer has use of the goods through this period, but does not become the legal owner until the final payment has been made.

hiring taking on new employees; *see also* recruitment.

hiring hall trade union facilities which attempt to match members needing work with current job vacancies.

histogram *see* bar chart.

historical cost original cost of an asset, or its value on acquisition.

historical cost accounting accounting process which takes the original cost of an asset as its starting point, and compares this with the realization value of assets.

historical cost convention accounting convention that asset values are based on their original cost of purchase or production.

historical costing the analysis of costs after they have been incurred.

hoarding accumulating or stockpiling goods beyond present need, usually in anticipation of a future shortage.

holdback portion of a loan that is not granted until some separate condition has been met.

holdback pay pay due to an employee but not yet paid.

holder of record shareholder whose name is assigned to shares in the company's share register.

holding company company which has been set up solely as a vehicle for managing the shares of other companies, which it either owns outright or in which it has a controlling interest.

holding pattern undesirable situation where an employee just returned from an overseas assignment is given no clear duties or responsibilities after repatriation.

holiday amount of leave from work to which employees are entitled annually; *see also* bank holiday; public holiday.

holiday pay 1 wages which continue to be paid to workers while they are on holiday; **2** alternatively, higher rates of pay which are paid for work on bank holidays or public holidays.

holism a focus on whole entities; the philosophy that the whole is greater than the sum of its parts.

holistic evaluation evaluation of a project or programme as a totality, taking into account its likely effects and impact on the environment.

hollow corporation corporations that concentrate on service provision and do little or no manufacturing.

home audit market research technique for gathering data on choice and volume in household consumption and purchasing.

home banking banking system where transactions can be carried out by the account holder from home, using the telephone or a computer terminal.

home market market for a product within the country where it is manufactured.

home nation the country where a multinational corporation is domiciled.

homeostasis condition where there is no change, used in modelling and experimental simulations.

home shopping systems for shopping for goods from home, using either printed catalogues and the telephone or on-line catalogues and ordering systems called up from a computer terminal.

home working the practice of carrying out some or all of a job in the employee's home, rather than at a separate workplace.

homogeneity sameness or similarity.

honour pledge or promise, sometimes accepted as security for a loan or performance of a contract.

horizontal expansion expansion of a business by acquiring further facilities which will increase the volume of its present business; as opposed to vertical expansion.

horizontal integration acquisition, amalgamation or reorganization of a number of formerly separate companies which extend activities into the same area; as opposed to vertical integration.

horizontal merger merger between two competing firms producing the same or similar goods and services.

hospitality management management techniques and skills associated with segments such as hotels, restaurants, travel and tourism.

host country nationals citizens of a country where a foreign business has established operations, who may be contacted in the form of customers or labour.

hostile in business, a climate where a firm's activities are opposed by other firms.

hostile bid offer to purchase shares which would give the buyer a controlling interest in a company, but where the company's senior management recommends that shareholders should not sell.

hostile takeover acquisition of a firm by another against the wishes and recommendations of the acquired firm's senior management.

hot money currency whose holders are anxious to sell quickly, usually in anticipation of an exchange rate fluctuation or devaluation.

Hotelling's Rule in environmental economics, the principle that the rate of depletion of non-renewable resources is such that extraction costs will rise at the same rate as the rate of interest.

hourly rate wage paid for an hour's work.

house in employee relations, term for a single place of work.

house claim pay claim made by employees of a single plant or company.

household savings rate nationally, the excess of disposable income over income actually spent on consumption.

household survey marketing survey of household buying behaviour.

house journal *see* house magazine.

housekeeping maintenance of a property, including maintaining general standards of cleanliness and attractiveness.

house magazine magazine published by a company for the information of employees and/or customers.

house mark *see* trademark.

house style 1 design and style issues associated with a company's image and brand; **2** visual standards for packaging, letterhead, promotional material, use of the company logo and so on; *see also* corporate image.

Howard–Sheth model detailed consumer behaviour model depicting some of the processes that go to make up consumer behaviour.

HPWS *see* high performance work systems.

hub and spoke routing system where airlines designate a few major airlines as 'hubs' and operate long-haul flights between them; passengers going on from these destinations then take shorter flights to nearby regional airports.

human asset concept that a firm's employees and management have skills and attributes which make them an asset to be valued rather than simply a cost.

human asset accounting accounting techniques which attempt to put a value on human assets.

human capital 1 the sum total of human assets held by a corporation; **2** the investment a firm makes in developing its employees.

human-centred manufacturing manufacturing systems which focus on the role played by human labour in the manufacturing process, in effect, designing systems to go around the people.

human engineering *see* ergonomics.

human interaction *see* relationship.

human motivation theory social and psychological theory concerning the factors which motivate human behaviour.

human relations management theory developed in the 1930s, which viewed businesses as primarily social organizations and attempted to serve as a counterweight to scientific management.

human relations department another term for employee relations department, human resources department, or personnel department.

human relations school school of industrial sociology which focused on relations between employees and management as a critical factor in improving productivity; *see also* human relations.

human relations theory systemic theory of organizations, taking the view that organizations function primarily as a series of human interactions.

human resource accounting accounting practice which reports on the contributions made by a firm's employees to its earnings and profits; *see also* human asset accounting.

human resource development overall programmes of training and career development for employees.

human resource flows inputs of labour, human knowledge, human capital and so on into the production process.

human resource management general term for the management functions required to manage human resources, including recruiting, employee relations, training, retention and redundancy.

human resource planning planning future human resource needs and associated recruitment and retention programmes.

human resources the people a firm employs, together with their associated skills, knowledge and capabilities.

human resource skills the skills required by managers of human resources.

human systems system involving human participation and interaction.

hurdle rate minimum acceptable rate of return on a project or development.

hybrid mixture of systems.

hybrid computer computer system combining features of both analogue and digital computers.

hydrocarbons contaminant released into the atmosphere by burning fossil fuels.

hygiene factors *see* dissatisfiers.

hype colloquial term for highly visible promotional activities that attempt to arouse consumer interest in a product or brand.

hypercommunication very high levels of communication.

hyperinflation inflation at very high rates, in excess of 100 per cent annually; *see also* galloping inflation.

hypermarket very large out-of-town retail outlet selling a broad range of products.

hypermedia systems databases combining text, sound, pictures and other forms of stored information.

hypothecation in banking, an agreement whereby if a loan is not repaid when required, any property put up as collateral can then be used by the lending agency.

I

ICF *see* investing cash flow.

ICOR *see* incremental capital–output ratio.

ICT *see* information and communications technology.

ideal capacity total capacity of a production system over a given time period, assuming there are no slowdowns or delays.

identity management management techniques involved in the creation and maintenance of corporate identity.

idle money money which is not invested.

idle time *see* downtime.

IE 1 *see* industrial economics; **2** *see* industrial engineering.

IEO *see* industrial economics and organization.

illegal contract contract which contains provisions which require one or both parties to violate the law, and which therefore is not legally binding.

illiquid assets which cannot be easily converted into cash; as opposed to liquid.

ILM *see* internal labour market.

IMACS *see* intelligent management assistant for computer systems.

image 1 the view of a person or organization taken by those around it; **2** the general feelings of people towards a person, government, business or organization.

image building in public relations, the deliberate creation of an image by communicating certain attributes to the target audience.

image making the design of an image, usually prior to a campaign of image building.

image study study of the representation of a company and its products held by customers and the public.

immediate objectives goals which can be accomplished quickly, often as a first stage towards the accomplishment of further, larger objectives.

immunity 1 protection from penalties or negative consequences of an action; **2** more specifically, exemption from certain regulations or taxes.

impact the effect of an advertisement or other communication on its target audience.

impact testing marketing and public relations research technique for measuring the extent of the impact of an advertisement, usually by focusing on what features of the advertisement can be recalled by the audience.

impairment the amount which must be deducted from a given capital sum through dividends, payments and losses.

imperfect competition competition where either buyers or sellers have the power to alter prices to suit themselves.

impersonality theory that rules and regulations apply to all impartially, and that managers have no power to bend rules to suit themselves.

implementation 1 putting a plan or concept into practice; **2** carrying out a plan.

implicit costs costs originating within the business and from the manner in which it is run.

import 1 to bring goods across a country's borders for sale in that country; **2** also, a good that is imported.

import controls general term for border controls affecting imports, possibly including the exclusion of some items and the imposition of tariffs on others.

import duty tax levied on imports; *see also* tariff.

import quota restriction on the quantity of a particular good that can be imported.

import substitution the replacing of imports with similar goods manufactured locally.

import tariff *see* tariff.

imposition demand for taxes due.

impost tax, usually in the form of a tariff.

imprest 1 advance or loan; **2** small sum of cash kept for immediate expenses; *see* petty cash.

improvement to make better or increase in value.

improvement curve graph showing the rate at which something improves; *see also* experience curve; learning curve.

impulse buying buying decision made on the spur of the moment, not as a result of a calculation of needs.

impulse goods *see* impulse merchandise.

impulse merchandise consumer goods which are usually purchased without planning by consumers; retailers usually place these in those locations in their stores where they will catch the consumer's eye.

impulse purchase a product or service purchased without prior thought.

imputed costs cost which is implied but not specified, usually incurred as a result of the basic functions of the business; *see also* implicit costs.

inactive account bank account where the number of deposits and withdrawals is very low.

inactive stock stock where the volume of shares traded is very low.

inalienable 1 good or property which cannot be sold or transferred to another party; **2** attributed of a good or property which cannot be separated from it.

incentive offer of money or other benefits which encourages customers to buy, or workers to work longer hours and/or increase productivity.

incentive pay bonuses offered as an incentive to workers, usually for increased productivity.

incentive payment scheme structured incentive pay which is included in a contract of employment; *see also* payment-by-results.

incentive plan *see* incentive payment scheme.

incestuous share dealing buying and selling by two companies of each other's shares, usually for tax advantages or other financial advantages (illegal in many jurisdictions).

incident event or occurrence which is analysed in an incident process or critical incident technique.

incident process case study where participants are required to collect further information at specific points in the case.

income money that is earned through work, the sale of goods and services, or as a return on investment.

income account account showing income flows only, without reference to expenses or outgoings.

income and expense statement summary of income and expenses over a given period, used mainly by non-profit organizations; *see also* profit and loss account.

income benefit insurance policy insurance policy which, in the event that the insured dies before the policy matures, provides an income for the insured dependents.

income, circular flow of *see* circular flow of income.

income distribution the way in which personal income is spent and thus continues to flow through the economy.

income effect effect on purchasing power caused by changes in personal income.

income elasticity of demand extent to which demand or sales volume of a good or service is affected by fluctuations in customers' income.

income–expenditure relationship in balance of payments, the assessment of the relationship between national income and national expenditure.

income fund investment fund, the prime objective of which is to maximize income rather than increase capital.

income segmentation form of segmentation which classifies potential customers into groups according to their income.

incomes policy government policy on personal income, usually aiming to limit or restrict pay increases with a view to restraining inflation.

incomes policy, voluntary situation where employees effectively set incomes policy by voluntarily agreeing to restrict their wage increases.

income statement *see* income and expense statement.

income tax tax on personal or corporate income.

in-company training training programmes held on the company's premises, organized by either the company itself or external consultants.

incompetence **1** inability to do a job or manage a function; **2** mistakes which lead to losses or damage.

incorporation process of forming a corporation, usually requiring the granting of a government charter.

incoterms general name for terms used by the International Chamber of Commerce in trade contracts.

increasing returns describes a situation where increasing input (of money, resources, labour and so on) leads to a proportionally larger increase in output.

increment 1 salary increase within a particular pay grade, often awarded annually or as a result of achieving seniority; **2** more generally, a limited increase or change.

incremental capital–output ratio (ICOR) increase in capital stock, divided by the increase in output of goods and services, over a particular period.

incremental costing *see* marginal costing.

incrementalism management approach which considers a number of alternatives and then tests these by implementing them one at a time.

incremental model model of planning which does not focus on long-term goals but instead makes reactive adjustments when new issues or problems appear.

incremental profitability increase in profitability over time, usually as a result of increasing levels of skill in the workforce.

increment tax tax levied on property which has increased in value, based on the value of the appreciation.

incumbent person holding a particular position or job.

incurred losses losses on investments or capital over a particular period.

indebtedness the extent of a person's or a company's debts and other liabilities.

indefinite tenure condition whereby someone holds a position for an unspecified period of time.

indemnify to compensate another party for losses they have incurred.

indemnity payment for damages or losses.

indemnity fund fund held in reserve by employers' associations to compensate firms for losses incurred during strikes.

indent order placed with an importer for the import of a good at an agreed price.

indenture 1 agreement setting out the terms under which bonds or indentures are used; **2** also, a contract between apprentice and employer.

independent agent *see* agent, independent.

independent audit audit performed by an auditor brought in from outside the company.

independent bank small, independently owned bank, usually operating in a single location.

independent retailer retail outlet not part of a chain, often managed by its owner.

index statistical record of economic indicators, showing changes over time.

indexation process by which inflation affects the determination of exchange rates.

indexing an investment strategy whereby a portfolio of shares is managed so that holdings are weighted to reflect the performance of a particular share index (such as the FTSE-100).

index linking adjustment of the value of wages, pensions and so on at a rate reflecting national increases in prices or inflation.

index method in marketing forecasting, the calculation of increases in demand based on index figures (such as population growth or increases in income).

index number measure assigned to a factor in an index, giving an indication of overall change in that factor over a period of time.

indicative planning planning using a broad consultative process and securing agreement from all those affected.

indicators factors which, while not significant in themselves, indicate larger or more important trends.

indifference curve graphic illustration of how individuals make choices between goods and services, showing their ideal preferences.

indirect cost cost incurred during manufacturing but which cannot be attributed to a particular product; as opposed to direct cost; *see also* factory cost; overhead costs.

indirect demand demand for a product which is not a finished good but is required as a component for another product; as opposed to final demand.

indirect labour labour which is not directly productive but nonetheless performs functions necessary to keeping the business in operation; as opposed to direct labour.

indirect labour cost wages and other costs associated with indirect labour.

indirect liability liability incurred by a third party who serves as guarantor or endorses a note.

indirect materials cost cost of materials and components required by the business but which do not directly form part of a finished product.

indirect production manufacturing machinery or equipment required to produce other goods.

indirect review review of quality through feedback from customers rather than through direct inspection of products.

indirect taxation taxes on goods and services, usually applied at the point of sale or purchase; *see also* sales tax; value added tax.

individual brand brand name which is applied to a single product; as opposed to family brand.

individual freedom extent to which people can make their own choices without constraint from external forces.

individualism theory that individuals are unique actors who should be allowed to conduct their own affairs freely.

individuals in business terms, persons considered in their own right rather than as part of an organization.

individual theory in organization behaviour, the set of theories which describe the behaviour of individuals in an organization context.

individual training training provided to an individual on a one-on-one basis, rather than as part of a group.

indivisibility the point at which labour can no longer be realistically divided, as the production system would no longer function.

induction the process of integrating newly joined employees into the company.

induction training training provided to newly joined employees; consisting of an explanation of the company and their expected roles in it.

industrial accident accident suffered at work.

industrial action collective action taken by workers in support of a demand or to draw attention to a grievance; *see also* go slow; strike.

industrial and labour relations *see* industrial relations.

industrial arbitration conciliation, usually conducted by a third party, aimed at resolving disputes leading to industrial action.

industrial bank bank offering financial services primarily to employees of a particular firm or in a particular industry.

industrial capital goods industrial buildings, plant and equipment.

industrial classification system of classification which classifies firms by the industrial activities in which they are most prominently involved.

industrial clusters geographic regions with high concentrations of firms in particular industrial sectors.

industrial concentration measure of the extent to which activity in an industrial sector is concentrated in the hands of a few large companies.

industrial conflict disputes between labour and management leading to industrial action.

industrial democracy philosophy of worker participation, aimed at increasing such participation and giving workers a greater say in managerial policy and decision making.

industrial development the growth of a nation's industrial capacity.

industrial development agency government or government-sponsored agency established to promote local economic development.

industrial disease illness contracted through exposure to hazardous working conditions.

industrial dispute disagreement between workers and management over issues such as pay and working conditions; *see also* industrial conflict.

industrial distributor distribution company dealing in industrial goods.

industrial dynamics *see* system dynamics.

industrial economics (IE) *see* industrial economics and organization.

industrial economics and organization (IEO) the application of theories derived from economics to industrial organization.

industrial engineering (IE) branch of engineering dealing with the design and construction of industrial systems, plants, machinery and so on.

industrial espionage the acquisition of secret or confidential information about a company by its rivals.

industrial estate area, usually on the edge of an urban centre, set aside by local planning laws for the development of factories and depots.

industrial goods machinery or components sold to manufacturers; as opposed to consumer goods.

industrial health and safety practices designed to ensure the health and safety of employees while performing their jobs.

industrial injury injury suffered in the workplace as a result of an accident, usually involving machinery or equipment.

industrialist owner and employer of capital which is invested directly in industry; sometimes synonymous with capitalist.

industrialization the conversion of an economy from being primarily agricultural to being primarily industrial.

industrial market market for industrial goods.

industrial marketing marketing of industrial goods to industrial customers; *see also* business-to-business marketing.

industrial market research branch of market research focusing particularly on industrial markets.

industrial organization (IO) *see* industrial economics and organization.

industrial organizations businesses engaged in industry.

industrial park *see* industrial estate.

industrial policy national policy concerning the advancement and growth of industry.

industrial product *see* basic product.

industrial psychology branch of applied psychology focusing on the behaviour of people in the workplace.

industrial reform the transformation of older industrial structures to meet modern conditions.

industrial relations **1** relations between companies and their employees, including actions by the company to influence positively employee morale, motivation and so on; **2** often refers specifically to relations between management and unions.

Industrial Revolution the period in the eighteenth and nineteenth centuries which, in Western Europe, was characterized by rapid industrialization and the widespread mechanization of production processes.

industrial sabotage refers to a wide range of actions which may be taken by workers during an industrial dispute to delay production or to damage goods and machinery.

industrial societies national societies or cultures where industrialization is complete and where industry provides a high proportion of national employment and income.

industrial sociology application of the principles of sociology to industrial organizations.

industrial strategy national strategy concerning industrial growth and development.

industrial trade union a trade union whose membership is restricted to workers in a particular industry.

industrial training training for employees working in industrial sectors.

industrial tribunal body set up to arbitrate disputes between workers and management, often dealing with cases of unfair dismissal or illness and injury claims.

industrial union *see* industrial trade union.

industries, manufacturing *see* manufacturing industries.

industries, service *see* service industries.

industry **1** general term for business, particularly that portion of business which is involved in manufacturing; **1** alternatively, a particular sector where companies are involved in broadly similar business, such as the mining industry, the pharmaceuticals industry and so on.

industry-wide agreement nationwide collective agreement negotiated between all employers and unions in a particular industry.

industry-wide bargaining bargaining process leading to an industry-wide agreement.

inelastic demand situation where demand for a product or service changes slightly or not at all in response to a change in price; as opposed to elastic demand.

inelastic supply situation where the supply of a product or service changes slightly or not at all in response to a change in price.

inequity conditions leading to unfairness or unequal treatment.

inertial forces forces which tend towards inertia.

inertia selling sales method where goods are delivered directly to potential customers who are then invoiced for the goods, the assumption being that customers will find it easier to pay than to return the goods.

inference engine in expert systems, software used to make inferences from a knowledge base.

inflation in economics, the situation where money supply expands faster than the supply of goods and services, driving up prices and thence wages; *see also* cost-push inflation; demand inflation; wage inflation.

inflation accounting accounting practices which factor the likely effects of inflation into estimates of revenues and costs.

inflationary gap the amount by which private and public spending exceeds the level required to maintain stable prices.

inflationary spiral the combined effects of wage and price inflation, with higher wages leading to higher costs and thence higher prices in a continuous cycle.

influence in marketing, a person who is held in esteem by others, and whose behaviour can affect the buying decisions of others.

influence market marketing term for groups of individuals or organizations that influence or put pressure on the company and its operations.

infobahn seldom-used term, synonymous with 'information superhighway'.

informal groups groups which cohere naturally rather than being formally defined.

informal leader individual who takes up a position of leadership in a group by the unspoken consent of its members, rather through formal appointment.

informal organization organization which evolves through relationships between individuals rather than being formally defined or structured.

informant in marketing research, a person who provides information as part of a survey; *see also* respondent.

information records of facts and opinions, both qualitative and quantitative in format, which can be transmitted and stored.

information age term for the modern period, reflecting the increasing importance of and value placed on information by companies and individuals.

information and communications technology (ICT) general term for technologies, usually computer-based, used to retrieve, store, analyse and transmit information and for communications; the same basic technology is often used for any or all of the above purposes.

information and knowledge industry industrial sectors which trade information and knowledge as commodities.

information asymmetry situation where one individual or group is better informed or has access to more information than others.

information bias particular slant or focus in information which leads to an interpretation which may not reflect the true situation.

information complexity nature of information which can lead consumers to have difficulty assimilating that information and so lead to information asymmetry.

information economy economy where information has value and is traded as a commodity.

information engineering use of information systems to integrate management activities.

information flows the movement of information within and between organizations.

information gathering collection of information as part of a research programme, prior to analysis.

information highways routes taken by information flows.

information overload situation caused when so much information is available that no one has time to digest or analyse it all.

information processing the storage and analysis of information, usually on a computer system.

information resource management general term for the management of information using databases, management information systems, decision support systems and so on.

information retrieval the use of computer-based systems to retrieve information stored in a database.

information revolution term describing the period in the late twentieth century when, in the developed nations, the rapid dissemination of information and communications technology resulted in an equally rapid increase in the speed and volume of information flows.

information storage facilities where information is stored for future analysis and use, ranging in technology terms from filing cabinets to computer databases.

information superhighway popular term in the early 1990s for the global communications network, referring primarily to the Internet.

information systems systems designed for the collection, storage, management and retrieval of information, usually based around computer databases.

information technology *see* information and communications technology.

information technology applications specific programmes or software used in information and communications technology, such as databases, e-mail, web browsers and so on.

infrastructure the basic physical structure of transportation and communications networks, public services, property and so on, on which a nation's economy depends.

infringement violation of a trademark, patent, copyright or similar, usually by reproducing material covered by the above without obtaining consent.

in-house training training provided by the company using its own resources and its own staff as trainers; *see also* in-company training.

initial mark-on retailer's initial display price less the cost of goods as delivered from the manufacturer.

injection **1** the addition of new capital into a company; **2** more broadly, a deliberate increase in purchasing power in the economy.

injunction ruling by a court of law preventing a named party from undertaking a certain specified action.

injury **1** physical harm caused to a person; **2** more generally, any damage suffered by a person or organization as a result of actions by another.

injury benefit compensation paid to an employee who is prevented from working as a result of an injury sustained in the workplace.

in kind the value of a good expressed in other similar goods, rather than in cash; *see also* payment in kind.

innovation the development of new technologies, products, processes and systems, and the implementation of these in business operations.

innovation diffusion the spread of a new innovation through the market so that it gradually becomes accepted as the norm.

innovation-intensive industries industrial sectors, such as electronics and biotechnology, characterized by constant and continuous innovation.

innovation management management techniques involved in stimulating innovative behaviour and in translating innovations into real advantage in terms of products and processes.

in play colloquial, refers to a company that is the target of a takeover bid.

input **1** materials and resources which go into a production process, leading to an output of finished goods; **2** in computing, the raw data or information which are analysed in information and decision-making systems.

input buffer device in a computer which makes it possible for more than one input device to operate.

input device in computers, a device which translates input from outside the computer (such as that typed in by a human operator at a keyboard) into the computer's own language.

input–output analysis market research technique used to identify trends in sales and purchases.

input–output models forecasting technique based on the theory that one industry's outputs are another's inputs.

insert stand-alone advertising leaflet or document which is then packaged with a newspaper or journal, which can be pulled out and read separately by readers or subscribers.

insertion an advertisement which is to be placed in a print publication.

insertion charge payment made to a newspaper, magazine, etc. for the insertion of an advertisement.

insertion order instruction made by an advertising agency to a publication, specifying the advertisement to be inserted and the fee to be paid.

in-service training training programmes undertaken while the employee is at work, and which do not interrupt his or her duties.

inside–outside approach strategic approach which first looks at the company's capabilities and then at opportunities or threats within the operating environment.

insider one who has access to special or privileged information.

insider trading in financial markets, term describing a case where someone has access to confidential knowledge about a company and uses that knowledge to make a profit from trading in the company's shares; illegal in many jurisdictions.

insolvency 1 technically, a business is said to be insolvent when liabilities exceed assets; **2** more practically, insolvency occurs when a firm or individual is unable to pay debts when they come due.

insolvency practitioner consultant who advises insolvent businesses and their creditors on how to reach accommodation over disposal of assets and payment of outstanding debts.

insolvent 1 being in a condition of insolvency; **2** being unable to pay debts when due.

inspection examination of finished goods to ensure they meet stated quality standards.

instalment one of a regular series of payments made to clear a loan or complete a purchase made on credit.

instalment buying purchasing goods on instalment, with the full purchase price paid off over a period of time, rather than handing over the full purchase price at the time of sale; *see also* hire purchase.

instalment credit credit granted to buyers for the specific purpose of making purchases on instalment.

instalment purchase *see* hire purchase.

instant business term meaning 'the current month'; often abbreviated as 'inst.'

institute non-commercial organization formed for purposes such as research or consulting.

institution 1 bank, pension fund, insurance company or other large organization which holds very large investments; *see also* institutional investor; **2** more generally, used as a synonym for organization and applied to any large business.

institutional advertising *see* prestige advertising.

institutional authority the authority which institutions can exert over those within their jurisdictions.

institutional change change which affects an entire institution, including its processes, personnel and strategies.

institutional decisions *see* organization decision making.

institutional economics the study of institutions as economic actors or agents.

institutional factors significant aspects of the organization structure of an institution.

institutional investor company or other organization with very large shareholdings in large public companies, which makes investment decisions with a view to maximizing its own profits.

institutionalism *see* institutional theories.

institutionalization to bring a person or good into or within the framework of an organization or institution.

institutional theories theoretical concepts concerning the nature and behaviour of institutions.

in stock goods which are available now and ready for delivery or sale.

instruction 1 order to carry out a certain task; **2** synonym for teaching.

instruction code *see* machine code.

instrument the written form of a legal contract.

insubordination deliberately disobeying an order given by a senior manager.

insufficient funds term for when a cheque is drawn on a bank account for a sum larger than the balance of the account; literally, there are not sufficient funds to honour the cheque.

insurable something which can be insured.

insurance provision against risk or possible loss, where payment is made into a common fund from which repayment is made if or when the loss occurs; *see also* assurance.

insurance broker agent who arranges insurance policies, acting between companies providing insurance and those companies and individuals who wish to buy it.

insurance company company that acts as an insurer, writing insurance policies for clients.

insurance coverage the amount of insurance provided for an organization, person or good in event of loss.

insurance management general term for the management of the provision of insurance including actuarial assessment, policy writing and underwriting.

insurance policy a contract between an insurance company and a client, specifying the amount of premium to be paid, the circumstances in which compensation will be paid, and the amount of compensation to be paid.

insurance underwriter member of an insurance company or a syndicate engaged in assessing and writing insurance policies.

insured in an insurance policy, the beneficiary to whom compensation will be paid according to the terms specified in the policy.

insurer in an insurance policy, the party (usually an insurance company) who pays compensation to the insured according to the terms specified in the policy.

insuring clause clause in an insurance policy stating that the insurer agrees to compensate the insured in event of loss.

intangible asset asset with no physical existence, but which nonetheless has value and is included on a balance sheet; examples include patents and goodwill.

intangible rewards rewards that have no monetary value or tangible nature, such as satisfaction.

integer programming (IP) mathematical programming technique, involving rounding off sums to the nearest whole number.

integral job evaluation job evaluation method comparing jobs in a holistic manner, rather than by individual elements of the job.

integrated circuit miniaturized electronic circuit, usually printed on a single microchip.

integrated data processing computerized data processing system that brings together data from a number of different sources.

integrated learning system educational or instructional programme which combines a variety of methods of instruction.

integrated marketing the integration of direct marketing and other forms of marketing within a single marketing programme.

integrated materials value chain logistics, production and marketing system which defines the movement of materials and products as a single continuous process.

integrated package software package that includes several different applications, typically word processing, graphic design, spreadsheets and database.

integrated services digital network (ISDN) high-technology telecommunications network.

integration combining of a number of different elements into a single system.

integration, backward *see* backward integration.

integration, forward *see* forward integration.

integration, horizontal *see* horizontal integration.

integration, vertical *see* vertical integration.

integrative bargaining non-adversarial bargaining which seeks to maximize the advantages for both sides.

integrative growth expansion of a business by acquiring the assets of other firms.

integrator employee or manager whose primary function is to coordinate the efforts of others.

intellectual capital knowledge generated by or contained in a company, either as a result of acquired learning or generated internally through research and development; more generally, the stock of knowledge and skills to which a company has access; *see also* intellectual property.

intellectual property any form of knowledge generated by the firm and formally registered through copyright, patents, trade marks and so on.

intelligence 1 generally, synonymous with knowledge; **2** of people, the measure of their general ability to think and reason.

intelligence test psychological tests of various kinds, used to measure intelligence.

intelligent management assistant for computer systems (IMACS) artificial intelligence system used in manufacturing control.

intelligent scheduling and information system (ISIS) artificial intelligence system used for job scheduling.

intelligent support systems (ISS) artificial intelligence system used as a decisions support system.

intelligent systems *see* artificial intelligence.

intelligent building building or plant, many of whose functions are controlled by computer systems which can in turn be easily controlled or monitored by human users working in a single system.

intelligent computer computer which has the ability to make judgements and recommendations.

intelligent terminal computer terminal with some integral processing ability, which can perform some functions without reference to a central processing unit.

intensive distribution distribution strategy which uses a very large number of channels and outlets.

interaction the mutual effect of two or more people or processes on each other.

interaction analysis research technique for measuring the extent and nature of interaction through observation of groups at work.

interaction matrix design tool used for physical positioning of machinery, equipment and so on, based on the interaction between different parts of the manufacturing process.

interactive behaviour behaviour between members of a group.

interactive programming general term for computer software used in decision-making processes.

interactive skills general term for skills used when interacting with others in a group, in either business or social situations.

interactive technology technology which allows a high degree of user control and machine feedback.

interactive video video programmes which can be directed to some extent by the viewer in order to select the desired information.

interbank market market where banks trade financial instruments and lend to each other.

interchangeable parts parts made on an assembly line which can serve as components for a machine of a similar type; components which are identical to one another.

interchangeability extent to which jobs and functions are similar or complementary, allowing workers to move between jobs without substantial retraining.

intercorporate stockholding ownership of shares in corporations by other corporations or companies; unlawful in some instances.

intercultural communication *see* cross-cultural communication

inter-dealer broker trader or agent who acts for market makers, usually with the intent of allowing the latter to remain anonymous.

interdepartmental conflict conflict or dispute about jurisdiction, resources and so on, between two departments of the same organization.

interdependence condition where two or more organizations, people, etc. rely on each other to some extent for the performance of tasks or the achievement of goals.

inter-entity transaction accounting term for an event when assets and/or money pass between two accounting entities.

interest 1 fee paid to the lender when borrowing money, or for the use of capital more generally; *see also* dividend; **2** in marketing, the point at which a consumer has become aware of a brand or product and is now actively trying to learn more about it before making a purchase decision.

interest cover ratio of the total of interest payments due to creditors, to total pre-tax profit, over a given period.

interest groups group of people held together by a common interest.

interest inventory survey technique which aims to uncover the full range of an individual's interests.

interest rate rate of interest charged on borrowed capital, usually expressed as a percentage of the sum lent.

interest rate contract contract to borrow or lend a sum of money at a stated sum of interest.

interest rate future *see* interest rate contract.

interest rate risk risks posed by unstable interest rates which could impair or harm the company's operations.

interest rate swap financial derivative, where fixed rate debt is traded for floating rate debt.

interest rate yield *see* yield.

interest test test used to gather information about people's personal interests.

interface connection between two organizations or processes; link between human and computer systems.

interference pay payment made to employees as compensation for lost production bonuses, when their work has been interrupted so that they have been unable to achieve production targets.

inter-firm relations contacts and linkages between companies, both formally through employer associations and industry associations, or informally through personal networks.

intergovernmental expenditure payments from one government to another for services or transferred goods.

intergovernmental revenue money received by one government from another in exchange for services and goods.

interim manager manager filling a position on a short-term or temporary basis, usually in advance of another more permanent appointment.

interim payment provisional or temporary payment made in lieu of the full payment due.

interlocking directorate position where a person is a director of several corporations which are themselves related; for example, when a director of a holding company is also a director of a subsidiary company.

intermediary a third party who assists in negotiations or business dealings, dealing simultaneously with the two principals.

intermediate-term credit credit which is extended for the medium term, generally for 3–5 years.

intermediation practice by financial institutions of placing funds which have been deposited with the institution into other institutions.

intermittent process process which is not continuous but varies from task to task.

internal audit audit carried out by members of the firm on its own accounts or processes.

internal bank division within a large corporation which provides banking functions to other divisions.

internal check checks which are built into a process or project, ensuring consistency and accuracy.

internal control measures taken within work teams or departments to ensure accurate reporting, scheduling, budgeting and so on.

internal customer person or unit who purchases goods or services from within the same organization; *see also* internal market.

internal forecast forecast developed within a company, concerned with its future operations.

internal investment the investment of profits in assets within the company.

internal labour market (ILM) labour market which exists within a company, that is, the extent to which employees can be re-employed elsewhere in the company.

internal market system whereby parts of an organization sell goods and services to each other, with funds credited to or debited from internal profit centres.

internal memory computer memory which is part of the central processing unit, used primarily to store data related to the basic operating configuration.

internal rate of return (IRR) rate of return on investment as measured by discounted cash flow techniques.

internal revenue tax proceeds levied by a government within its borders.

internal users people within an organization who use a service or good produced by that organization.

internalize to bring inside or into an organization.

international accounting accounting practices common to most developed countries.

international advertising *see* advertising, international.

international alliances alliances between countries domiciled in different countries.

international banking facility type of US bank whose sole business is to accept foreign deposits.

international bond markets bond markets open to buyers and sellers from other countries.

international business general term covering business which is done across borders around the world.

international business elites managers and executives who are skilled and experienced at doing business on an international basis.

international business negotiations negotiations between businesses domiciled in or operating in different countries.

international company *see* multinational company.

international competition competition between companies from different countries, possibly in a large number of markets around the world.

international consultancies consulting firms that operate internationally.

international contracts contracts between countries domiciled in different countries, which have to take different regulations and legal codes into consideration.

international corporation *see* multinational corporation.

international credit club reciprocal lending agreements between financial institutions for the purpose of financing imports and exports.

international currency markets currency markets open to buyers and sellers from other countries.

international debt markets debt markets in which players from different countries are involved.

international economic integration term for the gradual harmonization of tariffs and trade regulations accompanied by increasing globalization of business.

international equity markets *see* international stock markets.

international expansion expansion of a company's operations into countries other than the one where it is domiciled.

international finance the flow of finance capital across borders.

international financial management management techniques involved in managing international finance.

international financial markets financial markets in which there is participation by major financial institutions around the world.

international human resource management techniques involved in managing human resources in multinational companies.

international investment position statement showing a country's assets abroad and its liabilities to non-citizens.

international investments investments outside one's home country.

internationalism management philosophy which sees expansion into other countries as the key to the company's future.

internationalization expansion of a company's business into international markets.

International Labour Organization (ILO) United Nations-sponsored organization which sets standards for and collects information on working conditions, labour relations and so on.

international management management of international companies or corporations.

international marketing marketing into more than one national market.

international markets markets which exist in more than one country.

international migration movement of people, including workers, from one country to another.

International Monetary Fund (IMF) organization related to but not part of the United Nations, the purpose of which is to promote international trade, exchange rate stability and good financial management by governments.

international money markets *see* international currency markets.

international operations operations such as production and distribution which are conducted simultaneously in several different companies.

international payments payment flows between countries as reflected in the balance of payments.

international portfolio investment theory economic theory concerning international investments as an aspect of the international flow of capital.

international relations contacts between different countries, usually at the level of national governments.

international representative representative or agent of a company outside the company where it is domiciled or operates.

international reserves reserves held in gold or internationally accepted currencies.

international securities markets markets in which securities are traded by buyers and sellers around the world.

international stock markets stock markets open to buyers and sellers from around the world, such as the New York Stock Exchange, the Tokyo Stock Exchange and the International Stock Exchange in London.

international strategy strategy guiding the international marketing, operations and so on of a multinational business.

international technological gap difference between the technological capabilities of the advanced nations and those of less developed countries.

international trade imports and exports between countries.

international trade relations relations, including agreements and disputes, between governments concerning trade between their countries.

international trade secretariat (ITS) association of national trade unions from different countries, usually representing a particular industry or sector.

international workforces employees who are able to move between countries and work in different cultures.

Internet the global computer network which, using telecommunications technology, can be accessed by any modem-equipped computer; *see also* e-mail; World Wide Web.

internship training period for new employees, used most commonly in professional services, where performance is reviewed at the end of the period and, if satisfactory, an offer of longer term employment is then made.

inter-organizational relationships linkages, networks and personal relationships between companies and organizations.

interpersonal skills the skills required to manage and deal with other people.

interpreter 1 person who translates from one language to another in the course of a meeting or conversation; **2** computer software which translates computer languages into machine code.

interrogation 1 questioning a subject to elicit information; **2** preliminary analysis of data held in a database to see what classes and types of data are held.

interval measure financial ratio relating available assets to daily expenditure.

intervening bank bank which acts as an agent for an overseas bank in a local business matter.

intervention 1 process whereby an external agent intervenes in a process and makes changes; **2** deliberate adjustment of otherwise self-managing mechanism; **3** action by a third party such as an arbitrator to solve disputes between two others.

interventionism managerial philosophy based on intervention by senior managers in the affairs of lower managerial levels; usually associated with centralization and top-down control.

intervention price fixed price at which the European Commission buys some agricultural produce from farmers in order to keep overall prices at the level of the official target price.

interview verbal discussion between two or more people, for the purpose of gathering information by one party about the other(s); often used in recruitment and assessment.

interview, exit *see* exit interview.

interviewing procedures general term for methods of conducting and controlling interviews.

interview, structured interview based on a previously defined set of questions.

interview, unstructured interview in which questions and format have not been previously determined and the person being interviewed can to some extent guide the direction of the conversation.

in the black colloquial term meaning profit making or in profit; as opposed to in the red.

in the money colloquial term meaning in a highly profitable or lucrative position.

in the red colloquial term meaning loss making or in debt; as opposed to in the black.

intra-corporate trading business conducted between different parts of a corporation, sometimes through internal markets.

intra-firm contract any contract which obligates members of a firm to the firm, the most common example being contracts of employment.

in transit goods which are in the distribution channel and are currently being transported from one location to another.

intrapreneurship philosophy of encouraging managers to behave as entrepreneurs within their companies.

intrapreneurship model *see* intrapreneurship.

intrinsic reward satisfaction which is inherent in something; when used of jobs, refers to the sense of accomplishment and achievement which comes from doing the job itself.

intrinsic value value inherent in raw material or components prior to manufacture.

introduction process the introduction of a new product into a market.

intuition instinctive sense or belief that is not based on logic or analysis.

inventions new concepts or products developed as a result of innovation.

inventory stock actually in store at a given point in time; also used to describe raw materials currently in stock and being processed, and goods currently in the process of manufacture; can be used more generally to mean a list of all of a certain type of asset (inventory of skills, of human resources, and so on).

inventory control techniques used to control stocks of goods, materials, work in progress and so on.

inventory management general term for management of current inventory with the aim of achieving optimal efficiency.

inventory model production control model that tells managers the quantities of materials that are needed at a given time.

inventory shortage *see* shrinkage.

inventory turnover rate at which inventory turns over (that is, needs to be replaced) during a given period.

inverse demand pattern phenomenon whereby sales of a product increase in volume when the price rises.

investment the employment of capital in a way that is designed to increase its value.

investment adviser professional who acts as an adviser to people or institutions wishing to invest surplus capital in other companies.

investment appraisal analysis of a potential investment to determine factors such as potential risks and the rate of return.

investment bank *see* merchant bank.

investment banking branch of banking specializing in providing capital to business enterprises.

investing cash flow (ICF) cash flow which goes outwards into investments.

investment club group of people who pool their investment funds in a single investment portfolio.

investment company company whose primary purpose is to invest capital in other companies; usually such companies serve as vehicles, investing capital contributed by other companies or individuals.

investment counsel *see* investment adviser.

investment decision the decision to commit a certain amount of capital to a particular investment.

investment portfolio the investments held by a person or institution.

investment risk the potential for a particular investment to lose money.

investment trust *see* investment company.

investment yield *see* internal rate of return.

investor person or institution contributing capital as an investment.

invisible hand term used by Adam Smith, describing the tendency of markets to maximize benefits for both buyers and sellers, assuming conditions of perfect competition.

invisibles imports and exports which, unlike manufactured goods, are not tangible; most commonly used to refer to financial services.

invisible trade *see* invisibles.

invoice document which describes goods which have been delivered and the price of each.

invoicing systems for regular sending of invoices to customers, and monitoring their return.

involuntary bankruptcy state of bankruptcy which is forced upon a person or individual by their creditors.

involuntary unemployment condition of unemployment where people wish to work and have the ability to do so, but where no vacancies for employment exist.

IO *see* industrial organization.

IP *see* integer programming.

iron law of oligarchy perceived phenomenon whereby, in trade unions, power tends to concentrate in the hands of senior union officials.

iron law of wages theory that wages will always tend to equal what the worker needs for bare subsistence.

iron rice bowl in Chinese state enterprises prior to reform, the practice of providing housing and a full range of social benefits to workers throughout their lifetimes.

IRR *see* internal rate of return.

irredeemable money money which cannot be converted or redeemed.

irrelevance position theory that the value of a firm is unaffected by its dividend policy.

irritation strike industrial action where workers do not actually stop working, but instead work slowly and produce poor-quality work.

ISDN *see* integrated services digital network.

ISIS *see* intelligent scheduling and information system.

Islamic banking banking practices observed in Islamic countries, a common feature of which is that no interest is charged on loans.

IS-LM model macroeconomic model devised by John Richard Hicks, showing the relationship between supply and demand of both commodities and money.

ISS *see* intelligent support systems.

issue general term for securities sold by a company to investors; shares newly released for sale are referred to as 'an issue'.

issue by tender practice of inviting bids for shares to be issued and then selling to the highest bidder.

issued capital total of all securities issued by a company.

issued stock total of shares issued to shareholders; *see also* issued capital.

issuing house financial institution which serves as an intermediary for companies issuing shares, handling the actual issue and sale of the shares.

item an individual unit; the smallest indivisible component of a group.

itemized adjective meaning that all units in a group have been listed individually.

iteration repetition, usually of the same process or thing but with minor variations each time.

itinerant worker worker who travels from place to place as opportunities for work present themselves; *see also* migrant worker.

ITS *see* international trade secretariat.

J

J-curve graphical representation of the impact of currency devaluations on balance of trade; the latter usually continues to decline for some time after devaluation, before turning up again.

jig machine tool set up to perform a set task.

JIT *see* just-in-time.

job 1 group of related tasks carried out by an employee; **2** more generally, the position an employee holds and the related tasks, pay and benefits, place of work and so on.

job analysis examination of the tasks which make up a job and the circumstances in which they are carried out; *see also* job classification.

job and finish work system in which workers can go home as soon as they have completed their production targets, rather than waiting for the end of a pre-set work period.

job applicant person applying for a specific job.

jobber middleman or intermediary who sells goods in job lots.

jobbing cells manufacturing cells involved in jobbing production.

jobbing production *see* job production.

job centre *see* employment exchange.

job characteristic theory set of theories focusing on how jobs can be redesigned to become more effective.

job classification following job analysis, ranking of jobs according to complexity of tasks, skills involved and other factors, setting levels of seniority and pay.

job cluster groups of jobs which are similar in task or function.

job content the tasks and responsibilities associated with a job.

job definition *see* job description.

job description statement, usually written, of the duties, tasks and responsibilities of a job.

job design process of designing jobs so that they are as efficient as possible in terms of individual and unit productivity.

job diagnostic survey tool for analysing employee needs and perceptions of their jobs.

job dilution the division of tasks in such a way that the most complex are carried out by the most skilled employees, and vice versa.

job efficiency job design which leads to an efficient use of labour.

job engineering adapting existing jobs by changing procedures, equipment used and so on, so as to improve productivity and/or increase employee motivation.

job enlargement increasing the responsibilities and/or tasks associated with a particular job, effectively making the job more complex; usually accompanied by suitable training for the employee.

job enrichment restructuring jobs in such a way as to increase levels of motivation and intrinsic reward for employees.

job environment the conditions in which a job is carried out, including the physical workplace setting, social and psychological conditions and so on.

job evaluation techniques for establishing the nature of and work required for individual jobs; *see also* job analysis.

job family group of jobs of a similar nature.

job feedback information about job performance which is related back to the worker and/or managers.

job grading system of classifying jobs according to tasks required, skills required, levels of responsibility and so on, for the purpose of determining seniority and pay levels.

job hopping rapid movement between jobs, usually with different companies.

job lot bulk merchandise, often of mixed content.

job mobility *see* labour mobility.

job number in jobbing production, a code assigned to each job or batch for identification purposes during the production process.

job order order for the production of a specified quantity of manufactured goods.

job–order costing costing method whereby each job or batch produced is costed separately.

job orientation *see* induction.

job performance measurement techniques for measuring how well employees carry out the jobs they are assigned.

job price contract contract which sets a fixed price for a contract, irrespective of the time or costs involved in completion.

job pricing setting pay or remuneration for a job.

job production production of a single product at a time; as opposed to batch production, mass production.

job progression movement from one job to another with progressive increases in seniority and rates of pay.

job ranking *see* job grading.

job reductions cutbacks in the number jobs available, usually leading to redundancies.

job requirements skills and abilities required by a worker to perform a particular job.

job restructuring modification of a job and its tasks and responsibilities, usually so as to achieve greater efficiency.

job rotation scheme where employees are regularly moved from one job or place of work to another, so as to increase their experience and knowledge.

job satisfaction extent to which an employee is or is not satisfied with his or her job, usually a result of the combination of pay and intrinsic rewards which he or she receives.

job security contractual assurance that an employee will not lose his or her job.

job sharing practice whereby two or more employees share a job, usually by dividing the hours to be worked among themselves.

job shop production facilities specializing in jobbing production.

job shop scheduling scheduling of production work in job shops, characterized by the need to continually switch resources between jobs.

job shop scheduling software computer software programs used in job shop scheduling.

job specification written statement of the duties, responsibilities and requirements for a particular job; *see also* job description.

job splitting job sharing arrangement where work is divided between two or more people but in such a way that their individual work does not need to be coordinated.

job standardization practice of developing sets of standard procedures which are meant to reduce variations in job performance.

job stress psychological pressure created by conditions inherent in a job or the place of work more generally.

job subsidy *see* employment subsidy.

job swapping practice whereby two employees agree to exchange jobs.

job time time required to complete a job.

job training training for employees taking up a particular job, aimed to acquaint them with the tasks, responsibilities, duties and so on associated with that job.

job transition process of moving from one job to another, and adjusting to the different demands of the new job.

joint account bank account to which two or more people or organizations have access, including the ability to make deposits and withdrawals.

joint agreement statement of agreed terms of pay and conditions of employment, signed by both management and employees or their representatives.

joint consultation consultation process within organizations that seeks to gather the views of a large number of people, including both managers and employees.

joint contract contract where two or more people are named together as either the parties promising to deliver a good or service, or the parties who are to receive a good or service.

joint cost cost that must be assigned to two or more cost centres or production processes.

joint demand demand from customers for two or more goods which are complementary, such as the components needed in manufacturing.

jointly and severally legal term covering more than one party to a contract.

joint product products which require the same raw materials and production processes.

joint production costs costs incurred where two or more products are made using the same production process.

joint regulation process whereby two or more parties agree to the regulations that all will follow; used most commonly to describe agreements between management and unions to accept commonly agreed regulations.

joint stock bank *see* commercial bank.

joint stock company early term for company, where investors hold shares and have limited liability.

joint tenancy situation where two or more people have title to property.

joint ventures business arrangement where two or more people or companies form a partnership for a specific purpose, and which will be terminated when that purpose is achieved.

journal original record of transactions, including amounts and sources.

journal entry individual line in a journal, recording a specific transaction.

journeyman skilled craftsman or worker who has completed an apprenticeship.

judgement an individual's assessment of a situation based on all available information.

judgement rates in insurance, rates established by an underwriter based on his or her judgement.

judgemental formats performance appraisal techniques which rely on the subjective judgement of the appraiser.

judgment decision of a court concerning a suit.

judicial review legal examination of the facts of a matter by a court of law.

junk bond *see* bond, junk.

jurisdiction limits of authority of a person or organization.

jurisdictional dispute dispute between trade unions as to which has the right to organize to represent a particular group of workers.

just-in-time production and purchasing philosophy which focuses on producing and delivering products as and when they are needed, thereby reducing inventory levels and associated costs.

just-in-time manufacturing manufacturing philosophy and systems which aim to produce products as they are demanded, instead of producing them in advance and then holding them in inventory.

justified price market price which an informed buyer is willing to pay.

K

KBDSS *see* knowledge-based decision support systems.

kaizen Japanese term meaning continuous improvement.

kanban Japanese control system used in just-in-time management.

keiretsu Japanese term referring to groups of companies linked by formal commercial relationships or other networks; *see also zaibatsu*.

key 1 in management, adjective meaning most important or essential; **2** in computing, a single button on a computer keyboard which sends a command to the computer through whatever software programme is then running.

keyboard device for inputting data and issuing commands to computers, consisting of rows of keys which are programmed to issue different commands.

key date particularly important date, usually representing a deadline which must be met.

keyed advertisement advertisement that is coded in such a way that the advertiser can use the coding to measure consumer response to the advertisement.

key factor factor on which other factors depend; most important element in a situation; most important factor to be considered when making a decision.

key factor scoring in decision making, the identification of key factors of importance and then scoring the key factors of each alternative.

key industry industry which is of vital importance to a national economy.

key jobs most important jobs, in terms of the efficient and effective running of the company.

Keynesianism economic system developed by, or at least attributed to, John Maynard Keynes, based on the concept that employment and national income are affected by consumer spending.

key operation in work studies and flowcharting, an operation on which other operations depend, and which must be completed before work can proceed to the next stage.

keypad a small, hand-held keyboard, usually with fewer keys.

key task the central or most important task which must be performed as part of a job or operation, and on which other related tasks depend.

key task analysis analysis which sets out the key tasks and the methods of checking how well they are actually performed.

kickback payment made by a seller to a buyer in exchange for the latter having placed the order, usually used to covertly influence a market where many sellers are competing for the buyer's attention (illegal in some jurisdictions).

kicked upstairs colloquial term for removing an unsuitable employee from one position by promoting him or her to a more senior position.

killer application a computer software program which becomes the industry standard, not only driving competing programs out of the market but becoming a necessity to run other current generation applications.

killing colloquial term for very high profits, as in 'to make a killing'.

kilobyte (KB) a unit of computer storage capacity, consisting of 1024 bytes.

kind property or goods used in an exchange; 'payment in kind' means payment in goods rather than in cash.

kite another term for a bad cheque; also, rarely used term for an accommodation note.

kite mark mark or stamp on a product confirming it meets quality standards; originally referred to the mark of approval by the British Standards Institution.

kiting manipulation of share market price by market makers to artificially high levels.

knocked down 1 temporarily reduced or lowered price; **2** auctioning term for the price at which an item is actually sold; **3** also, a product which is supplied with its components packed separately, with the buyer responsible for assembling them.

knocking copy advertisement which makes unfavourable comments about competitors.

knowledge the range of what is known about a subject, based on a combination of analysed data, personal experience and intuition.

knowledge-based system *see* expert systems.

knowledge-based decision support systems (KBDSS) decision support system based on expert systems.

knowledge capital asset value inherent in a person, organization or artefact, by reason of information, skills etc. resident there.

knowledge engineering the conversion of knowledge into formats suitable for a database.

knowledge-intensive firms companies that make the collection, utilization and dissemination of knowledge and information a key part of their activities, particularly as these relate to innovation.

knowledge worker employee whose greatest personal asset is his or her knowledge, including skills and experience.

knowledge works Japanese form of business organization which aims to maximize the potential for knowledge and innovation.

K-strategists organizations relying on efficient production strategies.

K-type management management system indigenous to Korean companies.

kyoryoku kai Japanese term for a supplier association.

L

label panel of printed information on the outside of the good, containing information for the consumer and also any brand name or logo associated with the product.

labelling the design and production of labels.

labour in economics, one of the three factors of production, being the total input of human effort required in production; more generally, a term for work carried out by people.

labour-augmented technical change technical change that raises output without more labour being needed in the process.

labour bank bank owned by a labour union and run for the benefit of union members.

labour code regulation or law which defines the limits of the powers and rights of employers and employees with respect to each other.

labour costs total expenditure on employee pay and benefits.

labour courts special courts set up in some countries to hear legal disputes between employers and employees or unions.

labour dispute disagreement over pay, working conditions and so on between employer and employees, which can lead to one side or the other taking action such as strikes and lockouts.

labour, division of *see* division of labour.

labour economics specialized field in economics concerned with the study of labour as an economic force.

labour force **1** generally, the number of people in work or actively seeking work; **2** more specifically, a synonym for workforce.

labour, free movement of *see* free movement of labour.

labour intensive adjective describing projects or processes which require very large amounts of labour proportional to output.

labour law legislation dealing with industrial relations, working practices and conditions, and relations between employers and employees.

labour market the market in which labour is acquired by employers; the quantity and quality (in terms of skills, experience and so on) of labour available in a given area at a given time.

labour market analysis study of labour markets for the purpose of calculating present and future supplies of labour.

labour mobility extent to which workers can or will change jobs, either by changing occupations or moving to work in the same occupation in another region or country.

labour movement general term for organized labour in the form of unions and other associations.

labour officers term for managers working in labour relations.

labour pool group or population of workers from which an employer can recruit through the labour market.

labour process the process by which labour transforms a raw material into a product.

labour productivity measurement of output per worker.

labour relations general term for relations between employees and employers; *see also* industrial relations.

labour-saving equipment machines or tools which can substitute in part for human labour, by performing tasks which would otherwise have had to be done by hand.

labour stability index measure of the rate of turnover among employees, showing the proportion of leavers to those who remain in employment; *see also* labour turnover.

labour theory of value classical economists' theory of the value of labour.

labour turnover measure of the rate at which workers join or leave an organization, usually shown as a proportion of numbers of leavers to numbers of employed.

labour union organized body of workers with elected representatives who handled employee–management relations; often constituted nationally or across a particular industrial sector; *see also* trade union.

labour value theory *see* labour theory of value.

lag indicators economic indicators that follow changes in the economic cycle.

Laffer curve graphic depiction of A. Laffer's principle that higher taxation ultimately results in a decrease in government revenue.

laissez-faire 1 system free of external interference; **2** in economics, a free economy which operates without control or interference by government.

lame duck 1 a failing business, which is making little or no profit and is not expected to do so; **2** a member of a stock exchange who is expelled for failing to meet debts; **3** a manager or executive who has lost the confidence of colleagues or employees and is unable to function effectively.

LAN *see* local area network.

land 1 landed property or real estate; **2** in economics, one of the three factors of production, along with labour and capital.

land bank bank whose primary business activity is providing loans and mortgages for the purpose of buying landed property; *see also* building society.

land economy economic activity conducted in land markets.

landed property property which consists of a geographically defined portion of land and any structures built on that land.

land law legislation covering the market for and use of landed property.

land management branch of management specializing in the management of real estate and landed property.

land markets markets in which landed property or real estate is bought and sold.

language means of verbal or written communication between people, or between people and computers; *see* computer language.

language laboratory specialist teaching facility used in language training.

language training training programme, the object of which is to learn or increase fluency in another language.

Laplace criterion in decision making, theory whereby the decision maker assigns equal probabilities to all possible outcomes.

lapping form of fraud in which thefts are covered up by means of false entries in accounts.

lapse termination of a right through either disuse or the expiry of a previously determined period of time; *see also* exhaustion of rights.

laptop a small, portable micro-computer.

laser acronym for light amplification by stimulated emission of radiation, a device producing a beam of coherent light which has many uses as a design and production tool.

last in, first out (LIFO) in valuation, concept whereby the most recently acquired asset is the one used for setting a standard value for other similar assets.

latent defect defect in a product which was built in but which only appears after the product has been in use for some time.

lateral communication 1 communication between people on the same level of hierarchy within an organization; **2** communication between departments of an organization.

lateral relationships relationships between different departments or divisions of an organization.

launch the first release of a new product or brand into the market, usually accompanied by specially designed advertising and public relations campaigns.

law 1 a body of binding rules of conduct enacted by governments, with penalties for non-compliance; any single rule or regulation which forms part of this body; **2** in economics, immutable 'natural' forces which always occur in given conditions.

law of diminishing returns *see* diminishing returns.

law of increasing costs phenomenon whereby unit costs increase as volume increases; *see also* diminishing returns.

law of the situation concept developed by Mary Parker Follett, stating that conflicts between two parties should be resolved by reference to the facts of the situation, and not to the relative power the parties may have over each other.

lawyer professional who practises law, advising and representing companies and individuals on legal matters.

layaway practice whereby a retailer may, once a purchase has been made, hold a good for the consumer until a later date when the latter pays the purchase price and takes possession of the good.

lay day in shipping, day in which a ship is allowed to stay in port without being charged a fee.

layoff suspension of employment by the employer, usually because there is a lack of work.

LDCs *see* less developed countries.

lead 1 a contact or potential customer; **2** more generally, 'to lead' means to direct or give leadership to; *see* leadership.

leader person who commands, directs and/or controls the actions of others, usually with responsibility for coordinating and integrating the work of others so as to direct the organization towards its goals.

leadership the exercise of command, direction and control by a leader over an organization and its members.

leadership style the way a leader approaches the task of leadership, based on the task in hand and the leader's own skills and personal characteristics.

lead indicator economic indicators that precede changes in the economic cycle.

lead market in marketing and especially in advertising, the first market where a particular product or concept is tried; if successful, the product or concept is then disseminated into other markets.

lead rate higher wage paid to an employee who takes on more than ordinary responsibilities.

lead time in planning and scheduling, time which must be allowed for a process to be completed.

leakage dissipation of resources through waste, natural decay or pilferage.

lean manufacturing *see* lean production.

lean organization organization which has been stripped of its extraneous functions and is concentrated on its core business.

lean production Japanese model of efficient manufacturing originally developed by the Toyota corporation.

lean supply model supply chain model developed by L. R. Lamming, which aims to capture elements of relationships between buyers and suppliers.

leapfrogging in labour relations, phenomenon whereby a pay rise given to one group of employees tends to stimulate claims for similar or greater rises by other groups.

learning the acquisition of skills and knowledge.

learning, continuous *see* continuous learning.

learning company company that functions as a learning organization.

learning curve graph illustrating the rate at which people learn.

learning, double-loop *see* double-loop learning.

learning organization organization which makes learning and the acquisition of new knowledge and skills a central priority, encouraging not only learning by all managers and employees but the dissemination of that learning across the organization.

learning plateau temporary flat period on the learning curve, usually a result of the learner pausing to consolidate existing knowledge.

learning resource centre facility which provides aids and materials for learning.

learning time time set aside specifically for learning purposes.

learning theory in consumer behaviour, conceptualizations of how consumers gather and use information.

lease temporary rights of use of property, equipment, vehicles and so on in exchange for the payment of rent; a popular alternative to purchase where the use of capital goods is needed but it is not essential to have the ownership of these goods.

leaseback practice of selling property, equipment, vehicles and so on and then leasing them back from the new owner.

leasing activities involved in granting or obtaining a lease.

leave of absence time for which an employee is allowed to be absent from normally schedule work, sometimes without pay.

ledger written summary of all transactions affecting a particular account.

ledgerless accounting *see* slip system.

legal adjective describing something which is allowed by or within the bounds of the law.

legal entity any individual, organization or association such as a company or partnership that is recognized by law and has the right to make contracts.

legal holiday US term for a public holiday, equivalent to bank holiday.

legal interest maximum rate of interest permissible by law.

legal reserve funds which a financial institution are required by law to hold in reserve in order to meet obligations.

legal system national system of laws and mechanisms for their enforcement and judgment of individual cases.

legal tender any money which is recognized as such in law; in most jurisdictions, creditors and sellers are obliged to accept all forms of legal tender.

legislation written enactments by government setting out the terms of the law.

leisure personal time which is not occupied by work or necessary personal duties.

lend to give or loan money, property and so on to another, on the expectation that it will be returned; *see also* loan.

lender one who lends to another.

lender of last resort one of the functions of a central bank, whereby it lends money to other banks when required.

lending the act of making a loan.

lending institution financial institution which acts as a lender.

length of service the length of time that a worker has been continuously employed by a firm.

less developed countries (LDCs) countries whose economies are still largely agricultural or who have just begun the process of industrialization.

let 1 to rent unused property or equipment to another party; **2** to contract out work rather than doing it in house.

letter-box company holding company with no formal premises beyond a postal address, usually established in countries with low tax rates; *see also* offshore company.

letter of credit instrument issued by a financial institution certifying the credit of the bearer and allowing him or her to obtain credit or funds from another institution.

letter of hypothecation document held by a bank which lists goods pledged as collateral for a loan, and gives the bank the right to take possession of these should the loan go into default.

letters patent written documentation certifying the holding of a patent.

letter stock unregistered stock which has not been formally underwritten.

level-by-level planning method of materials planning which establishes gross and net levels of requirement for each level of the process, the net level of each process being the gross level for the next process and so on.

level of aspiration personal goals or desires which individuals work towards or seek to achieve.

level of authority hierarchical position within an organization, showing whom the manager has authority over.

leverage 1 *see* gearing; **2** more generally, any advantage a firm has over its rivals which can be put to use.

leveraged buy-out acquisition where loan capital is used to meet the majority of the purchase price.

leveraged firm firm with a high level of debt.

leveraged marketing marketing where a company is able to capitalize on existing products or processes to create and market very profitable new products at little additional cost.

leveraged recap tactic whereby a firm recapitalizes itself by converting most of its equity into debt, thereby discouraging potential takeovers.

leveraged takeover *see* leveraged buy-out.

leverage ratio *see* gearing ratio.

leveraging *see* leverage.

levy required contribution of funds, either as a tax or as a fee paid to an association or company.

liabilities total of all existing liability.

liability 1 any form of debt owed to others; **2** also, the extent to which an individual or company may be held responsible in law for their actions or those of others.

liability insurance insurance which compensates the policyholder for any damages for which he/or she is held liable in law.

liability limits maximum compensation which will be provided under the terms of liability insurance.

liaison general term for establishing and maintaining formal contacts with other individuals, divisions, departments and so on, often beyond what is required by the formal hierarchy of the organization.

liaison unit unit within an organization that has responsibility for maintaining liaison with and between other units.

liberalization deregulation; opening up of a market to free trade; the abolition of restrictive practices.

library searching researching data and information from published and publicly available sources.

licensed lender any organization authorized under local law to make loans to others.

licensing arrangement whereby one company authorizes another to use its intellectual property in exchange for payment, usually of royalties.

lien legal right to take possession of another's property as security against unpaid debt.

lieu days holidays taken as a substitute for unpaid overtime.

life assurance assurance or insurance policy paying compensation to the dependents of the policyholder in the event of the latter's death.

life cycle *see* product life cycle.

life cycle analysis analysis which aims to determine the length of a product life cycle, including the length of each stage.

life cycle, professional the stages through which a professional's career passes, from first recruitment to retirement, reflecting the skills and experience which the professional acquires along the way.

life expectancy **1** actuarial calculation of the average number of years that a person can expect to live; **2** in marketing, the time that a product or brand can expect to remain profitable before demand drops away; **3** in production, the time that a machine or tool can be expected to function before needing to be replaced.

life insurance *see* life assurance.

lifelong learning rolling programme of learning and knowledge acquisition which lasts throughout an employee's or manager's career.

lifestyles the tastes, attitudes, activities and behaviours of consumers, which dictate to some degree their purchasing choices.

lifetime education *see* lifelong learning.

lifetime employment contract of employment which ensures that the employee may remain with the company through his or her entire career.

lifetime value (LTV) value of a product or asset over the course of its productive life.

LIFO *see* last in, first out.

limited company company which is registered according to law; the term 'limited' refers to the fact that shareholders are not personally liable for the actions of or losses suffered by the company.

limited distribution choice of a small number of distributors who will give maximum distribution coverage for the lowest cost.

limited function wholesaler wholesaler who does not provide any marketing functions, usually being limited to physical distribution only.

limited liability condition whereby shareholders are not personally liable for debts incurred by the company whose shares they own.

limited life partnership established for a limited period of time, which is dissolved at the end of that time.

limited-life consortium joint venture by a number of partner businesses to develop and exploit a single product or market, which dissolves once its immediate objectives have been achieved.

limited-line stores retail stores that carry only a limited number of product lines in each product category.

limited order order where the customer has placed restrictions on volume and/or price.

limited partner member of a partnership who does not have liability for debts incurred by the partnership as a whole; *see also* limited company.

limited problem solving (LPS) problem-solving behaviour focusing on a simple or limited problem.

limiting factor any factor which constrains or the production or sale of a product or service.

line 1 in manufacturing, that portion of the firm directly involved in production; **2** more generally, a term denoting channels of authority and communication, as in 'line of command'; **3** in retailing, a product or brand stocked by a retailer.

linear programming mathematical technique used to solve some types of decision-making problems.

linear responsibility responsibility up or down the chain of command.

linear trend data presented in time sequence which are represented on a graph by a straight line.

line authority authority held by a manager over direct subordinates.

line item any item posted on a separate line in a profit and loss statement.

line management level of management which directly supervises line functions, taking direction from senior management and transmitting these as specific directions to subordinate workers.

line manager manager of a line function, who receives orders from superiors and transmits them in more detailed form to subordinates.

line of command *see* chain of command.

line of credit agreement whereby a company agrees to allow customers credit up to a certain level at any point in time.

line of discount credit which a bank will advance to a business customer on the basis of the latter's accounts receivable.

line organization company structure in which all authority flows down from the top, and where each subordinate employee or manager reports to only one superior.

line pricing pricing strategy where all products of a similar nature are priced at the same level.

linked subcontracting one name for the practice of making employees redundant from their permanent jobs, and then rehiring them as independent subcontractors.

liquid adjective for an asset which either exists in cash form or can be easily converted into cash.

liquid assets assets which either exist in cash form or can be easily converted into cash.

liquidate 1 to convert assets into cash; **2** to pay off a debt; **3** to terminate a company by selling off its assets and using the resulting income to pay creditors.

liquidating dividend dividend payable to shareholders when a firm is closed down and its assets are liquidated.

liquidation legal process involved in terminating a company's existence, including the selling off of all assets.

liquidation value *see* break-up value.

liquidator official appointed to oversee the liquidation of a company.

liquidity measure of the cash on which a company can easily draw, in the form of either cash savings or assets which can be easily liquidated; often used as a general measure of financial solvency.

liquidity preference theory of John Maynard Keynes that people prefer to hold their savings in cash rather than in investments which might be difficult to liquidate.

liquidity ratio *see* cash ratio.

liquidity trap Keynesian economics term for the phenomenon whereby the demand for cash becomes more elastic as interest rates rise.

liquid ratio ratio of current assets (not including stocks) to current liabilities; *see also* current ratio.

list building the acquisition and enlargement of a list of names and addresses which can be used for direct mailing.

list price 1 the quoted price of a good; 2 the retail price of a product or service as suggested by the manufacturer, before retailer's discounts.

list renting acquiring the use of a mailing list for direct mail on a temporary basis; in practice, the holder of the list arranges for the mailings to be made, rather than releasing the names directly to the client.

literacy ability to read and write in one's native language.

literature academic term for a body of books, journal articles and so on which cover a specific subject and which should be referred to when discussing this subject in detail.

livery company one of the professional guilds still active in the City of London.

liveware in computing, colloquial term for the people who manage and maintain computer systems.

load a consignment of goods being shipped.

load chart graphic illustration of the distribution of work in a plant or on a particular production line.

load–factor pricing varying the price of a product, for example on a seasonal basis, so as to maximize use of production facilities.

loading the adding of overheads and administrative costs to prime costs, usually stated as a separate charge.

loading charge premium charged by some types of investment fund to cover selling costs.

load levelling scheduling practice which ensures that the workload is spread as evenly as possible.

load up to make an investment which brings one to the limit of one's financial resources.

loan agreement whereby one party agrees to lend money or goods to another party; a fee may sometimes be charged; *see also* lend; interest.

loan capital capital which is invested in a company in the form of a loan, rather than through the purchase of equity, and which is entitled to payment of interest regardless of company performance; *see also* equity capital.

loan-closing payments payments which cover costs incurred when a loan terminates or matures.

loan crowd members of a stock exchange who lend to investors who have sold short.

loaned employee employee transferred temporarily from one division to another, or even one company to another, to meet particular labour or skill requirements.

loaned flat stock which is loaned with no interest due; *see* loan stock.

loan fee charges made to borrowers, usually to cover service costs associated with making a loan.

loan interest interest paid on a loan by the borrower.

loan rate rate of interest which lenders charge to borrowers.

loan stock securities loaned to a broker who has sold short and must borrow in order to fulfil a contract.

loan value amount of money that can be borrowed using a life insurance policy as security.

lobbying 1 campaigning with the aim of influencing a key decision maker, usually in government, towards or away from a certain course of action; **2** expression of the wishes and desires of an interest group.

lobbyist professional in the public relations field who specializes in lobbying key figures in government and industry.

local US term for a local branch of a trade union, usually based in a particular plant or site.

local area network (LAN) computer network which covers a relatively small area, usually a building or plant, linking all computers and computer-controlled devices on the site.

local government regional or district government, at one or more levels below national government; in many jurisdictions, local government has the principal say on issues such as planning.

localism business and management philosophy which concentrates on developing different strategies in each locality where the company does business, tailored to different cultural and environmental conditions.

localization marketing and advertising strategy which tailors branding, communications and so on to local market conditions.

local option decision which managers on site can make for themselves, without having to refer to central authority.

local regulations government regulations affecting a specific area.

location place or site.

lock-away a security which is purchased with the intent to hold it for a long term.

lockout the physical barring of employees from the workplace, used by employers as a tactic in industrial disputes.

lockup colloquial term for securities that have been withdrawn from circulation.

logging on process of switching on a computer terminal and connecting it to a system; usually involves giving a password, an identity code and several other commands.

logic bomb type of malicious computer code that, upon activation, destroys other computer programs.

logic tree *see* decision tree analysis.

logistics management of the flow and storage of goods and services from point of orign to point of delivery.

logistics requirement planning integrated system combining materials requirement planning and distribution requirements planning, so as to create an integrated logistics chain.

logo a graphic emblem which serves as a badge or name for a brand or for a company; its primary purpose is to serve as an immediately recognizable visual cue which signals to customers and others the presence of the brand or company.

long US colloquial term for owning shares; being 'long' on a particular share means the speaker owns shares in the issuing company.

long lease lease with an extraordinarily long term, typically for more than one person's lifetime.

long-lived assets assets which will hold some portion of their value for a number of years.

long position holding shares or other securities in advance of an anticipated increase in value; *see also* bull position.

long-range planning planning activities directed specifically at the intermediate and long-term future, setting the framework for more detailed strategies and outlining the path the company will take towards its goals.

long run *see* long term.

long service a lengthy period of continuous employment with the same company.

long service awards public recognition by a company of the long service of particular employees.

long tail term of UK origin, referring to an economy where a large percentage of firms are performing below acceptable standards, or below the mean of performance.

long tail claim insurance claim where liabilities continue to occur for some years after the claim is first made.

long term a time span, typically of two years of more, which is used to define strategies, investments and so on.

long-term contract collective agreement which is negotiated for periods of two or more years; any contract between two parties which is intended to last for a period of several years.

long-term debt debts which are not due to be fully repaid until two or more years have elapsed.

long-termism *see* long-term orientation.

long-term liability liabilities which will not have to be met until two or more years have elapsed.

long-term operational assets assets which are acquired with the intention of permanent use, rather than for resale.

long-term orientation philosophy of planning and thinking towards the long term and being proactive towards the future.

long-term unemployment continuous unemployment for more than twelve months.

long ton unit of measure, consisting of 2240 pounds.

loose rate work situation where workers can earn productivity bonuses with comparative ease; as opposed to tight rate.

Lorenz curve graph showing distribution of income and wealth in target population.

loss excess of income over expenditure; the opposite of profit; the destruction of an asset.

loss expectancy in insurance, an estimate of the monetary value of damage caused should the event being insured against actually occur.

loss leader product or service which is sold at a loss, but which has the effect of drawing customers to purchase other, profit-making goods and services.

loss on disposal loss incurred when an asset is disposed of for less than its book value.

loss ratio in insurance, ratio of premiums paid in to compensation paid out.

loss reserve financial reserves held by insurance companies, usually by statutory requirement, to meet unexpected claims.

lot administrative grouping of goods for transport or sale.

lot-sizing determining the optimum size for a lot.

low grade poor quality or inferior.

low-context cultures culture where, in communication, everything is spelled out and little is left unsaid.

low-risk strategies strategic options chosen primarily to minimize risk.

loyalty commitment by members of an organization to that organization and its goals, including a willingness, to a degree, to put the organization's interests before their own.

loyalty, customer *see* customer loyalty.

LPS *see* limited problem solving.

LTV *see* life time value.

Luddite colloquial term for employees who are opposed to and actively resist technological change; the name comes from an eighteenth-century anti-technology movement in Britain.

lump sum single aggregated figure, with no breakdowns or sub-divisions.

Lutine bell bell sounded at Lloyd's Register of Shipping in London upon important occasions, especially when a ship is reported lost.

luxury goods goods or services which enhance quality of life but are not strictly necessary for survival.

luxury tax tax imposed in some jurisdictions on luxury goods and services.

M

machine ancillary time machine running time which is devoted not to production but to such necessary purposes as set-up or calibration.

machine bureaucracy organization structure that concentrates on efficiency and standardization.

machine code in computers, the system of codes which, when activated, cause the computer's mechanical functions to operate.

machine downtime time when a machine is shut down and not working for any purpose, usually due to breakdown or shutdown for maintenance.

machine hours (MH) hours of running time required by a machine or machines to carry out a particular stage of a production process.

machine idle time time when a machine could be running but is not, usually because there is a lack of available inputs (raw materials, labour and so on).

machine intelligence artificial intelligence programmed into machines.

machine loading and scheduling scheduling techniques which aim to ensure that, in a given process, machines run with the maximum possible efficiency and reach production targets.

machine-level control in manufacturing systems, control systems that operate at the level of the individual machine.

machinery general term for machines or mechanical devices of any kind which are used in production or for ancillary purposes.

macro large or large scale; usually used as an adjective.

macroeconomic factors those factors which contribute to macroeconomic performance.

macroeconomics study of entire economies and the factors and forces contributing to and affecting overall economic performance.

macro-environmental trends large-scale trends which affect the environment across the world or over a very broad region.

macromarketing in macroeconomics, study of the exchange process as it takes place across an entire economy.

made work work which is deliberately created, usually by government initiative, with the aim of providing employment for the long-term unemployed.

magnetic storage general term for electromagnetic storage devices used by computers to store programs and data, including disks and tape.

MAID *see* media analysis and information databases.

mailing lists lists of names and addresses used in direct marketing and other promotional activities where material is posted to customers' homes.

mail order the purchase of goods using a catalogue; purchases are then shipped by post to the customer's home.

mail order house retailer who sells by direct mail.

main bank system name given to the Japanese practice whereby the bank which holds the largest amount of a company's debt is also one of its largest shareholders.

mainframe a large central computer, now largely obsolete.

maintained mark-on selling price of goods less their delivered cost.

maintenance work which is done to machinery, tools and so on to keep them in prime operating condition; money paid for any purpose or any person to enable them to maintain their present condition.

maintenance factor *see* dissatisfiers.

maintenance shift in shift work, a shift which is devoted to the maintenance of machinery rather than production activities.

maintenance systems systems and procedures for ensuring effective maintenance.

majority shareholder shareholder who owns more than 50 per cent of the shares of a company.

make good to finish work or prepare raw materials; to discharge an obligation.

make or buy strategic choice centring on whether to produce a product, component, service, etc. in house, or to buy it from an outside supplier.

maker the manufacturer of a component or product.

make-ready to set up a machine to do a particular job or task.

make-work *see* made work.

malfeasance criminal wrongdoing.

malfunction breakdown or failure of equipment or of a system.

malicious code in computer systems, code deliberately implanted in a computer as a form of sabotage that destroys or damages stored data; *see also* logic bomb; virus.

malpractice case where a professional service results directly in damage or loss to the client.

malpractice insurance insurance policy taken out by some in professional services against legal claims for damages in cases of malpractice.

Malthusian theory idea posited by Thomas Malthus in the nineteenth century that the population would increase beyond its capacity to feed itself.

managed change changes which are instituted and controlled by the organization.

managed costs costs where management has some degree of discretion or control.

managed currency currency where exchange rates and monetary value are regulated by the government.

managed exchange rates exchange rates which are controlled by government rather than dictated by the market.

managed expenditure expenditures over which management has some degree of discretion or control; *see also* managed costs.

management **1** general term for the coordination and direction of resources, capital and labour to ensure the organization meets its goals; **2** also used to refer to the body of managers and executives responsible for management.

management access time time elapsed between the point when a manager requests information and the point when he or she receives it.

management accounting accounting function which collects, analyses and presents financial data for the primary purpose of supplying financial information to all levels of management.

management audit systematic appraisal of management performance, capabilities and effectiveness.

management board in German two-tier systems, the board of directors which handles day-to-day management; *see also* supervisory board.

management buy-in (MBI) the acquisition of a complete company or division of a company, including its management, by outside investors.

management buy-out (MBO) the acquisition of a complete company or division of a company by its present management from its previous owners.

management by crisis management style that is highly reactive, concentrating on managing problems as and when they emerge.

management by exception management practice which looks for deviation from normal standards and concentrates on analysing and, if necessary, rectifying these; in such systems, subordinates are usually only required to inform managers of progress when exceptions occur.

management by objectives management philosophy which sets a series of objectives for company, division and individual performance, concentrating on actually meeting the objectives rather than on the processes used to meet them.

management by walking about management philosophy which focuses on communication between management and employees, by means of managers making frequent personal visits to the shop floor and other areas of the firm.

management company company which manages the assets of others, in exchange for a fee or a share of the profits.

management consulting professional service which advises companies on planning, strategy, operations and so on, sometimes assisting in information collection and analysis and/or in the implementation of solutions to problems.

management development general term for the provision of training and experience to managers which enhances their capabilities and makes them suitable for greater responsibility and/or promotion.

management discretion the extent to which managers are free to exercise their own judgement rather than referring matters to superiors.

management education education programmes through which managers learn the principles and techniques of management.

management education programme an individual programme of management education.

management expertise collective skills and experience required for effective management.

management functions series of basic activities which managers must perform as part of their task, including planning, decision making, supervising, leading and controlling.

management information system (MIS) information systems, usually computer-based, which provide managers with the information they need, on demand, to develop plans and make decisions.

management philosophy the mental approach to the tasks and goals of management used by an individual manager or the overall management of a firm.

management practices the approaches and techniques used by managers to carry out management functions, often strongly influenced by management philosophy.

management prerogative traditionally, exercising of complete authority by management, an authority that might become qualified during collective bargaining.

management process the means by which managers perform their functions and reach their goals; *see also* management functions.

management process school theory of management which focuses on the management process as the best way to improve management performance.

management ratio relationships between sets of data which serve as indicators of company and management performance, such as profit to sales or direct costs to indirect costs.

management research formal research into the problems and issues affecting the management of organizations.

management science the application of scientific techniques, particularly quantitative techniques, to the study of management.

management skills expertise or capability in performing the tasks associated with management.

management style attitude of management to areas such as leadership and supervision, the exercise or delegation of authority, and communication with other managers and staff; usually a reflection of management philosophy.

management succession planning planning which aims to ensure that there is a sufficient supply of qualified junior managers who can succeed to senior positions.

management support systems (MSS) general term for computer-based databases, information systems, decision support systems and expert systems.

management systems basic classification of management styles developed by R. Likert.

management teams teams of managers brought together to manage a complex function or project, or to solve a problem.

management theory theoretical appreciation of the role and nature of management.

management threshold term for the stage in a manager's career when he or she progresses from specialist technical functions to a more general managerial role.

management trade union trade union whose members are managers of firms, rather than lower-ranking employees.

management training training of the skills required to be a successful manager; *see also* management development; management education.

manager anyone within a firm who bears responsibility for planning, direction and controlling the work of others.

managerial accounting *see* management accounting.

managerial behaviour general term for the attitudes and actions exhibited by managers in particular sets of circumstances.

managerial control the monitoring and controlling activities carried out by managers with the aim of ensuring that schedules are adhered to and targets met.

managerial grid technique developed by R. R. Blake and J. Mouton for defining and measuring leadership styles with reference to the three elements of grid theory; *see also* grid theory.

managerial performance extent to which managers meet or exceed the goals and targets set for them, or which they set for themselves.

managerial responsibility the responsibility taken by managers for making decisions, and for accepting the consequences of those decisions in the event of failure.

managerial role general term for the tasks, behaviours, responsibilities and activities expected of a manager.

managerial style *see* management style.

manager's letter written instrument which sets out the extent of a manager's responsibilities, either for a particular task or in general.

managing director chief executive officer of a company, who coordinates the work of other directors and senior managers; *see also* president.

mandate written instructions by an organization to an agent or representative, setting out limits of responsibility and the policies to be followed.

manifest in shipping, a document stating the contents of a particular lot or load of cargo.

manpower general term for available labour, either within a company or in the labour pool from which the company can draw.

manpower analysis analysis of the firm's present manpower situation, creating a summary of employees and their attributes.

manpower budgeting estimates of future labour needs and resources.

manpower deficit situation when there are not enough workers to fill all available jobs.

manpower planning plan which projects future manpower needs as well as potential sources of manpower.

manpower ratios methods of measuring costs and effectiveness of the firm's workforce, such as sales per employee or net profit as a percentage of payroll costs.

manpower surplus situation where there are more workers, or would-be workers, than there are jobs available.

man-to-man rating performance appraisal system whereby each person in a unit is compared with each other person in the unit.

manual 1 document which provides instructions for how to use a particular piece of machinery or follow a certain procedure; **2** also, term for something which is done by hand rather than by machine.

manual labour labour which is carried out by hand rather than by machine.

manual skill the ability to do manual tasks.

manual work *see* manual labour.

manual worker worker employed in manual labour.

manufacture to make or assemble a product or component, usually in quantity.

manufacturer's agent agent who represents a manufacturer, usually in either a selling or purchasing capacity.

manufacturer's representative *see* manufacturer's agent.

manufacturing the process of converting raw materials into components and/or components into finished goods.

manufacturing costs all costs incurred during manufacturing, including both direct costs and overhead costs.

manufacturing industries general term for industrial sectors primarily involved in manufacturing.

manufacturing inventory goods held in stock by a manufacturing business, ranging from raw materials to finished goods.

manufacturing management branch of management specifically concerned with the techniques and processes of manufacturing.

manufacturing overhead overhead or indirect costs incurred by a manufacturing operation.

manufacturing resource planning general term for planning and forecasting the nature and amounts of inputs required for a production process; *see also* material requirements planning.

manufacturing scheduling scheduling of manufacturing functions to ensure that each stage of the manufacturing process is completed in an efficient manner.

manufacturing strategy strategic choices as to which products to make and when.

manufacturing structure the capacity, facilities, technology and so on which make up a particular manufacturing process.

manufacturing systems general term for the facilities needed for manufacturing operations, including machinery, plant layout and architecture, human resources and supporting services.

manufacturing teams groups of employees tasked with carrying out a particular function of set of functions within the manufacturing process, usually working on an autonomous or semi-autonomous basis.

margin short for margin of profit; also, especially in securities trading, the amount paid by a buyer when using credit rather than paying the full purchase price in the first instance.

marginal 1 literally, 'on the edge'; **2** issue which is not of central importance; **3** a very small change to the existing situation.

marginal analysis analytical method which examines the impact of small incremental changes in a given situation.

marginal borrower borrower who is discouraged from borrowing by a rise in interest rates.

marginal buyer buyer who is discouraged from making a purchase if the cost of goods or services increases.

marginal cost increase in production costs that results from the production of a single additional good.

marginal costing method of costing which separates fixed costs from the remainder, which are then termed marginal costs.

marginal efficiency of capital *see* internal rate of return.

marginal efficiency of investment rate of return on a unit of investment compared with the return on a comparable amount of alternative investment in a given time period.

marginal lender lender who is discouraged from making a loan by a decline in interest rates.

marginal pricing pricing strategy where the market price is based on the marginal costs associated with the goods to be sold.

marginal producer 1 producer who sells goods at a price which covers the costs of production but with little profit; **2** alternatively, a producer who sells only small quantities of a product and has little power in the market.

marginal productivity the proportional rate of increase in productivity compared with the size of the workforce.

marginal products volume of products created by increasing any factor of production by a unit of one.

marginal profit increase in profit created by increasing the volume of production by one unit.

marginal propensity to consume percentage of any increase in personal income which is spent on consumer goods and services.

marginal propensity to invest percentage of any increase in personal income that is invested.

marginal propensity to save percentage of any increase in personal income that is saved.

marginal rate of tax result of any change in total personal income tax, divided by the amount of total taxable income.

marginal revenue increase in revenue generated by the sales of one additional unit of a particular good.

marginal seller seller who will be discouraged from selling if the market price declines.

marginal tax rates *see* marginal rate of tax.

marginal trading situation where buyers make purchases partly on credit, rather than using their own money in the first instance.

marginal utility increase in satisfaction which results from the purchase or consumption of one more unit of a good.

marginal worker worker whose wage exactly equals the value of his or her productive work.

margin call demand by a broker or financial institution for a buyer to increase the margin paid.

margin of profit measure of the difference between revenue and costs.

margin of safety, cost–volume–profit measure of the extent to which revenue or profits exceed the break-even point; the amount of revenue remaining after the payment of fixed costs.

margin payment in futures contracts, payments required by the clearing house to cover actual or potential losses.

marine insurance specialist branch of insurance devoted to insuring ships and their cargoes.

markdown any reduction in the original selling price of goods, as in a sale, or when stocks are revalued in a declining market.

market 1 geographical or other defined area in which there exist a number of potential customers for a product or service; **2** more generally, the sum of potential demand for a product or service; **3** alternatively, the largely invisible mechanism by which goods and services are traded between buyers and sellers; **4** finally, a defined location where both buyers and sellers come to trade specific commodities.

marketability 1 the extent to which a good is suitable for trading in an open market; **2** also, the extent to which an asset can easily be bought or sold.

marketable anything which can be bought or sold in a market.

marketable securities securities which can be traded easily and quickly in most markets.

market analysis market research term for the identification of the size, scope and characteristics of a particular market.

market assessment evaluation of the nature and potential of a market.

market audit *see* marketing audit.

market capitalization total of all shares issued by a company, multiplied by their current price.

market demand total of actual or potential demand for a product within a particular market.

market diversification marketing strategy in which a firm attempts to sell products into various different markets or market segments.

market economy economic system which focuses on the market as the principal mechanism for distributing goods, services and money.

market equilibrium state of balance occurring when prevailing prices match the expectations of both buyers and sellers and price fluctuations then cease.

market estimation assessment of the total volume of demand for a given product, brand or service in a market.

market exploration research into the potential of a market which has not been previously exposed to a particular product or brand.

market factor derivation the identification of particular factors which might cause a change in the levels of demand for a particular product or brand.

market failure situation where a market is not operating efficiently and is therefore not meeting the needs of buyers.

market fit *see* fitness for use.

market follower 1 a product or brand which is intended to compete with existing products, as opposed to market leader; **2** a company which chooses to enter established rather than new markets.

market forecasting analysis and prediction of likely future demand and other trends in markets.

market identification in market research, the identification of markets or segments which offer potential for the company's products and services.

marketing 1 the provision of goods and services to customers which meet their needs while earning a profit for the seller; **2** the management function responsible for this activity, including analysing the needs of customers, designing products and processes to meet those needs, and communicating the availability of these to the customer.

marketing audit analysis of the effectiveness of a firm's marketing activities.

marketing board agencies, usually government owned or backed, which serve as centralized intermediaries especially in the agricultural sector, buying from producers and then selling to retailers.

marketing campaign structured programme of marketing activities centred around a particular good or brand.

marketing channel route by which products and services are delivered from producer to consumer; *see also* channel of distribution.

marketing communications communications which are intended to inform consumers about the availability and features of products and services.

marketing concept view that marketing activities ought to be the central focus of other business activities; *see also* market orientation.

marketing control system of monitoring and control of marketing activities, ensuring that they stay on schedule and on budget and meet targets.

marketing cost analysis analysis which sets out the costs incurred during the marketing process.

marketing culture company culture which focuses the efforts of all employees on markets and marketing; *see also* market orientation.

marketing database stored data which is used in marketing, most commonly, contact details and known attributes of past, present and potential customers.

marketing decision making specific branch of decision making concerning marketing activities, such as which markets to enter and which products or services to sell.

marketing department sub-unit of organization responsible for the marketing function.

marketing, direct *see* direct marketing.

marketing distribution *see* distribution.

marketing environment generally, the market in which marketing activities take place, including customer profiles, income, demand and so on.

marketing ethics application of ethics to marketing activities, with the aim of preventing marketers from treating consumers unfairly.

marketing forecasting overall forecasting of likely future developments and trends in marketing; *see also* market forecasting.

marketing foundations fundamental principles on which marketing is based.

marketing function the processes of marketing, usually managed from within a marketing department.

marketing game variant of business game which focuses on marketing decisions.

marketing, green *see* green marketing.

marketing information information which is of use in marketing, including not only market information but also information about new processes, innovations and so on.

marketing information system information system, usually computer-based, which assembles and collates information about products, customers and transactions, which can then be used in marketing decision making.

marketing information technology devices for collecting marketing information, such as databases, point of sale scanners and so on.

marketing intelligence branch of the marketing function concerned with market intelligence and information gathering.

marketing, international *see* international marketing.

marketing management general term for the management of the marketing function, and for the managers within the marketing department who are responsible for such management.

marketing mix the elements of marketing, traditionally known as product, place, price and promotion, which are combined in different forms to appeal to different markets; *see also* four Ps.

marketing, not-for-profit *see* not-for-profit marketing

marketing objectives the goals of a particular marketing programme, usually expressed in terms of desired share of market, volume of sales, and so on.

marketing opportunities situations which appear to offer particularly favourable opportunities for marketing, for example, where there is a perceived high level of demand for a product.

marketing orientation generally, synonymous with market orientation; also used pejoratively of companies where the marketing department is dominant and where there is an excessive focus on the marketing function itself, rather than on customers.

marketing planning the planning of marketing activities.

marketing promotion promotional activities undertaken for marketing purposes.

marketing research research on issues of importance to marketing management, including market research, research on new products and processes and so on.

marketing risks factors which could impair or negate marketing activities, potentially leading to the failure of a product or brand in the market.

marketing segmentation *see* segmentation.

marketing strategy strategy which defines how an organization will seek to meet its marketing goals, including markets and products where attention will be concentrated and money which will be spent on marketing functions.

marketing theory body of theory covering such areas as consumer decision making and buying behaviour.

marketing tools techniques which marketers use to attempt to influence customers, including advertising, public relations, price changes, product features and so on; *see also* marketing mix.

market intelligence the gathering of data and information about current and potential markets.

marketization the introduction of markets into economies or sectors where markets had not previously existed, most commonly in the public sector.

market leader 1 dominant company in a particular market, usually meaning that it has the largest share of revenue or sales volume; **2** can also mean a company that is first into a particular market, as opposed to a market follower.

market liberalization making markets more free through deregulation.

market maker trader in securities or commodities who buys and sells as a principal rather than as an agent.

market offering product or service which is available for purchase in the market.

market order instruction to buy or sell commodities or securities at the price then prevailing.

market orientation philosophy which involves a company focusing on its customers, in particular on collecting information about customer needs and wants so as to design products and services which will provide customer satisfaction.

market penetration extent to which a company's market offerings have been taken up by the market, usually expressed in terms of market share.

marketplace physical or notional location where goods and services are bought and sold.

market potential potential demand for a service or good within a market or segment, expressed in terms of either volume of units or monetary value.

market power extent to which any party in a market, either buyer or seller, can dictate prices and terms to other parties.

market presence extent to which a company is known and involved in a market, often a reflection of its market position.

market price 1 price of a good which is established in the market through the interacting forces of supply and demand; **2** the price at which sellers agree to sell a good and buyers agree to buy it.

market profile collective information about a particular segment or group of customers, including demographic and socio-psychological traits.

market prospect a likely potential customer.

market rate *see* market price.

market regulation restrictions imposed on the conduct of parties in a market, either through self-regulation by industry associations or, more commonly, through government legislation.

market research general term for information collection and analysis about current or potential markets and the customers within them, with the aim of finding the best marketing opportunities for the company.

market research agency company which specializes in providing market research services to other companies.

market saturation extent to which the total of a product or service sold in a market approaches the limits of total possible demand for the same.

market segmentation analysis which seeks to identify groups of consumers within a market who share common characteristics, thus allowing the company to tailor its marketing efforts more closely to supposed consumer needs.

market segment capacity total volume of a product or service that a particular market segment is capable of purchasing.

market share ratio of a company's own sales to the total of sales of all similar products within a particular market or segment.

market sharing agreement agreement between two or more companies to share marketing activities within a particular market or segment; in many jurisdictions, where such agreements are deemed to be anti-competitive, they are illegal.

market skimming *see* skimming.

market stability extent to which demand for a particular product or service is likely to remain constant or rise progressively, with no unpredictable fluctuations.

market strategy strategy adopted by a company in its approach to a particular market; *see also* marketing strategy.

market testing experimental offering of a new product or service in order to gauge consumer response.

market–to–book ratio in financial statement analysis, the relationship between the market value of a company and the value of its net assets.

market valuation estimate of the value an asset would realize if it were to be sold.

market value price that a commodity would command if it were to be sold on the open market.

mark-on **1** retailer's margin on goods sold to consumers, reflecting the difference between the cost of acquiring the goods and their sale price; **2** more generally, the margin added by any member of the value chain as goods are transferred on to a new owner.

Markov process stochastic process with the property that, if the present state is known, additional information about past states will not affect future states.

mark-up **1** *see* mark-on; **2** more generally, an increase in the price of products or services.

Maslow's hierarchy *see* hierarchy of needs.

Marxism political and economic philosophy based on the works of Marx, usually including central economic planning, regulated markets and communal ownership of the means of production.

mass communication communication to a very large audience using print and broadcast media, outdoor billboards and so on.

mass marketing marketing programmes aiming to sell very large volumes of a product to large and loosely defined markets; as opposed to targeted marketing.

mass media media which have very large audiences, including television, radio and national newspapers and, potentially, the Internet.

mass production continuous production of very large volumes of products using mechanized assembly lines or flow lines.

mass unemployment widespread unemployment affecting a large proportion of the working population, usually occurring as an effect of economic depression.

master activity programming procedures based around those activities which have been observed and identified as the most important or critical tasks; the nature of those activities serves as the basis for procedure definition.

master agreement agreement covering a number of parties, with provision for subsidiary agreements between these parties; in industrial relations, large-scale agreement between a number of companies and unions.

master budget overall budget which coordinates departmental or divisional budgets.

Master of Business Administration (MBA) postgraduate degree in business and management, often regarded as an essential basic qualification for a career in management.

master production schedule overall production schedule which sets out times for completion of the product and its major components.

master record index *see* build schedule.

master sample set of data which is frequently used for analysis and comparison, and from which smaller limited samples can be drawn.

master schedule overall schedule which incorporates a number of more focused schedules; *see also* master production schedule.

master unit part of a computerized system which controls the activities of other parts of that system; *see also* central processing unit.

matched and lost situation in stock markets where two simultaneous bids are made for the same stock and where there is only sufficient stock on the market to meet one bid.

matched bargain situation in stock markets where shares offered can only be sold if there is a purchaser immediately available.

matched sample in research, two samples which are statistically identical and which, unmodified, should produce the same result when analysed.

material control inventory control systems for raw materials.

material cost cost of the raw materials required to make a product or provide a service.

materiality the extent to which an idea or fact is relevant to the present situation.

material requirements planning (MRP) management information and control system dealing with the materials and components required in production processes.

materials handling 1 the physical movement and storage of materials around a place of work; **2** the techniques involved in such movement and storage which aim to achieve optimal efficiency, safety and so on.

materials management the management of materials handling.

maternity rights benefits, including paid leave of absence, which are due to female employees during and after pregnancy.

mathematical model model of a real or theoretical situation using mathematical techniques.

matrix rectangular array, composed of two or more rows and columns.

matrix organization organization where a specific work unit or project team may be performing two or more functions simultaneously, and may therefore be accountable to two or more managers.

mature economy economy which has reached a stage of full industrialization and high mass consumption.

maturity 1 completion of a contract; **2** in finance, the point at which a loan, bill or note is due for payment.

maturity date date at which a contract, loan, etc. reaches maturity.

maturity stage stage in national economic growth which results in the achievement of a mature economy.

maturity value value of a bill, loan or note upon reaching maturity.

maxim commonly understood precept or law.

maximax rule decision-making rule whereby the option which provides the maximum possible outcome is always chosen.

maximin rule decision-making rule whereby the option which provides the highest value from the minimum possible outcome is always chosen.

maximization strategic option which aims to achieve the best possible result from a given situation.

maximum distribution the effective limits of the range of distribution, such as the largest possible number of shops that can stock a particular product or brand.

maximum foreseeable loss estimate of the maximum amount of damage that could result from a given accident; *see also* normal foreseeable loss.

maximum/minimum control inventory control technique which sets a maximum and minimum level for quantities of components and materials to be held in stock; when current inventory reaches the minimum level, stocks are re-ordered up to the maximum level.

maximum work area maximum extent of the physical space which a worker can reach in order to use tools, equipment and so on at a given workstation.

MBA programme educational programme leading to a Master of Business Administration Degree.

MBI *see* management buy-in.

MBO *see* management buy-out.

mean mathematically calculated average point.

mean audit date in auditing where more than one unit or department is to be audited, the mean date on which the average unit is likely to be audited.

means–end chain hierarchy of objectives in which each goal becomes part of the means to achieve another, higher order goal.

means–ends analysis approach to decision making which begins with the desired goals and then analyses the alternative means for achieving these.

mean variance average level of variance within a given set.

measure representation of quantity or extent.

measured daywork system whereby workers are paid at a rate which varies according to whether they have reached or exceeded daily productivity targets; *see also* payment by results.

measurement the process of measuring the quantity or extent of a particular object, group of objects, event, phenomenon, etc.

measurement principles financial accounting principles of measurement.

measurement system system of units of measurement such as the metric system, imperial system and so on.

measure of value method of gauging the results of activity by assigning a monetary value to those results.

mechanical ability test test used to ascertain an employee's ability to use machinery and tools.

mechanical aptitude test *see* mechanical ability test.

mechanistic organization organization which is strongly hierarchical, with defined and regulated functions and communication limited to the chain of command.

mechanistic structure *see* mechanistic organization.

mechanization the replacement of and/or enhancement of manual labour by machines.

media means of transmitting messages; used colloquially to refer to newspapers, television and radio.

media analysis analysis of the effectiveness of a particular media as a venue for advertising or other communications.

media analysis and information databases (MAID) marketing research database in the UK.

media director in advertising, the manager responsible for selecting a media channel and coordinating the placement of the advertisement.

median mid-point in an array, where exactly half the points in the array have a higher value and half have a lower value.

media research analysis of the reach of particular media channels in terms of the number and type of readers/listeners/viewers they attract.

media testing media research techniques for testing the nature of response from different types of advertising media.

mediation *see* conciliation.

mediator third party who intervenes in a dispute in an effort to reconcile the disputing parties.

medium singular of media, a means by which a message is transmitted.

medium-term liability liability which must be met in a few years time, but not immediately.

MEDSS *see* model-embedded decision support systems.

meeting gathering of two or more people, either in person or using telephone/video technology, to discuss a particular issue or group of issues.

mega- prefix meaning very large.

megacorporation very large corporation with multinational interests and a turnover measured in hundreds of billions of dollars.

megatrend large-scale, long-term trend usually affecting all, or a large portion of, the world.

member bank US, a commercial bank or clearing bank.

membership formal participation in an organization such as an association or trade union.

membership group type of reference group used to study consumer behaviour, composed of people who belong to members of a common group.

memorandum 1 document which records terms of an agreement; **2** alternatively, written message circulated internally within an organization.

memorandum of association written statement signed when a company is first formed, stating the nature of its business and the amount and classes of shares to be issued.

memory the data storage capacity of a computer.

mentor an experienced senior employee who advises and coaches trainees or junior employees, often on a one-to-one basis.

menu list of available options, used in computing to show the range of possible commands that can be issued to the computer at a given time.

menu-driven term used of computer software programs which offer menus to users at every stage, allowing them to choose the commands they wish to give.

mercantile adjective relating to trade or commerce.

mercantile agent agent who engages in trade on behalf of another party, buying and selling goods on consignment; *see also* agent.

mercantilism economic policy based on the acquisition of precious metals or currency, common in Europe in the seventeenth to nineteenth centuries.

merchandise goods which are offered for sale; *see also* consumer goods.

merchandise charge costs such as shipping which are added to the base cost of merchandise before the mark-on is calculated.

merchandise transfer the transfer for accounting purposes of merchandise from one department to another.

merchandising general term for activities relating to the marketing and selling of merchandise in retail outlets.

merchant business person who buys goods and then sells them on, either as a wholesaler or a retailer.

merchant bank bank which specializes in providing services in financial markets, including arranging venture capital or loan capital, handling share issues, dealing in currency and commodity markets and so on.

merchant house company whose primary purpose is to engage in merchant trading, as a wholesaler and/or retailer.

merchant wholesaler merchant or merchant house acting as a wholesaler.

merger situation where two or more companies combine their assets to create a distinct and separate company.

merit quality deserving of recognition.

merit pay additional pay given to an employee in recognition of services of outstanding value.

merit system system where promotion is based on the demonstrated merit or worth of the employee to the firm.

message the content of a communication or advertisement.

meta- prefix meaning beyond or of a higher order.

meta-databases database consisting of information on other databases.

meta–information system systems which links a number of existing information systems, offering the ability to transfer between these systems.

meta-rationality higher order rationality.

meta-system general system which includes a large number of sub-systems.

methodology science of methods; the methods used in conducting a particular study.

methods engineer technician who designs and carries out method studies.

methods–time measurement (MTM) form of motion study which assigns times to each work activity and uses these as standards for assessing performance.

method study the observation, analysis and recording of methods of working.

metrification conversion from non-metric to metric standards of measurement.

mezzanine finance short-term or intermediate-term finance, usually loans.

M-form *see* multidivisional form.

MH *see* machine hours.

micro-business very small business, usually employing fewer than five people and with a very low turnover.

microchip in electronics, small integrated circuit manufactured on a single wafer, or 'chip', of silicon or other material.

microeconomics study of economics at the level of the individual or organization.

microelectronics miniaturized electronic components, and the products which require these in order to function.

micromarketing in microeconomics, the study of exchanges at the level of the individual or organization.

micro-political risks political risks inherent in political events happening at a local level.

microprocessor integrated circuit or circuits which can process information and carry out instructions.

mid-career plateau situation where a manager finds that there are no apparent opportunities for further promotion.

middleman intermediary such as a wholesaler or agent who occupies a position in the channel of distribution between the manufacturer and the retailer.

middle management level of management below top management, responsible for executing instructions passed down from the latter.

migrant manager manager who lives and works in different countries in succession, either by moving between companies or through overseas postings for a single company.

migrant workers workers who travel to other countries to obtain work but who have no right of abode in that country; *see also* guest workers.

migration large-scale movement of people from or to a country or region.

military–industrial complex term for the links between national armed forces, government and companies manufacturing products for military use.

military management management techniques derived from and used in military organizations.

minimax rule decision-making rule whereby the option which minimizes the actual or potential loss is always chosen.

minimization strategic option which aims to reduce or minimize the impact of a particular situation or event.

minimum charge the lowest rate charged for a service, regardless of the amount of service actually consumed.

minimum earnings level *see* minimum wage.

minimum entitlement the minimum pay which an employee will receive under a variable pay scheme, regardless of other conditions.

minimum lending rate in the UK, interest rate at which the Bank of England lends to other banks.

minimum manufacturing quantity the lowest production volume which it is economically viable to produce.

minimum rate *see* minimum charge.

minimum stock *see* buffer stock.

minimum wage lowest permissible rate of pay for any employee, usually determined by law.

minimum wage agreement agreement reached through collective bargaining concerning the minimum wage that an employer will pay.

minority interest a holding of shares or other assets insufficient to give the holder a majority or controlling interest in the company.

minority investment specifically, a shareholding which amounts to less than 51 per cent of the company's shares; more generally, a shareholding which does not obtain a controlling interest.

minority shareholder shareholder whose total shareholding in a company amounts to a minority, or non-controlling, interest.

mirror principle principle that people will respond to an action in a manner similar to the action itself, i.e., bad treatment will result in bad behaviour.

MIS *see* management information system.

misconduct improper conduct, an abuse of one's position or responsibility.

misperceptions theory in economics, the theory that business cycles are to some extent caused by asymmetric information among economic actors.

misrepresentation to represent the facts of a situation incorrectly, or to claim that a statement is true when it is in fact false; deliberate misrepresentation can in some cases be considered fraud.

mission general term for the broad aims and goals of an organization.

mission statement written statement setting out an organization's mission.

mix the number and quantity of raw materials that go to make up a product; *see also* marketing mix.

mixed benefits scheme pension scheme providing retirement benefits in the form of both a lump sum on retirement and an annuity in succeeding years.

mixed capitalism economic system which consists of a mix of private and state-owned companies.

mixed cost cost which includes elements of both fixed and variable costs.

mixed economy economic system where both private and public sectors own large portions of the means of production and compete together in the market.

mixed model production production system developed by Toyota whereby small quantities of a number of different models can be produced within the same system.

mobility the ease with which goods, currency, people and so on can move from one physical location to another.

mode value of a variable which corresponds to its greatest frequency of occurrence.

model in design, representation of an object at less than actual size; in management theory, a diagram or other representation of how a system or process works.

model building the process of creating a model; *see also* modelling.

model embedded decision support systems (MEDSS) decision support systems based on mathematical models.

modelling the techniques used in creating models, including mathematical techniques and computer software programs.

models of development examples of particularly successful economic development which are studied in order to learn about economic and business success.

modem device which allows a computer to transmit and receive data along a telephone line.

modernization upgrading systems and technology to reflect current standard practice.

modern portfolio theory approach to investment decision making which seeks to maximize gain and minimize risk by selecting an appropriate investment portfolio.

modular design design of products, systems, etc. which seeks to incorporate common elements through standardized modules, around which the final product or system is built.

module distinctive part of a system, often a stand-alone component which is integrated into a larger system; in management education, a part of a training programme that focuses on a specific subject.

modus operandi recognizable methods and style of operation; *see also* management style.

modus vivendi arrangement between two parties in a dispute whereby they agree temporary procedures prior to the settlement of the dispute.

monad system composed of a single unit.

monetarism economic philosophy which focuses on controlling the supply of money as the means of managing the economy.

monetarist economist or other who believes in or practices monetarism.

monetary aggregate total of all measures of money supply.

monetary assets cash or assets which potentially exist in cash form, such as accounts receivable.

monetary base aggregate of money held in banks, either as personal savings or by the banks themselves.

monetary items assets which are valued at a fixed price.

monetary measures government measures to control money supply or the amount of purchasing power in the economy, usually by raising or lowering interest rates; *see also* fiscal measures.

monetary policy government policy concerning money supply in the economy at large.

monetary principle in financial accounting, the underlying assumptions about the stability of the primary currencies in which the company trades.

monetary reserve money which must be held in reserve by financial institutions as security against possible future liabilities.

monetary union system where two countries agree to merge their currencies, and the financial institutions that support those currencies.

monetary value the value of a good if converted into money, often used in areas such as environmental economics in order to place cash values on non-tradable goods.

money primary instrument of economic exchange, either circulating as currency or represented by cheques, bills of exchange, bank balances, credit balances and so on.

money at call any loan or other debt which must repaid on demand by the lender.

money broker financial institution specializing in money market operations.

money income income which is received in the form of money.

money manager executive who manages funds invested.

money market market where financial instruments such as loans, credit and currency are bought and sold.

money markets collective term for markets where money is traded; *see also* money market.

money measurement concept theory that as money is the primary unit of exchange, only those things which can be measured in monetary terms should be accounted for and included in economic analysis.

money supply amount of money currently circulating in an economy.

money wages wages received in the form of money.

monitor 1 management role whereby managers search for and assemble information about their own business unit and the environment in which it operates; **2** also, visual device used for displaying computer data; *see also* visual display unit.

monitoring observation of a process or project in order to collect data and to check whether schedules and budgets are being adhered to.

monochronic time schedule (M–time) in cross–cultural management, the concept that some cultures visualize time as linear and compartmentalized, placing great value of preset schedules; *see also* polychronic time schedule.

monopolistic competition situation in a market where each competitor's offering differs from all other offerings to such an extent that switching is not possible.

monopoly exclusive control of a market, asset or commodity by a single person or organization; market condition where there is only one seller of a particular product or service.

monopsony market condition where there is only one buyer for a particular product or service.

Monte Carlo simulation simulation or business game where random elements are introduced to provide for an uncertain outcome.

moonlighting holding a second job, often at night, in addition to a primary day job.

morale mental state of employees and managers, composed of a mixture of satisfaction, confidence and willingness to work.

moral hazard risk which arises from the potential carelessness or misconduct of an employee, manager or agent.

moral suasion pressure applied to force one party to comply with a contract or regulation without resort to legal means.

moratorium artificially imposed delay in a process or period of non-activity.

morphological approach research into human decision-making processes, used for example in design management and marketing.

mortality rates 1 proportion of the population which can be expected to die during a given time period; **2** of companies, that proportion of firms which can be expected to cease trading during a given time period.

mortgage loan made using landed property as security for the debt, most commonly made to enable the mortgagee to purchase the property.

mortgage banker bank specializing in the provision of mortgages.

mortgage bond *see* bond, mortgage.

mortgage broker organization that arranges mortgages by bringing potential lenders and borrowers together.

mortgage debenture *see* debenture.

mortmain perpetual ownership of landed property or real estate vested in an institution or an individual and his or her heirs.

most-favoured nation status granted by one trading nation to another, usually meaning a reduction in tariffs and trade restrictions.

motion in meetings, a proposal put to the group which requires their approval for further action.

motion study study of physical movements of materials and people in the production process, with the aim of identifying movements which need to be corrected or eliminated.

motivate to ensure that people make the choices and carry out the roles, tasks and functions assigned to them or desired of them.

motivation factors which motivate people and which induce desired behaviours or actions; *see also* incentive.

motivational needs personal needs and wants which serve as motivating factors.

motivation–hygiene theory theory developed by Frederick Herzberg, identifying working conditions leading to satisfaction or dissatisfaction.

motivation incentives *see* incentive.

motivation study research which aims to understand motivation needs and other motivators, used in market research to understand consumer buying decisions.

motivation theory psychological theories concerning human motivation.

motivators individual factors which provide motivation.

motives impelling force which induces a person to act; reason for taking an action.

motor activity combination of nervous and muscular activity required to make physical movements.

motor industry general term for motor vehicle manufacturers (including makers of components), distributors and retailers.

motor insurance insurance provided for motor vehicles, their cargoes and their passengers.

motor skills skills requiring motor activity; generally, any skill requiring physical strength, dexterity or coordination.

mouse computer input control device, used as a substitute for or complement to a keyboard.

moving annual total forecast of sales, profits, turnover, and so on which is regularly updated in light of new information.

moving average average which is continually recalculated as data change over time.

moving parity method of setting exchange rates which fixes the rate on a monthly basis as a moving average of the rate over previous months.

MRP *see* material requirements planning.

MSS *see* management support systems.

MTM *see* methods–time measurement.

mudarabah instrument of participatory finance used in Islamic banking, in which banks invest directly in businesses.

multi–channelling selling or distributing a product simultaneously through two or more channels.

multicultural societies societies which incorporate elements from two or more cultures.

multidivisional form form of corporate organization in which activities are separated out into divisions which have local autonomous control.

multidivisional structure *see* multidivisional form.

multi-domestic markets situation where a company is marketing into a number of different markets within its own country of origin.

multi-employer bargaining collective bargaining encompassing more than one employer; *see also* industry–wide bargaining.

multi-grade salary structure payment system based on a number of different salary bands.

multi-industry anything which affects or is present in more than one industrial sector.

multi-lateral trade negotiations negotiations on issues concerning trade between many different countries.

multi-level distribution *see* pyramid selling.

multimedia integrated use of audio and visual technology, usually with an interactive function.

multimedia technology computer-based technology used to deliver multimedia programs.

multinational anything which affects or is present in more than one country.

multinational company company which has operations in more than one country.

multinational corporation corporation which has operations in more than one country.

multinational enterprise *see* multinational company.

multi-plant company company which has more than one plant or factory.

multiple 1 more than one; **2** in retailing, a retail firm with a number of very similar outlets selling similar product lines.

multiple banking the offering of a variety of different banking services to customers through the same bank outlet.

multiple branding the marketing of the same product under different brand names.

multiple exchange rate situation where more than one exchange rate exists for the same currency.

multiple management form of democratic management which includes employee and management committees which have input into strategy and policy.

multiple offer bundling of several products as a single offer with a single price.

multiple pricing price discount which is offered if multiple units are ordered or purchased at the same time.

multiple regression analysis statistical technique which allows for the prediction of dependent variables based on their relationship with other variables.

multiple task role job or position that involves a variety of different tasks.

multiplier in economics, relationship between spending and investment to aggregate income.

multiplier principle principle which defines changes spending and investment in terms of changes in aggregate income.

multiprocessing operating a number of computers from a single point of input or control.

multiprogramming ability of a computer to run more than one program at the same time.

multiskilling simultaneous use of more than one skill.

multi-user more than one user.

Murphy's Law 'what can go wrong, will go wrong'.

musharakah instrument of participatory finance used in Islamic banking, in which the bank and the company establish a new partnership in which both invest.

mutual assent agreement by all parties in a negotiation or contract.

mutual company company which is owned by its customers, to whom profits are distributed; *see also* cooperative.

mutual fund investment portfolio managed on behalf of a group of joint owners; *see also* unit trust.

mutual gain bargaining philosophy of bargaining which seeks to achieve a result beneficial to both sides, eschewing adversarial or confrontational bargaining.

mutual goal setting management practice of defining employees' personal goals through discussion and consultation with employees.

mutual insurance where the insured pay into a common fund from which any indemnifications are made.

mutuality 1 principle whereby an issue is agreed to be negotiable between the parties involved; **2** agreement that an issue is subject to common interest.

mutual rating method of employee evaluation based on ratings of performance by peers.

mutual savings bank bank which operates for the benefit of depositors, to whom profits and dividends are distributed.

myopia, organizational tendency among thinkers in organizations to see and believe only such information as confirms their previously held views; *see also* cognitive biases.

N

NAFTA *see* North American Free Trade Agreement.

NAIRU *see* non-accelerating inflation rate of unemployment.

name in the Lloyd's insurance market, a member of a syndicate who has invested personal funds.

named insured person or organization named in an insurance policy as the primary beneficiary.

named vote vote which records the names of all present and how they voted, providing a record which can be published later.

name screening in market research, process of checking that proposed names for a product or brand have not been used previously and convey the correct image to customers.

narrow market market where demand is very limited.

NASDAQ New York-based stock market which also operates overseas, trading in over-the-counter securities.

nation-state independent country with an established government and legal system.

national accounting accounting by government which reports on national income and resources.

national aggregate inventory total of all goods held in inventory by manufacturers, distributors and retailers within a country.

national agreement collective agreement which covers all firms and industries in a particular industry across the country.

national bank US, privately owned bank which is regulated under the Federal Reserve System.

national brand brand which is distributed very widely, through numerous outlets.

national community the whole of a nation, including population, organizations, institutions and so on.

national context the framework or environment provided by a particular nation, a combination of its cultures, customs, laws and so on.

national culture culture which is common to a particular nation.

national debt total of all government liabilities.

national economy the economic system operating in a particular country.

national environment environmental conditions prevalent in a particular country.

national income total of all personal income in a country over a given period.

national insurance government-run health and unemployment insurance plan, financed in part by mandatory premiums from all in employment.

nationalism political philosophy dedicated to the advancement of the interests of a country and its people, possibly at the expense of other countries and peoples.

nationality statement of national origin or belonging, usually the country in which a person or organization is permanently domiciled.

nationalization **1** taking business activities formerly in the private sector into government hands; **2** converting private companies into state-owned companies.

national plan overall economic and development plan formulated by government.

national policy central government policy affecting an entire country.

national wealth total of assets and money in a national economy.

natural capital naturally occurring factors of production, primarily land.

natural environment the naturally existing environment in which a firm operates, including geological, geographical and biological features.

natural monopoly **1** monopoly that occurs naturally, where a service cannot be divided between more than one producer; **2** in economics, condition where lowest production costs occur when there is only one producing firm in the market.

natural price in classical economics, the level towards which prices gravitate given free competition.

natural resources naturally occurring raw materials which can be extracted from the environment, such as water, petroleum, minerals and so on.

natural selection theory developed from evolutionary theories of biology, that those firms which survive are those that are strongest and best equipped to do so.

natural wastage practice whereby firms reduce the numbers of people employed by not replacing those who leave or take retirement.

nature essential or innate qualities of a thing or person.

near money assets which can be easily converted into cash.

needs **1** in consumer behaviour, personal requirements which serve as motives for behaviour; **2** also necessary requirements before process can be carried out (resource needs) or before an employee can function effectively (training needs).

needs analysis programme of analysis which serves to define precise needs in terms of resources, training and so on.

needs assessment analysis of present and future requirements for a particular asset or resource.

negative cash flow situation where expenditures exceed income.

negative demand **1** situation where the level of demand for a good is less than the quantity of supply; **2** alternatively, situation where the majority of the potential market for a product has rejected it.

negative elasticity theory that demand moves in the same direction as price, i.e. that an increase in price will stimulate an increase in demand.

negative income tax income tax system which sets a certain minimum income threshold, assesses and collects tax from individuals whose income is above this level, and makes compensatory payments to those whose income is below this level.

negative sum game situation where aggregate losses will always exceed aggregate gains.

negligence failure to use due care or to follow correct and expected procedures, which can result in loss or injury.

negotiable asset or instrument which can be sold or transferred.

negotiable instrument document representing certain rights, liabilities and so on which can be transferred between parties and which can be bought or sold; examples include promissory notes, bills of exchange and bearer bonds.

negotiated price price which is reached through negotiation between buyer and seller, rather than simply being set by the seller.

negotiation procedure by which two parties meet to reach agreement over issues such as wages, prices, mergers and so on.

negotiation skills skills required to negotiate successfully and ensure that any negotiated agreement meets one's own goals.

negotiation strategies planned methods for achieving success in negotiations.

negotiation tactics methods used during negotiations to ensure that one's own goals remain part of the agenda and are focused upon by all parties.

negotiator one who acts as an agent for others in negotiations.

nemawashi in Japanese business, the practice of securing informal consensus from all parties involved in advance of making a decision.

neo-classical economics school of economics which developed in the late nineteenth century, focusing on issues such as allocation and capital; has remained the dominant school in economic thinking throughout the twentieth century.

neo-Confucianism synthesis of Chinese philosophical schools which took place in the twelfth century AD and lasted until the twentieth century; sometimes used in the media to refer to the apparent melding of Confucian philosophy and business acumen in the late twentieth century.

neo-Keynesianism economics school based on the works and views of John Maynard Keynes, focusing on the effects of government income and expenditure on economic forces.

nepotism practice of hiring relatives or close personal friends into positions of power and authority.

net sum remaining after deductions (e.g. for expenses) have been made.

net assets assets remaining after all obligations have been met.

net asset value total of all current assets less all outstanding liabilities.

net avails in discounting of notes, the face value of a note less the value of the discount.

net book value value of a fixed asset after depreciation, as shown on the company's books.

net cash flow net value of cash flow over a given period, that is, incomes less outgoings.

net change difference between the daily opening price and closing price of a security, regardless of fluctuations in the interim.

net cost gross cost less all income or profits resulting from that cost.

net current assets total of all current assets less all current liabilities.

net current asset value working capital divided by the number of shares currently outstanding.

net debt total of all liabilities less any reserves earmarked for the repayment of liabilities.

net domestic product gross domestic product less depreciation on capital goods.

net earnings gross earnings or income less tax deducted.

net effective distribution the actual range of distribution, such as the number of shops actually stocking a particular product or brand.

net income total income less costs, expenses, depreciation and other allowances.

net interest *see* pure interest.

net investment gross investment less depreciation on the capital goods invested.

net long-term debt total of long-term liabilities less any reserves earmarked for the repayment of liabilities.

net loss total of all losses over a given time period, less any profits accrued during the same period.

net margin *see* net profit.

net national product gross national product less depreciation and capital consumption.

net–net income synonymous with net income; money remaining after all income has been paid.

net present value (NPV) difference at a given point in time between the value of the investment and the value of the return on investment, calculated using discounted cash flow techniques.

net price final price after all deductions and discounts.

net profit total of all profits over a given time period, less any expenditures or losses accrued during the same period.

net revenue *see* net profit.

net sales total of all sales over a given time period, less any returns.

net tax liability gross tax owing less any allowances or deductions.

net terminal value the terminal value of an investment less costs and expenditures over the course of the investment.

net trade position *see* balance of trade.

network **1** generally any arrangement of objects, systems or people connected by real or notional lines; **2** in management, any situation where diverse organizations or parts of an organization are connected directly to each other by lines of communication; **3** in computing, a system whereby a number of computers and peripherals are interconnected, can communicate with each other and can function simultaneously.

network analysis form of critical path analysis which observes the parts of a network and how they function together.

networking 1 using a network to achieve a particular purpose; **2** colloquial term for establishing and maintaining personal relationships in a business setting.

net working capital total of working capital remaining after current liabilities have been deducted.

network management 1 management techniques which use networks in order to achieve managerial goals; **2** alternatively, management techniques for creating and maintaining networks.

network marketing marketing operation which uses a network of small sales operations, which coordinate their activities in the field.

network planning planning techniques which use a network as a method of coordination and control of the planning process.

net worth total equity of a business; total of current assets less current liabilities.

net yield total return on investment less any incurred costs or losses over the course of the investment.

neural net *see* neural network.

neural network computer network which attempts to mimic the functions of the human brain.

neuroscience branch of biological science focusing on nervous systems and activity.

New Economics *see* Keynesianism.

new issue a security which is being offered for sale for the first time.

new technology technological innovations which have only recently been introduced.

newly industrialized economies (NIE) economies which have just reached a state of industrialization, and which still contain substantial agricultural sectors.

newsgroup Internet-based discussion group which provides a forum for the exchange of information on specific subjects.

niche *see* niche market.

niche market very tightly defined market, with a small number of customers exhibiting proportionately high levels of demand for a carefully specified product or service.

niche width the size of market which a product or service may be sold or, more generally, in which a company trades; broad niches contain large populations with general needs, while narrow niches tend to have small populations with specific or specialized needs.

NIE *see* newly industrialized economies.

noise trading in securities or currency trading, trading based on non-standard techniques for valuation and analysis, thereby introducing excess volatility or 'noise' into market prices.

nominal existing in name but not necessarily in fact.

nominal capital sum of the nominal value of all the shares in a company.

nominal partner partner whose name is registered with a partnership or company but who in fact takes no personal role in running the business.

nominal price **1** very small price which serves to signify only that a transaction is taking place, and not the value of the good being transferred; **2** in securities, an estimated price given to a security which is traded too infrequently to have established a market price.

nominal value *see* face value.

nominal yield yield from a security calculated on the basis of its face value.

nominee person who is nominated by another to act in the latter's interests.

nominee holding shares held in a company by a nominee, thus allowing the real owner to conceal their identity.

non-accelerating inflation rate of unemployment (NAIRU) rate of unemployment in an economy which does not increase wage inflation; if unemployment falls below this rate, then wage inflation will increase.

non-bank depository institution financial institution which is not technically a bank but is nevertheless allowed to accept funds on deposits.

non-cash transaction any transaction which does not involve the exchange of cash, for example, using credit or barter.

non-contributory pension pension plan where the employer makes all the necessary investment and the beneficiary is not required to make contributions.

non-current accounts all accounts apart from working capital accounts.

non-current assets assets which the company intends to hold for the long term and which it does not intend to (or cannot) dispose of quickly.

non-current liabilities liabilities that will not become due in the short term.

non-durable goods goods which are consumed and wear out fairly quickly, requiring frequent replacement.

non-employment condition in which people are unable to work even though there may be suitable job vacancies; *see also* unemployment.

non-executive director director of a company who is not an employee and has no functional responsibility; as opposed to executive director.

non-financial compensation benefits apart from wages and money which are provided to an employee by the employer; *see also* employee benefits.

non-interventionism policy of leaving matters to take their own course, or of not intervening in the decisions and practices of subordinates.

non-linear programming mathematical techniques used to solve some types of decision-making problems.

non-monetary items assets or goods to which a monetary value cannot be easily assigned.

non-participation refusal to participate in an activity.

non-performance failure to complete a task or contract as scheduled or promised.

non-price competition competition between rival sellers where prices remain relatively stable and competition focuses on the other three elements of the marketing mix.

non-profit activity which is deliberately intended not to make a profit.

non-profit company *see* not-for-profit company.

non-profit marketing *see* not-for-profit marketing.

non-profit organization *see* not-for-profit organization.

non-qualified stock option in the US, a stock option which is exempt from capital gains tax.

non-recourse finance loan or credit arranged in such a manner that the party applying for the credit is not responsible for any failure to repay it.

non-recurrent transactions one-off transaction which is unlikely to recur, such as the purchase of a major capital good.

non-recurring charge a one-off charge or expense which will not be incurred again.

non-renewable resource natural resources which are totally consumed and cannot be replaced by similar resources.

non-stock corporation corporation which has no issued share capital.

non–store retailing retail selling through channels other than stores, for example, home shopping and electronic shopping.

non-tariff barriers barriers to trade such as quotas, which do not involve the use of restrictive tariffs.

non-taxable income income which is exempt from taxation.

non-traceable costs costs whose sources cannot be ascertained, and which are assigned to cost centres on an arbitrary basis.

non-union sector industrial sector in which there is no trade union organization or representation.

non-unionized company company whose employees are not members of a union.

no par value shares shares which do not have a par value or face value.

no-poaching agreement agreement between two companies that neither will attempt to recruit employees, customers, resources etc. that belong to or are regarded as part of the territory of the other.

no-raiding agreement agreement between trade unions to the effect that neither will attempt to recruit workers who are already members of the other.

norm average or normal expected standard.

normal foreseeable loss estimate of the normal amount of damage that could result from a given accident.

normal good any good which, given the same price, will be consumed in greater quantities when income increases.

normal price price of goods in a market under normal conditions.

normal profit ordinary minimum rate of profit which an investor will expect from a given investment.

normal time standard time period required to complete a process or task, assuming no accidents or interruptions.

normal working area normal physical space which a worker can reach in order to use tools, equipment and so on at a given workstation.

normative that which can be treated or regarded as a norm.

normative decision models models which show managers how decisions should be made given normal conditions.

normative economics study of economics in which it is accepted that the economist establishes normative standards for the subject under discussion.

normative forecasting technique forecasting technique which defines a normative or desired future and then forecasts the likely changes and developments which would be required to reach that point.

norming establishing a norm or standard.

North American Free Trade Agreement (NAFTA) free trade agreement including Canada, the USA and Mexico.

north–south dialogue discussions on resolving the trade imbalance of the north–south divide, often sponsored by organizations such as UNCTAD.

north–south divide in economics, the phenomenon whereby the countries of the northern hemisphere, especially its more northerly regions, control the bulk of the world's wealth, while those of the south have the bulk of the world's population.

no-strike clause clause in a collective agreement preventing strikes by workers.

nostro account foreign currency bank account maintained by a bank in the country of the currency in question (i.e. a US dollar account held in an American bank by a British bank).

notary public official who may serve as a witness to certain legal documents, including depositions and oaths.

note written instrument that serves as a recognition of a liability or debt, containing a promise to pay a certain sum by a certain date; *see also* promissory note.

note issuance facility type of Euronote, which allows a firm to borrow capital at a predetermined interest rate.

note of hand *see* promissory note.

notepad very small hand-held computer.

note payable note which the borrower is obliged to pay at a specified time.

note receivable notes which a lender has issued and on which he or she may demand payment.

not-for-profit company company which exists to provide certain goods and services for primarily social ends, and does not seek to make a profit.

not-for-profit corporation corporation which exists to provide certain goods and services for primarily social ends, and does not seek to make a profit.

not-for-profit marketing the marketing of services and goods on a not-for-profit basis.

not-for-profit organization organization whose prime purpose is to deliver goods and services to a target market, and which does not intend or expect to make a profit from doing so; *see also* not-for-profit corporation.

not-for-profit sector general term for sectors such as charities, education, some types of healthcare and other services which are offered as social goods and where the providing institutions do not seek to make a profit.

not sufficient funds situation where a cheque has been presented to a bank but there is not enough money in the account to cover the cheque.

NPV *see* net present value.

nuclear energy electricity generated by nuclear power plants.

numerical aptitude test test used to determine a person's ability to use numbers or numerical systems.

numerical control control of machine operations through a series of numerical codes; *see also* direct numerical control; computer numerical control.

nursery finance loans made to companies planning to go public, to enable them to meet the associated costs of doing so.

O

objective rationality decision-making approach in which the option selected is the one that will, according to rational analysis, maximize the return to the firm or individual.

objectives specific aims or goals.

objectives, corporate *see* corporate objectives.

objectives, management by *see* management by objectives.

objective test test whose results can be scored unambiguously by any marker (for example, a multiple choice test).

objective value the price for which a good can be sold, that is, taking account of the prices of competing goods in the same market.

obligation the responsibility of one party to another as defined in terms of a contract; more specifically, a debt owed to another.

OBS *see* off-balance sheet banking.

observation principles in financial accounting, the principles by which accounting procedures define the entity to be accounted for.

obsolescence condition of being obsolete, occurs when a product or technology has been superseded by more advanced forms.

occupation 1 the work a person does to earn a living; 2 trade or profession.

occupational accident accident causing harm to machinery or employees which occurs at work.

occupational analysis analysis of the nature of and tasks involved in particular occupations.

occupational bargaining *see* industry-wide bargaining.

occupational capacity redevelopment retraining of workers to render them suitable for employment in different occupations.

occupational classification classification of occupations by common features (e.g. professional, vocational, trade and so on).

occupational guidance advice given to individuals as to the occupation for which they are best suited.

occupational health practices adopted to prevent illness or accidents stemming from conditions in the workplace.

occupational illness illness resulting from a particular condition to be found in a person's place of work.

occupational mobility ease with which employees can change jobs or occupations.

occupational pension pension scheme set up for all employees involved in a particular occupation, regardless of the company they work for.

occupational profile description, following occupational analysis, of the traits and skills required for a particular occupation and the tasks involved when working in that occupation.

occupational psychologist licensed practitioner in occupational psychology.

occupational psychology branch of psychology which studies the psychological processes of people working in different occupations.

occupational stress stress induced by conditions in the workplace.

occupational union trade union recruiting members from one occupation or profession.

odd pricing psychological pricing tactic which sets prices at a figure just below a round number (e.g. 49p rather than 50p; £1.99 rather than £2.00).

OECD *see* Organization for Economic Cooperation and Development.

OEM *see* original equipment manufacturer.

off-balance sheet banking (OBS) banking activities that do not appear on a balance sheet.

off-balance sheet financing raising money in forms that do not result in liabilities appearing on the balance sheet.

off-board securities trading outside the main exchanges.

offensive flexibility strategic position which emphasizes flexibility over the long term, allowing the firm more easily to exploit emerging strategic options.

offer 1 bid or request to purchase a product or service, usually accompanied by a statement of the price the buyer is willing to pay; **2** alternatively, an offering of goods, commodities, etc. in the market to prospective buyers; *see also* offering.

offering product or service which a company offers for sale to consumers; any issue of securities through the financial markets.

offer for sale *see* offering.

office 1 physical workplace in which managerial or clerical work is usually done; **2** alternatively, a term which describes the holding of a particular executive position (i.e. 'to hold office').

office automation the use of mechanical or computer-based systems to perform many basic office tasks.

office automation system technical and computer systems used in office automation.

office management skills required to ensure efficient and effective management of an office.

Office of Fair Trading UK government agency responsible for enforcing legislation concerning market activities by firms.

office planning planning the physical layout and distribution of tasks in an office environment.

office technology information technology and applications used in offices, including computers and peripherals, information systems, word processing software, databases, Internet browsers and other software programs.

official 1 in government or regulatory activities, any person appointed to carry out a particular task; **2** adjective used to describe any communication or directive which has been approved by senior management or by government and to which all are required to give their attention.

off-line condition where a computer or machine has been shut down for maintenance or repair.

offset to counterbalance; to measure or weight one factor against another.

offshore bank bank located in a foreign country which takes deposits in a variety of currencies and offers the benefits of offshore banking.

offshore banking system whereby individuals and corporations use banks located in foreign countries, whose liberal banking laws allow banking transactions which would be difficult or costly to conduct through domestic banks.

offshore company company or subsidiary domiciled in a country other than the one where it has its primary operations, usually for regulatory or tax reasons.

offshore financial centre country which has deliberately chosen to adopt very liberal tax and regulatory regimes in the hope of attracting offshore banking and financial activity.

offshore market market in which goods or commodities are traded outside the country where the traders are domiciled.

off-the-books payment payment made but not recorded in the company's accounts.

off-the-job training training programmes delivered outside the physical setting of the workplace, usually at a specialized training facility.

oil 1 petroleum and some of its byproducts, used as source of energy and raw materials; **2** colloquially, to make payments or give favours as a bribe to hasten a process.

oil crisis problems associated with a sudden shortage of oil and its byproducts.

oil crisis price shock economists' term for the rapid rise in prices caused by the oil crisis of the early 1970s.

old boy network colloquial term for system whereby hiring companies give first preference to close friends or former colleagues of managers already with the firm.

oligarchy organization or society tightly controlled by a small group of people.

oligopoly market which is dominated by a small number of producers.

oligopoly price price for products or services in a market dominated by an oligopoly, where the producers have the power to increase prices.

oligopsony market which is dominated by a small number of buyers.

oligopsony price price for products or services in a market dominated by an oligopsony, where buyers have the power to drive prices down.

ombudsman third party appointed to handle grievances which cannot be dealt with through normal channels.

omikoshi **management** Japanese term meaning 'bottom-up management'.

omnibus motion motion containing a number of different sections or clauses, each pertaining to a different subject.

omnibus survey survey of a type used in market research, covering a range of different topics in the same questionnaire.

on account purchase where the price is charged to an account held by the customer with the seller, which the former will settle at a later date.

on consignment the holding of goods by an agent who attempts to sell them on behalf of their owner.

on cost *see* indirect cost.

on demand condition of a bill of exchange meaning it must be paid whenever the holder presents it.

one-line consolidation summary of an account in a single entry or line in the account books.

one-stop banking provision of all banking services through a single outlet.

one-stop shop shop which provides a full range of necessary goods and services.

one-time rate in advertising, rate paid for a single insert which will not be repeated.

on-line condition of a machine or computer system where it is running and functioning normally.

on-line library any database which can be accessed immediately by a computer, either from internal storage or through the Internet.

on-line search search program which selects relevant data from a computer database.

on-line storage computer data storage facility which can be accessed directly at any time.

on margin the purchase of securities using a downpayment only, with the purchaser borrowing the rest of the price from the broker.

on stream active function or process.

on-the-job training training programme which is delivered in the workplace, possibly using workplace situations as examples of problems to be solved.

OPEC *see* Organization of Petroleum Exporting Countries.

open account credit offered by sellers to customers allowing any number of purchases up to the limit of the account, with accounts to be settled after a stated period of time.

open cover insurance policy which insures goods without specifying a limit to the amount of compensation to be paid.

open-circuit television television which is broadcast and can be received on any television set within range.

open credit credit which is extended without prior proof of creditworthiness.

open door policy government policy which allows free movement of goods and people from another country across its own national borders.

open economy *see* free economy.

open-end agreement agreement or contract between two parties, the exact terms of which are spelled out later.

open ended agreement, contract, process or initiative that has no specific structure and which can be defined at a later date by mutual agreement between those involved.

opening job which is currently vacant and for which applications are being accepted.

opening purchase initial purchase of a particular security by an investor.

open learning *see* distance learning.

open-loop control engineering term referring to systems where it is assumed that process control affects output quality but not vice versa; as opposed to closed-loop control.

open order 1 order for goods that does not specify the price to be paid; **2** in securities trading, a buy or sell order to a broker that has not yet been executed.

open plan office office layout where internal walls and barriers have been removed.

open position *see* bear position.

open prospectus prospectus that leaves open the terms of the investment to be made.

open rate rate charged for advertising that can be varied according to the frequency with which advertisements are placed.

open shop workplace in which unions represent many workers but where union membership is not a requirement of employment.

open stock stocks of goods which are retained and held in storage for a long period.

open system computer system which can be easily accessed without security controls, and/or by using various different software applications.

open-to-buy in retailing, the quantities of stock which a retailer can order without exceeding planned inventory ceilings.

open union union that recruits generally, rather than focusing on a particular industry or profession.

operating the normal functioning of a machine, production facility, business unit, etc.

operating activities normal business activities.

operating budget budget which sets out the expected costs of operating a project or business unit over a stated period of time.

operating cashflow net cash flow from trading activities within a given financial period.

operating core the focus of the firm; the activities responsible for the main stream of production, distribution and marketing.

operating cycle general term for the pattern of business activity, where raw materials are purchased and processed into finished goods, which are then sold for cash.

operating expense expenses incurred in the course of running a business.

operating income income produced by business operations.

operating leverage ratio of fixed costs to total costs, representing the extent to which an organization can vary costs of operation.

operating loss loss sustained during the course of normal business operations.

operation process chart chart setting out the operations required to complete a particular process; *see also* flow process chart.

operating risk level of risk incurred in the course of normal business operations.

operational control control exercised by managers over the day-to-day operations of a firm.

operational flexibility extent to which a firm's operations can be reconfigured to meet new and changing needs.

operational goals intermediate level goals which are usually subsets of strategic goals; for example, reaching a certain level of production or profitability by a set date.

operational planning process **1** intermediate level planning which sets targets as intermediate steps to strategic targets; **2** setting plans which interpret strategic plans on a task and functional basis.

operational research *see* operations research.

operations general term for the day-to-day running of a business.

operations management management discipline that focuses on the management of production operations, including areas such as scheduling, materials handling and workflow management.

operations research (OR) scientific discipline devoted to understanding the problems associated with operations and then applying science-derived solutions.

operative worker responsible for a specific task; *see also* operator.

operator trained worker who operates a particular machine or system.

operator responsibility extent to which the operator of a machine or tool is responsible for it and for performance with it.

opinion former in consumer behaviour studies, term applied to a person who is respected by his or her peers and whose opinions and views are often mimicked or repeated by others.

opinion leader **1** synonymous with opinion former; **2** also, a member of an organization who as the ability to influence or determine the opinions of other members.

opportunism the seeking out and taking advantage of favourable opportunities.

opportunity cost measure of the profit that would have been obtained had a particular investment been made elsewhere; literally, the cost of missing or failing to take up an opportunity.

opportunity cost of capital expected rate of return on capital employed, assuming it is employed in the most effective manner possible.

optimal solution solution providing the best possible results.

optimal system design process of designing the most efficient and effective system for accomplishing a particular purpose.

optimization the process of defining the solution to a particular problem which will achieve the optimal or most satisfactory outcome.

optimum capacity balance in production systems between the highest possible output and the lowest possible unit cost.

optimum stock level stock level which balances the opposing needs of ensuring sufficient stocks for the running the business while incurring the lowest possible inventory costs.

option agreement which gives the buyer the right to make a purchase within a given time period, which the buyer may or may not subsequently do; used particularly in securities markets.

optional consumption consumption of goods that are not strictly speaking required for subsistence; *see also* luxury goods.

optional dividend dividend which can be paid in the form of either cash or shares, at the discretion of the recipient.

option contract contract giving the buyer an option to purchase a specific quantity of a security (call option) or to sell a specific quantity of a security (put option).

option dealing securities trading using options contracts.

option market market where option contracts are traded.

option spreading simultaneous purchase and sale of options, with a view to making a profit on the price difference between buy and sell options.

OR *see* operations research.

order 1 request by a buyer for goods, services, securities and so on, which will be delivered at some point in the future; **2** direct command to a subordinate which the latter is required to obey.

order acceptance acceptance by a seller of a bid placed by a buyer.

order–call ratio in direct sales, ratio of number of orders taken to number of calls made by the sales force.

ordering cost administrative costs associated with making an order.

ordinary income taxable income other than capital gains.

ordinary interest amount of interest earned or due over an annual period.

ordinary shares shares in a company which represent equity in the company and thus include rights of ownership.

ordinary stock *see* common stock.

organic anything which grows naturally, or which mimics the patterns which are found in nature.

organic organization organizational structure which attempts to mimic biological and societal structures, usually featuring high levels of decentralization, democracy, flexibility and good lines of communication.

organic structure *see* organic organization.

organism organized single body having a number of interconnected and dependent parts.

organization 1 any structured system, including a hierarchy of authority, chain of command and responsibility, and definition of particular roles and tasks; **2** alternatively, the process of organizing people and equipment to carry out tasks efficiently and effectively.

organizational behaviour *see* organization behaviour.

organizational change management strategy which attempts to change the structure and/or culture and climate of an organization to make its operations more efficient and effective.

organizational chart *see* organization chart.

organizational climate *see* organization climate.

organizational convergence trend identified by some observers whereby global organizations are becoming more similar in terms of structure and management.

organizational design *see* organization design.

organizational development *see* organization development.

organizational form *see* organization forms.

organizational goals *see* organization goals.

organizational learning concept which focuses on how organizations learn as groups, rather than on learning by individuals within such groups.

organizational memory accumulated past experience, contained within both physical records and personal memory, within an organization.

organizational models theoretical models which aim to explain how and why organizations are structured and function.

organizational multiplier factor by which the effect of change in a particular part of an organization on the rest of the organization can be calculated.

organizational norm standards of behaviour or performance which an organization expects of its members.

organizational units individual business or operation units which form part of a larger organization.

organization and methods analysis of the methods and modes of operation to be found in a particular organization.

organization behaviour the study of the attitudes, behaviour and activities not only of individuals within organizations, but of organizations themselves as independent entities.

organization budget budget which encompasses all of an organization's activities.

organization buying behaviour behaviour and decision-making processes exhibited by companies and organizations when taking the role of customers in industrial markets.

organization chart graphic depiction of the structure and hierarchy of an organization.

organization climate general term for the working environment within an organization, referring to physical, social and psychological characteristics of that environment.

organization control the controls required to keep an organization running efficiently and effectively.

organization control systems formal systems such as reporting and management hierarchies used to ensure organization control.

organization costs costs associated with the establishment and administration of an organization.

organization culture the common values and shared understandings present among members of an organization.

organization decision making decision-making processes within an organization involving, depending on the organization culture, some or all of its members.

organization design the process of planning and structuring organizational hierarchies and forms.

organization development programme of management and employee development which provides an overall framework for development.

organization ecology environment within which organizations exist and evolve; this concept, adapted from biology, suggests that principles such as natural selection are at work among organizations.

organization expense the costs involved in establishing an organization, such as fees to register a new company.

Organization for Economic Cooperation and Development (OECD) federation of industrial nations, including those of Western Europe, Japan, the USA and Canada, which promotes international trade and economic growth.

organization forms the different types of organization structure which can be employed (e.g. S-form, M-form, etc.).

organization goals the collective goals and targets which an organization sets for itself and its members.

organization inertia the tendency in organizations for things to remain the same, rendering change processes difficult and expensive.

organization knowledge the shared and pooled knowledge of members of an organization which is available to other members.

Organization of Petroleum Exporting Countries (OPEC) federation of the world's major oil producing and exporting countries who work together to set prices and production volumes.

organization planning process of designing an effective organization which is suited to carry out a particular set of purposes.

organization psychology branch of psychology which studies the mental processes of people within organizations.

organization research research into the forms, nature and conduct of organizations.

organization strategy strategy which defines how an organization will reach its goals.

organization structure the framework on which an organization is built, including such features as levels of hierarchy and lines of command.

organization subculture within an organization culture, a further set of shared values and assumptions common to a small group of members.

organization tree *see* organization chart.

organization types *see* organization forms.

organized labour groups of workers who form into organizations to undertake collective bargaining, the most common form of which is the labour union.

organizing the process of forming a union or a local branch of a union within a workplace.

orientation training provided to new employees to help them familiarize themselves with their tasks and the company as a whole; *see also* induction.

orientation programme *see* induction training.

original equipment finished components which are sold to manufacturers who assemble other, larger products; car engines are an example.

original equipment manufacturer (OEM) manufacturing firm which makes original equipment and sells it to other manufacturers.

original issue discount discounted selling price of a security at the time of issue.

Osgood scales type of multiple-choice questionnaire used in market research.

other revenue revenue from activities which do not form part of the company's major activities.

outbid to offer a bid of a higher value than other bids already received.

outcry market commodities market where bids asked and received must be called aloud on the trading floor.

outgoings expenditures or money paid out for any purpose.

outlay *see* outgoings.

outline process chart *see* operation process chart.

out-of-pocket expense expense paid by an employee using his or her own money, which is later reimbursed by the company.

out of stock product line requested by a customer of which all units have previously been sold.

out-of-the-money call option where the deal price is greater than the market price.

out of town retail outlet located away from the town centre, usually in a suburban area; *see also* shopping centre, out of town.

outplacement 1 assisting employees leaving the company to find new employment elsewhere; **2** professional services devoted to this purpose.

output total production yielded by a manufacturing process; in economics, the total of production in an economy over a given time period.

output-based performance appraisal performance appraisal which concentrates mainly on the volume of output generated per employee.

output budgeting *see* planning–programming–budgeting system.

output device computer peripheral which displays the output from a program or application, the most common forms being printers and VDUs.

output per man-shift estimate of average production per employee per shift.

outreach activities by an educational or training institution to increase the geographical range of its activities.

outside–inside approach approach to strategy which first examines the organization's environment and then its own capabilities.

outsourcing the contracting out of work instead of having it performed in house.

outstanding debts or issued credit which have not yet been repaid.

out-turn *see* output.

outwork work which is carried out on behalf of a company but outside its premises, for example, in employees' homes.

outworking *see* outwork.

overage excess quantity of goods over and above the lot size or order.

overall assessment rating summary of results of a personnel assessment, used as a guide to the individual's future potential.

overall market capacity volume of a good or service demanded by a market before reaching saturation point.

overall performance ratio measure of company performance based on factors such as revenue, profits and asset value.

overborrowing situation where a firm has borrowed so much money that it is very highly geared, with a consequent strain on profitability.

overcapitalization situation where a firm has been overcapitalized.

overcapitalize to place an excessively high value on an asset or property, or on the capital of a company; alternatively, to provide more capital than is required.

overdraft credit facility provided by banks to customers whereby the latter can draw limited amounts of funds over and above their current account balances.

overdue 1 a project which has run beyond its planned completion date; **2** a payment which has not been received by a specified date.

overextended 1 situation where an individual or company has received more credit than they can pay back; **2** borrowing beyond one's ability to repay; **3** expansion at too quick a rate, resulting in losses or debts.

overhead *see* overhead costs.

overhead absorption the allocation of indirect costs to various cost centres.

overhead costs costs incurred during the general running of the business and not directly attributable to a product or service.

overheating rapid economic growth, usually resulting in rising inflation.

overinsurance insurance policy for greater than the value of the property insured

overissue issue of stock which results in the total of issued stock exceeding the limit of authorized stock.

overlaid shift an additional shift which overlaps with existing shifts.

overmanning situation where a company has more employees than it needs to operate efficiently.

overproduction production of goods at a volume greater than can be profitably sold.

overqualification situation where an employee or manager has more qualifications or skills than are strictly necessary to do a particular job.

overrun volume of production, costs, etc. that prove to be greater than originally planned.

overseas assignments job postings which send managers to work in positions for the same company but in different countries.

overseas projects projects developed by a company in countries other than the one where it is domiciled.

oversold situation where goods, commodities, securities, etc. have been sold in quantities greater than the seller currently possesses.

overstaffing *see* overmanning.

oversubscribed share offer where buyers have offered to purchase more shares than are actually being issued.

over-the-counter market market for unlisted securities, usually shares in smaller firms.

overtime time worked beyond that required by the contract of employment, which is usually paid at a higher than normal rate.

overtime ban form of industrial action in which one side or the other forbids the working of overtime.

overtrading situation where a company has expanded rapidly and now finds itself short of working capital and experiencing liquidity problems.

overtraining training to a level which is in excess of what the job or task actually requires.

own brand consumer goods sold by retailers which bear their own brand name, rather than that of other producers, usually sold in competition with manufacturers' brands.

owner management company where the owners of a company are also its managers.

owner-manager entrepreneur who manages the company he or she owns.

owner-operator self-employed contractor who owns a piece of capital equipment and also operates the same on contract to clients.

owner's equity portion of the equity of a firm which is the personal property of the owners; *see also* stockholders' equity.

ownership possession of legal title goods or property.

own label *see* own brand.

ozone depletion reduction in the quantity of ozone in the upper atmosphere as a result of industrial and other pollution, said to have harmful effects on the global biosphere.

P

Pacific Rim the countries bordering the Pacific Ocean, including East Asia, Australasia and the west coast of the Americas.

pacing controlling flow production lines so that they move at a steady speed.

package term for the total compensation, including pay and fringe benefits, received by an employee.

package courses pre-prepared teaching programmes including a variety of learning materials.

package deal comprehensive agreement which settles a number of major points of contention simultaneously.

packaging protective covering surrounding products when they are shipped and sold, which is also often designed and printed so as to convey product information and brand name or logo.

pack test in market research, testing product packaging to ensure that it successfully conveys product information and brand image to the consumer.

paid-in capital *see* contributed capital.

paid-in surplus payments for shares in excess of the nominal value of those shares.

paid-up capital *see* share capital.

paid-up insurance insurance policy on which premiums have been fully paid up to date.

paid-up pension pension plan on which premiums have been fully paid up to date.

palletization warehousing system where goods are stored on wooden pallets.

panel discussion discussion, usually featuring questions and answers directed by an audience to a panel of experts.

panel interview interview where the candidate is questioned by a panel of interviewers rather than a single interlocutor.

panel methods market research technique involving panels of consumers providing opinions and information on goods and services.

panic sudden widespread belief that a company or even an entire economy is about to collapse, usually resulting in rapid divestment, devaluation of stocks and currency, and widespread losses among investors.

panoptic control overall control or complete control from a single point.

pantry check in market research, a form of home audit focusing specifically on patterns of purchase and consumption of foodstuffs.

paper general term for printed negotiable instruments such as notes and bills of exchange.

paperless item processing system (PIPS) accounting or money transfer system which can handle all transactions electronically without resorting to written documents.

paper money printed paper currency, complementary to metal coins.

paper profit profit that is recorded in a firm's accounts.

par equality or on an equal basis.

paradigm set of scientific principles and beliefs within which research is conducted.

paradigmatic technology a new technology which makes all related existing technologies obsolete.

paradox of thrift theory developed by John Maynard Keynes, that efforts to increase the level of savings result in a decrease in real savings.

parallel interface physical link between computers, using two or more wires or cables to maintain the link.

parallel pricing ensuring that prices for a company's products are broadly in line with those of competitors, and that all price increases are at roughly the same rate and at the same time.

parallel processing in computing, the ability of a computer to run more than one operation simultaneously.

parameter constant characteristic or feature which serves to define a thing or concept.

parent company company which owns another company, the latter being a subsidiary of the former; *see also* holding company.

Pareto diagram graphic representation of the Pareto effect.

Pareto effect phenomenon where a relatively small proportion of a company's business activities are responsible for the majority of its profits.

Pareto optimality situation where a distribution of resources means that no one has less resources and at least one person has more.

Pareto's Law states the 80/20 principle, i.e. that 20% of activity produces 80% of profits, or that 80% of capital is tied up in 20% of stock, etc.

pari passu term used to describe a share issue which is identical to the previous issue.

Paris Convention international agreement regulating the operations of airlines.

parity equality or equivalence.

Parkinson's Law 'work expands to fill the time available'.

parochialism attitude or outlook which is innately conservative, focusing on particular local issues and ignoring the wider perspective.

part component or subdivision of a larger unit.

partial loss partial damage or destruction of an asset which can be repaired or remain in service.

partial monopoly monopolistic situation where there is more than one seller but where each is sufficiently powerful to be able to control and set prices.

partial payment payment for goods or services of less than the full amount, the remainder usually being made at a later date.

participating retailer retailer who takes part in a particular promotional scheme and agrees to reduce prices, take promotional material, introduce special offers and so on.

participation in human resources, a philosophy which encourages involvement in the organization and its goals by employees and managers at all levels; usually accompanies democratization and decentralization.

participation loan loan, usually of large size, where several banks act as joint creditors, each contributing a portion of the funds lent.

participative management managerial style that stresses participation and consultation rather than direction and control.

participative planning *see* indicative planning.

participatory finance system whereby banks take a shareholding in companies to which they lend or otherwise take a stake in the business; *see also mudarabah.*

part method training method which teaches the component parts of a process separately rather than as an integrated whole.

partner person who has a share in a partnership.

partnership type of business organization where, unlike in a limited company, the partners who own the business do not have limited liability.

parts *see* components.

parts explosion in manufacturing planning, the process of working backwards from the finished product to generate requirements for all necessary components and sub-assemblies.

parts list in production, the list of components and raw materials required to produce the finished product.

parts sourcing establishing reliable and cost-effective sources for components required to produce finished products.

part-time employee employee who works only a limited number of hours per week, not enough to be considered a full-time employee.

part-time work work which does not require a full-time employee to complete, and can be done on a part-time basis.

party plan selling method where prospective customers are brought together in a social situation, often a private home, to see product demonstrations and listen to promotions.

par value 1 *see* face value; **2** condition of a negotiable instrument when its actual value equals its face value.

passbook book which records bank transactions on a particular account.

passed dividend any dividend which is scheduled to be paid at a particular time but is instead cancelled.

passive balance of trade synonym for an unfavourable balance of trade.

passive trust inactive trust, where the trustees have no direct function or authority but retain the ownership of whatever property is held in trust.

password code which, when given and recognized, allows someone access into a secure location or system; commonly used when logging on to computer systems.

past due payment which was required by a specific date, now past, but which has not been received; *see also* overdue.

patent legal recognition of an invention, which also grants sole right of manufacture and sale for commercial purposes to the patent holder; *see also* trademark.

paternalism management philosophy which is strongly authoritarian but also believes that management has a duty to see to the welfare of employees.

path–goal theory of leadership management theory that outlines the task of senior management as being primarily to set goals for junior managers and employees, outline the paths required to reach those goals, and then give the latter groups responsibility for proceeding to the goals.

patriarchal management management style based on family models of organization, with a senior (usually male) head of the organization who is both its absolute authority and the provider of members' welfare needs.

patronize to buy regularly from a particular retail outlet or service firm.

pattern bargaining collective bargaining strategy where unions base their claims on similar successful claims by other unions.

pawn to pledge personal property as collateral for a loan.

pay as you earn (PAYE) system of income tax payment where tax is deducted by the employer and paid into a tax office before the net pay is handed over to the employee.

pay as you go pension scheme where pensions are paid out of current, rather than past, contributions.

payback return on investment.

payback period period of time until the return on investment is fully realized.

PAYE *see* pay as you earn.

payee person or organization to whom payment is made.

payer person or organization making a payment to another.

pay deal wage agreement negotiated between unions and management.

pay differential differing levels of pay that exist between different grades of employee.

pay grade job grade that carries a different level of pay from other grades.

payment 1 any amount paid by one person to another as wages or fees for services rendered; **2** also used to describe individual instalments on hire purchase schemes, mortgages and so on.

payment by results wage system where part or all of an employee's pay is linked to productivity or performance in the workplace, according to previously calculated standards.

payment date date on which a payment falls due.

payment deficit in balance of payments, a situation where imports are valued higher than exports.

payment in kind payment which is made in goods and services rather than in money.

payment in lieu money payment made as a substitute for another benefit.

payment pause a temporary stoppage of payments; governments may sometimes institute payment pauses if public sector spending is out of control.

payment surplus in balance of payments, a situation where exports are valued higher than imports.

payment system basic system whereby employees' pay is calculated, usually based either on hours worked, on productivity, or on a combination of the two.

pay-off ultimate reward; *see also* yield; return on investment.

payola colloquial term for a bribe or kickback.

pay-out money which is paid, generally synonymous for expenditure.

pay package overall pay provisions including basic wages, bonuses, overtime and so on, negotiated as part of a pay deal.

pay period time period over which wages due to employees are calculated, with payment being made at the end of each period.

pay plan *see* payment system.

payroll total wage bill which a company faces at the end of each pay period.

payroll deduction any deductions made from employees' gross pay by the employer, including taxes, pension contributions and so on.

payroll giving plan whereby employees may contribute a regular sum to a charity of their choice by instructing this sum to be deducted from their pay and sent to the charity.

peak highest point in a cycle; the highest point of a rising trend, which then begins to decline once more.

peak capacity the maximum amount a system can produce under normal conditions.

peak loading point in a cycle at which workloads reach their highest level.

peak manning point in time when the largest number of employees is required to cope with higher workloads; occurs on a seasonal basis in some industries.

peak season time of year when demand for a particular product or service is highest.

peculation synonym for embezzlement.

pecuniary used to describe a thing which consists of money.

peddler salesperson, particularly one who carries goods and sells them door to door.

peer person of an equivalent social or workplace standing.

peer goal setting system whereby employees or managers in the same peer group jointly set goals for themselves.

peer group group of people of equivalent social or workplace standing.

peer-group pressure the phenomenon whereby peer groups put pressure on individual members to conform to the standards of the group.

peer rating in management education, assessment method whereby students or trainees assess each others' work and performance.

peg exchange rate of a currency as accepted by that country's central bank.

pegged exchange rates exchange rates which are fixed or set at a certain level against another currency (such as the franc or the US dollar); their value will still fluctuate as the currency to which they are pegged goes up and down in value.

pegging the act of fixing or setting an exchange rate.

penalty compensation, usually monetary, which must be paid if a contract is not adhered to or if standards are not met.

penalty clause clause in some contracts which provides that compensation must be paid by one party to another if contracted work is not completed on schedule.

penetration pricing low price attached to a product, service or brand when entering a market for the first time, in order to undercut existing competitors and gain market share.

penny stocks low-priced stocks, usually in small companies.

pension regular payments made to a person who has either retired or been forced to leave work permanently as a result of accident or illness.

pensionable salary portion of a person's wage which is used to calculate the rate of pension to be paid.

pensionable service length of time an employee has been with a company which is used to calculate the pension benefits to be paid from company pension schemes.

pension fund investment plan into which pension contributions are paid; these are then invested and the resulting income is used to pay pensions back to contributors.

pension plan organized scheme whereby a person pays contributions to a pension until the plan matures, at which point he or she begins to receive pension payments.

people and organization planning planning concept which includes management development and related issues such as training and career planning.

people skills general term for the skills required to communicate and interact with other people; sometimes also includes leadership skills.

per annum yearly; on an annual basis.

p/e ratio *see* price–earnings ratio.

per capita income average income per person.

per capita output average productive output per person, measured in monetary terms.

per capita tax average tax paid per person.

perceived equitable rewards in human resource management, the wage or benefits which workers feel are appropriate or equitable, given the jobs they are doing and the amount of labour or skills involved.

perceived risk levels of risk as perceived by, for example, a consumer when making a purchase; may vary from actual risk.

percentage of sales ratio used when calculating the relationship between total sales and some other factor.

percentage order in securities trading, a specific order to buy or sell a security once trading in that security reaches a certain level.

perceptual distortion in market research, the extent to which a consumer's view of a product, service or brand is affected by personal beliefs and values.

perceptual skills general term for skills which allow a person to see things clearly and understand their nature and implications.

per diem daily; on a daily basis.

perestroika term used to describe the reform process in the former Soviet Union begun by Mikhail Gorbachev.

perfect competition competitive situation where complete information is freely available to all in the market and where there are no restrictions on competition.

perfect information situation where all available information is known to all players in a market.

perfect market market situation involving perfect competition, where there no constraints on competition in terms of either regulation or information flows.

perfect monopoly a complete monopoly, with one person or organization controlling 100 per cent of supply or production in a particular market.

performance carrying out of a task or project in a satisfactory manner; more generally, the extent to which a person or company has met their goals over a measured period of time.

performance analysis system for measuring performance against a set of previously defined standards.

performance analysis service professional service which provides perfor mance analyses to other organizations and companies.

performance appraisal judgement of an individual's performance to date, with a view to seeing whether and how that performance can be improved.

performance criteria factors against which performance is measured and judged.

performance envelope limits of feasible performance in a given set of circumstances.

performance gap difference between expected and actual performance, when the latter falls short of the former.

performance guarantee contractual obligation to perform up to a specified quality standard.

performance improvement improvement of outputs from a process or system.

performance incentive pay or other benefits provided to employees to encourage higher levels of performance.

performance index statistically-based method of measuring performance, usually against an average of similar performance.

performance-linked pay *see* performance-related pay.

performance measurement process of defining actual levels of performance achieved against a previously defined standard.

performance monitoring ongoing measurement and analysis of performance.

performance objectives goals which have been set for performance, and which the person or organization is expected to achieve.

performance-related pay wage scheme where wages received are linked, in whole or in part, to measured performance, with pay increasing as levels of performance increase.

performance review *see* performance appraisal.

performance standard level of performance required.

performance target *see* performance objectives.

performance test experimental measure of how well something will perform in actual conditions, often used to test new products for faults before they are launched.

performance tolerance level of variance from performance standards which is allowable; often used when calibrating machines and/or measuring machine operators' performance.

period a measure of time used in scheduling, planning and accounting, used to calculate pay, productivity, revenue and so on.

period expense expense incurred during a specified period of time but not assignable as a direct cost.

periodic stock control form of inventory management whereby stocks are checked at measured intervals of time.

period of grace amount of time given to one party to a contract to meet their contractual obligations; often, this is time additional to that specified in the contract.

peripheral device a device linked to the central processing unit of a computer, such as s printer, keyboard, monitor and so on.

peripheral workers employees not involved in the core business activities of the firm, and sometimes employed on a part-time or casual basis.

perishable something which has a finite existence before it decays, dies or disappears.

perishable dispute industrial dispute where the original issue being disputed disappears or solves itself over time.

perishable goods goods, primarily foodstuffs, which spoil or decay over time and which require special packaging, warehousing and transport.

perks short for perquisites.

permanent income average income level throughout one's career, from first entering employment until retirement.

permissive leadership leadership style which permits and encourages subordinates to take responsibility and express their views of senior management policy.

perpetual inventory inventory system where continuous rotating checks are made on stock levels.

perpetuity permanent, or lasting forever.

perquisites generally synonymous with fringe benefits, but can also mean special rewards given for a particular task.

personal accident policy insurance policy under which the named insured or beneficiaries are compensated in event of accident or death to the insured.

personal computer small self-contained computer system accompanied by basic peripherals, usually a keyboard and a printer, which can function either on its own or as part of a network.

personal consumption expenditure total of expenditure which goes towards consumer goods.

personal credit credit allowed to or held by an individual consumer.

personal income that portion of national income which is distributed to individuals and households.

personal information manager electronic device, usually computer-based, that performs various functions such as diary, database, etc.

personality 1 distinctive individual features of a person's character; sometimes used anthropomorphically to apply to things, machines, goods (i.e. 'brand personality') and so on; **2** alternatively, term for a well-known and influential public figure.

personality profile personal assessment technique which summarizes all known traits of a person's personality.

personality promotion promotional tactic which involves endorsement of a product, brand or service by a well-known public figure.

personality test personal assessment tool for gathering information about personality traits.

personal loan any loan made by a bank or financial institution to an individual, usually excluding mortgages.

personal pension plan pension arrangement which is organized by the individual with a pension fund, rather than through a company or union.

personal property personal possessions which can be moved, thus excluding landed property.

personal records records containing personal data on employees which is held by the employing company.

personal savings personal income which is saved rather than spent on consumption.

personal selling method of selling whereby the salesperson visits the customer in person to offer goods or services.

personal tax tax paid by individuals rather than organizations.

personnel all persons employed by a company, department or division.

personnel agency *see* employment agency.

personnel assessment assessment of the performance and capabilities of a company's personnel.

personnel audit survey of company personnel at the present time.

personnel demand analysis summary of a company's personnel needs at the present time.

personnel department sub-unit within a company which is responsible for all aspects of relations with and management of the personnel of the company.

personnel management management function which focuses on the links between employees and their company; included in this area are such functions as recruitment, training, development, industrial and employee relations, health and safety in the workplace, retirement and redundancy.

personnel placement system of ensuring that employees are in jobs which fit most closely their own skills and abilities.

personnel planning analysis of future personnel requirements along with the setting out of a strategy for securing personnel resources to meet those requirements.

personnel selection in recruiting, the process of choosing the most qualified candidates for a job from among the total pool of applicants.

personnel specification description of the personal abilities and qualities needed by the holder of a particular job.

persuasion providing encouragement or motivation to a person in the hope that they will choose a particular course of action.

PERT *see* programme evaluation and review technique.

petition for bankruptcy formal statement of bankruptcy by a person or company.

petrodollars money invested or deposited with international banks by oil-producing nations.

petty cash small amounts of cash kept on hand to meet expenses.

phantom stocks rewards scheme where participants receive the benefits of shareholding even though they do not actually take title to any shares.

phases timed stages of a project or process, each usually requiring the attainment of some intermediate goal.

physical distribution the actual movement of goods and materials from their source to their destination.

physical distribution management the management of the physical distribution process, including issues such as warehousing, mode of transport and route planning.

physical distribution systems systems required to move goods and stocks from one location to another with the channel of distribution.

physical inventory inventory which is carried out by physically surveying stocks and itemizing each unit.

physiocracy government or management according to the natural order.

physiocratic school school of eighteenth-century economists who advised that the economy should be run according to natural principles and laws.

physiological needs needs relating to a person's physical condition, such as needs for shelter, safety, health and so on.

picket group of employees engaged in picketing a workplace.

picketing during industrial action, an action taken by the union which attempts to ensure that the workplace is closed and that no other employees can break the strike by going to work.

piece rate in payment-by-results systems, the wage paid for each unit of production achieved.

piecework pay system where pay is incrementally increased for each unit of work which the employee completes; *see also* payment by results.

piggybacking marketing one product, service or brand conjointly with another, to take advantage of the second product's superior market position and/or to save on marketing costs.

pilfering theft by employees and others from stores held in inventory.

pilot *see* pilot project.

pilot interview in market research, interview carried out to test interviewing techniques in advance of the main body of interviews.

pilot production test batch of production to give feedback on product quality and system performance before the main production commences.

pilot project small-scale test or experimental project carried out in advance of the main work.

PIMS *see* Profit Impact of Marketing Strategies.

pinch colloquial term for a shortage of money, caused by either a rise in prices or a reduction in income.

pioneer product product which is entirely new in terms of design and/or function.

pipage the distribution of liquid materials (such as water or oil) through pipes.

pipeline management another term for the management of the supply chain.

PIPS *see* paperless item processing system.

piracy the illegal copying, distribution and sale of intellectual property; most commonly used to refer to the illegal copying and sale of software.

pitch sales presentation, usually made in person.

placement 1 finding the right job for a person, one which best suits their skills and aspirations; 2 in securities trading, synonymous with placing.

placing the assignment of blocks of issued shares by the issuing company to a middleman; the latter then sells the shares on at a market price.

plain time rate pay system which pays a standard rate per hour or day, without bonuses.

plan statement of how a thing is to be done; written document setting out the activities, times and budgets required to meet a set of goals.

planned gap in planning and forecasting, the difference between the firm's goals and what it is likely to achieve, given current conditions.

planned obsolescence deliberate design of a product so that it will become obsolete after a limited period of time; *see also* built-in obsolescence.

planners managers and executives with specific responsibility for planning.

planning the process of formulating plans.

planning, central *see* central planning.

planning cycle period of time over which plans are held to be valid; period between the start of a planning process for one plan and the start of the planning process for the next plan which will supersede the first.

planning function 1 general term for the activities required for planning; 2 in large firms, the department(s) with special responsibility for planning.

planning–programming–budgeting system combined planning and budgeting system used for establishing forecasts and costs for large-scale programmes.

planning process the process by which plans are drawn up, amended and agreed.

planning, strategic *see* strategic planning.

plant an individual production facility, often synonymous with factory, but also used to describe raw materials processing facilities.

plant bargaining collective bargaining between management and the employees of a single plant or workplace.

plant, virtual *see* virtual plant.

plastic colloquial term for credit cards, debit cards and similar instruments of payment.

plateau a levelling off of a trend.

pledge promise or guarantee.

plough back to reinvest profits, converting them into capital assets.

plug colloquial term for the promotion of an organization or good, often informally as in the course of an interview or conversation.

plug and play computer software programs or applications which can be loaded automatically and are ready for immediate use, requiring no technical skill either to install or to use.

plunger private investor whose behaviour is characterized by high levels of risk taking, gambling large amounts of money on speculative investments.

plural executive group of managers exercising executive authority as a unit.

pluralism the simultaneous holding of more than one job or carrying out of more than one task by the same person.

pluralistic theory in industrial psychology, the definition and structure of common and divergent interests among employers and employees.

poaching 1 recruiting employees or managers who already hold jobs with other companies; **2** recruiting by unions of workers who are already members of another union.

point of equilibrium point at which a balance is reached between competing interests.

point of order question put to the chairman of a meeting concerning the manner in which the meeting is being conducted.

point of origin the depot or warehouse where goods are collected for transport to their destination.

point of sale place where goods are actually purchased, most notably, the till in a retail outlet.

point of sale material materials such as printed leaflets or signs which convey point of sale promotional messages.

point of sale promotion promotional tactic in marketing which delivers its message to the consumer at the point of sale.

point of sale terminal cash register or till where sales are registered and money is kept.

points rating evaluation technique involving scoring different attributes on a points scale, such as 1 to 10.

policy 1 stated aim or purpose; **2** also stated guidelines on particular issues (such as ethics or conduct of employees).

policyholder the named person who pays contributions towards an insurance policy and is, in most cases, the principal beneficiary.

policy instruments means which governments or organizations have at their disposal to enforce policies.

policy loan loan made by an insurance company using an existing insurance policy as collateral.

policy register insurance company's record of all current policies.

policy value in insurance, the value to be paid out when a policy matures.

political conflict **1** dispute or disagreement between two governments or organizations over policy; **2** in international terms, this occurs where policies conflict and can lead to sanctions, terrorism or war.

political risk the potential for political unrest, either domestic or international, to cause operating difficulties or losses for businesses.

political risk service professional analysis service that assesses political risk on behalf of other companies or governments.

political strike industrial action taken to support political ends rather than because of any dispute with the employer.

political union merging the governments of two or more countries or regions, including harmonization of their administrations and electoral assemblies, if any.

pollution artificial contamination of the biosphere, primarily through the emission of waste during production or consumption.

pollution, atmospheric the emission of gases or other substances into the atmosphere during energy consumption.

pollution control measures taken to reduce or eliminate pollution.

polychronic time schedule (P–time) in cross–cultural management, concept that some cultures visualize time in a non–structured way, placing more value on people and transactions than on schedules; *see also* monochronic time schedules).

Ponzi scheme form of fraud in which investors deposit money with an agent who promises to invest on their behalf but who instead steals their money.

pool common supply of commodities, resources, labour and so on from which a company can draw.

pooled interdependence term describing the relationship between parts of an organization, whereby each contributes in some fashion to a final product or outcome.

population total number of people in a given geographical area or, in research terms, total of people or items within a defined sample.

port in maritime shipping, a facility including a harbour and unloading and warehousing facilities where goods are loaded on to and off ships.

portability extent to which a good or concept can be transferred to another setting.

portable pension arrangement between company pension plans or occupational pension plans whereby employees changing jobs can move their pensions from one plan to another.

portfolio total of all investments held by an individual or institution.

portfolio analysis techniques for analysing the market position and future of prospects of products and services; *see also* Boston Box.

portfolio investment investment in a range of securities, thus diluting the risk of possible loss.

portfolio management branch of management concerned with the management of investments so as to yield the best possible return and/or minimize investment risk.

portfolio selection process of determining where money should be invested, i.e. whiteout investments should be added to the portfolio.

POSDCORB acronym for the management functions and roles defined by Henri Fayol: planning, organizing, staffing, directing, coordinating, reporting and budgeting.

position 1 the situation in which a company presently finds itself, in terms of its own internal capabilities and its relations with markets and the environment; **2** synonym for job or post.

position audit analysis of the company's current position.

position evaluation *see* position audit.

positioning movement towards a preferred or ideal position.

positioning statement *see* position statement.

position statement statement of current position in terms of competition, markets, environment and so on, used as a basis for goal-setting and planning; financial statement summarizing the contents of the balance sheet.

positive cash flow situation where income exceeds expenditure.

positive discrimination hiring policy which deliberately aims to hire members of minority groups, possibly setting a quota on the numbers of such persons who will be hired.

positive feedback information fed back from the outcome of a process which confirms that the process is working correctly and/or provides valuable information about how it could be improved.

positive reinforcement benefits or rewards which encourage certain desired types of behaviour.

post 1 job title, often used to describe the jobs of officials in organizations, institutions or governments; **2** to send or despatch.

postal questionnaire in market research, a printed survey form sent to a research sample by post, with responses also returned by post.

post audit audit carried out at the end of an accounting period, after all transactions have been recorded.

post-dated cheque cheque which bears a date later than the one on which it is written, and is therefore not negotiable until that date.

post-industrial society society where innovation and knowledge have superseded capital and labour as the primary economic resources.

post–industrialism economic and social condition where the exploitation of knowledge, rather than manual labour, is the prime generator of wealth.

post test survey carried out after a programme or project has finished in order to determine how effective it has been.

potential 1 latent capability; **2** possible achievements or results should a machine, system or person operate at maximum effectiveness.

potential acquisition valuation method technique for evaluating investment proposals, which can then be ranked in order of attractiveness.

potential appraisal appraisal method which assesses a person's potential, rather than actual, achievements.

potential demand estimated demand for a product or service which a market should be capable of absorbing.

poverty the state of being poor, in terms of money or other resources.

poverty trap in welfare provision, situation where people receiving welfare or unemployment benefits are discouraged from taking paid employment as this would result in their receiving less net income.

power the ability to act or exert influence over others.

power distance in Geert Hofstede's theories of organization culture, the extent to which power and authority are concentrated within organizations.

powerlessness inability to act or exert influence; as opposed to power.

power of attorney authorization for one person to act in all legal matters for another.

power structure the manner in which power is distributed through an organization.

practical capacity volume which a system can produce when operating at its most efficient level.

pre-audit auditing of accounts before transactions take place and are recorded.

preauthorized payment payment which has been authorized in advance of when it needs to be made.

preceding year basis system of calculating tax or other assessments on the basis of income in the preceding year.

predatory pricing pricing strategy which focuses on pricing lower than competitors so as to win market share.

predetermined motion time system work study method based on previously determined standard times for each action or activity; see also methods-time measurement.

prediction forecasting of possible future events.

predictive bargaining approach to collective bargaining which tries to anticipate future demands.

predictive research research which attempts to predict the future.

prefabricate partial preassembly of a product in sections which are then transported to another site and assembled quickly.

preference item good or brand most desired by consumers.

preference shares class of shares which takes precedence over ordinary shares in the paying out of dividends.

preferential creditor creditor who takes precedence over other creditors in the repayment of debt, particularly when a company has been terminated and its assets are being disposed of.

preferential hiring recruitment practice in unionized workplaces where an employer agrees to give preference to members of a particular union over other applicants.

preferential shop workplace where preferential hiring is in force.

preferential tariffs lower rates of tariffs for particular goods or for goods from a particular country of origin.

preferential trade agreement trade agreement between two or more countries allowing for favourable terms of trade including reduced tariffs and free movement of goods; see also most-favoured nation.

preferred debt 1 debt which must be repaid before others; 2 in instances of bankruptcy or the termination of a company, debts where the creditor has prior claim on assets.

preferred position advertising venue or space for which a higher price must be paid.

preferred stock *see* preference shares.

preliminary expenses expenses incurred before or during the setting up of an organization or project; *see also* organization costs.

premium 1 high-quality and/or high-priced goods or services; **2** instalment payments for insurance policies or pension plans; **3** in securities trading, the value of a security over and above its issue price.

premium pay wage system where workers are paid according to their ability to meet or exceed previously determined standard times for the completion of tasks.

premium payment additional bonus payment to workers at a higher than normal rate, for example, for working overtime.

premium plan a wage system linked to premium pay, but based on times to production targets rather than particular tasks.

premium pricing setting of prices at a high level so as to signal high quality and/or prestige value.

premium on stock positive difference between a stock or share's current market value and its issue price.

pre-packaging packaging which is added by the manufacturer rather than the retailer and which is present when the goods are distributed.

prepaid goods which are paid for before the customer takes delivery.

prepaid expenses expenses that are paid in advance.

prepay to pay for goods and services in advance.

prepayment to make payment before it is required, or before taking delivery of goods.

pre-publication before publication.

present value discounted value of an investment at a particular point in time in the future; *see also* net present value.

president US term for the chief executive of a company, equivalent to managing director.

press general term for newspapers and journals, sometimes also including television and radio.

press relations aspect of public relations that concentrates on effective communication with press organizations such as newspapers, television and radio.

pressure the exertion of force or influence on another to achieve a desired result.

prestige advertising advertising which is aimed primarily at enhancing the image or reputation of the product or institution being advertised.

prestige pricing *see* premium pricing.

pre-test experimental testing of a product or service prior to the formal launch, to gauge consumer reaction and to check for any faults.

preventive discipline disciplinary actions aimed at ensuring compliance with standards and regulations, rather than with punishing infractions.

preventive maintenance regularly scheduled maintenance with the aim of keeping breakdowns and machine faults to a minimum.

price amount of money asked by the seller for a good which is offered for sale; *see also* cost; value.

price controls government regulation of prices, usually involving setting prices for some commodities at a fixed level.

price convergence tendency for prices for the same or similar goods in different markets to converge over time.

price cutting reducing prices below those offered by competitors; *see also* predatory pricing.

price discretion extent to which the salesperson can vary the retail price of a good to meet customer requirements.

price discrimination charging different prices to different customers for the same product or service.

price–earnings ratio ratio of earnings per share to the current market price of the same share.

price elasticity extent to which the demand for a product changes in response to price increases or decreases.

price fixing practice whereby competitor companies agree to set a common selling price for similar goods (illegal in many jurisdictions).

price indices measures of current prices which can be compared to show the rate of price increase or fluctuation over time.

price inelasticity situation where demand for a good is not greatly affected by increases or decreases in price.

price leadership phenomenon whereby the price of the leading product or brand in the market is copied by most other brands, though without deliberate collusion between competitors.

price level current prices compared with a measured base price.

price lining pricing policy where a number of similar items are priced at the same level.

price mechanism interaction between buyers and sellers in a market which results in the determination of the final price for goods and services.

price out of the market to increase the price of a good to the point where demand declines sharply.

price plateau levelling off of price increases when it becomes clear that consumers will not pay more.

price rigidity condition where prices do not or cannot vary even if costs change considerably.

price ring agreement between competitors to fix prices; *see* price fixing.

price sensitivity *see* price elasticity.

price skimming *see* skimming.

price spreading in options trading, the simultaneous purchase and sale of options with different prices.

price stabilization government policy aimed at keeping prices at or near a desired level.

price strategies *see* pricing strategy.

price taker anyone who accepts a price offered by a seller.

price–volume curve graphic depiction of the impact of changes in the selling price of goods on the volume of goods sold.

pricing the establishment of a price for a good, based on factors such as the cost to produce the good, the amount the market will pay and so on.

pricing methods techniques used for determining the price at which a good is offered to the market.

pricing policy in marketing, the overall approach to pricing and view of the function which it serves.

pricing strategy overall approach to pricing which determines how prices for individual goods will be set.

primary distribution first level of distribution from the factory gate, usually to one or more wholesalers or other intermediaries.

primary labour market labour market for highly skilled workers.

primary offering principal or most important product offered in a particular market.

primary product products consisting of raw materials or resources such as timber or minerals.

primary research research with the intent of uncovering basic data or information about a subject which has previously been unknown.

primary reserves term for the monetary reserves which banks are required by law to maintain to cover liabilities.

prime cost *see* direct cost.

prime interest rate rate of interest at which central banks lend to other banks; alternatively, the starting rate used by banks for the calculation of interest on loans, which is then adjusted upwards to cover various levels of risk.

principal 1 any named party in a contract or agreement; in principal–agent relationships, the party for whom an agent acts; **2** the amount of money actually lent or extended in credit, the base sum on which interest is calculated.

principal–agent relationship situation where one person or institution employs another to act for them on a certain issue, for example, in selling goods or in negotiations.

principle of selectivity theory that in any given situation, a small number of agents within a population is responsible for the majority of productivity or results produced.

principles general precepts, tenets or standards of behaviour.

principles of management general guidelines as to how management should function and be performed.

principles of organization the common features and functions which all organizations exhibit to some degree, such as division of labour, levels of authority, defined responsibility for limited tasks and so on.

printout output of a computer program or database fed to a linked printer and printed out on paper.

prior charge debt which is considered to have priority over other liabilities when a company is wound up.

prioritize to arrange tasks or issues in order of priority or importance.

priority task or issue of primary importance or needing immediate attention.

private brand *see* own brand.

private carrier transport firm which carries goods on behalf of only a limited number of clients.

private company limited liability company which does not issue shares to the public.

private enterprise any business where the capital and means of production are owned by private individuals rather than the state.

private investor person who makes investments on their own account, rather than using an institution as intermediary.

private label *see* own brand.

private lender private individual who lends money to another.

private ownership ownership of goods or assets by an individual rather than by the state.

private rate of return rate of return on investments held by private investors.

private sector that portion of the economy that is in private ownership.

privatization the transfer of companies or assets from state ownership to private ownership; as opposed to nationalization.

proactive anticipating events and taking steps to deal with them; as opposed to reactive.

proactive management management philosophy which tries to anticipate change and take steps to prevent problems from occurring.

probability the likelihood that a thing will take place.

probability theory application of mathematical techniques to assigning probabilities to likely future events.

probable maximum loss in insurance, the maximum loss that can reasonably be expected.

probation preliminary period of employment during which an employee's skills and capabilities are assessed, before confirming the employment as permanent.

probationary period period of time when an employee remains on trial.

problem solving defining and implementing solutions to events or issues that threaten the efficient or effective running of the business.

procedures standard ways and means of doing things; series of established steps towards a particular goal.

procedural agreement separate agreement between management and unions outlining the procedures to be followed in the event of a dispute.

proceduralize to introduce procedures covering a certain course of action.

procedure statement documentation outlining procedures to be followed in case of a particular event.

proceeds income from a sale, roughly equivalent to revenue before deductions for costs and expenses.

process series of tasks which are required to be completed in order to reach a specific goal.

process analysis analysis of a process with a view to understanding the various steps and tasks it contains and ultimately making it more efficient.

process chart charts showing the steps taken during a process and the order in which they must be carried out.

process control system computerized systems for controlling and monitoring the manufacturing process.

process costing costing techniques which establish each process as a cost centre and attribute costs accordingly.

process inspection inspection or monitoring which takes place during a process, rather than before or after.

process mix in manufacturing, the balance between making components in-house and buying them in from outside suppliers.

process planning determining the steps to be taken, the order in which they should be taken and the time for each step.

process production production which requires a single continuous process rather than a large number of individual steps.

process technologies technology or machinery required to run manufacturing processes.

procurement *see* purchasing.

producer individual or company who makes finished products or components, or extracts and processes raw materials.

product 1 the end result of a manufacturing process, usually either a process, raw material or finished good; 2 in marketing, a physical good which is purchased and used by the consumer, as opposed to a service.

product acceptance extent to which the market uses and is willing to purchase a particular product.

product adaptation the partial redesign of products to make them more suitable for other markets, primarily export markets.

product assortment all the various brands or products in a particular category which are on sale at a given time.

product comparison market research technique in which respondents are asked to compare a range of products and select the ones they would purchase.

product concept initial idea for a product, which leads to the research and development of the physical or actual product.

product cost cost of manufacturing or producing a product.

product costing the process of assigning product costs, usually by first defining which costs are attributable to which products and then by deciding how overhead costs will be assigned.

product development the creation of new products and services.

product design the process and specification by which new products are conceived of and brought to market.

product differentiation identification and development of unique or special product features, which will serve to distinguish the product in the minds of consumers.

product diversification in marketing strategy, the development of new products to take advantage of existing strengths and/or opportunities.

product features aspects of a product, either its functions or aesthetic features, which serve to differentiate the product and which provide value to consumers.

product image general view that consumers have of a product.

production the fabrication and assembly of products.

production, assembly line *see* assembly-line production.

production bonus extra wage paid to employees upon the completion of production targets.

production budget budget of project costs for a particular production process or the production of a particular product.

production capacity volume of production which a production system can achieve in a given time period.

production cell decentralized production unit, usually integrated with other such cells as part of an overall production process.

production control the means by which production is controlled and regulated to ensure maximum efficiency of all parts of the production process.

production costs costs incurred during production, including both direct and indirect costs.

production efficiency condition in which production systems are operating efficiently in terms of both cost effectiveness and volume and quality of production.

production engineering the design and installation of production processes.

production flow the flow of materials and components through a production line, resulting in a finished product at the end.

production flow analysis analysis of the production flow for the purposes of achieving greater production efficiency.

production inputs capital, labour and materials which are consumed in the course of production.

production, lean *see* lean production.

production line physical route which materials and components take through a plant or factory during the production process; *see also* flow line production.

production-oriented company company which focuses on its own production processes, tending to manufacture what is best for the company's own purposes rather than what is best for its customers.

production planning overall term for planning and scheduling of production activities with the aim of achieving production efficiency.

production possibility frontier the extent to which a country or economy can develop new products, based on available technology and resources.

production process the process through which production takes place, being the aggregate of a number of subordinate tasks or processes.

production schedules predetermined time sequences according to which various steps in the production process are to be completed, and targets set for volume output.

production scheduling the process of designing and setting production schedules.

production sharing **1** system whereby two or more companies are involved at different stages of a production process; **2** alternatively, system where different stages of a production process take place in different countries.

production technology machinery and systems which are used to substitute for manual labour in the production process.

production workers employees directly employed in production processes.

productivity total production compared with inputs or consumption over the same period of time, which serves as a measure of whether the firm's production processes are working efficiently.

productivity agreement collective agreement on the issue of productivity.

productivity bargaining collective bargaining which aims to link worker productivity to pay and other rewards.

productivity barriers factors which prevent any increase in productivity.

productivity breakthroughs sudden and rapid increase in productivity, usually the result of new technologies or processes.

productivity differential differences in productivity at two specified points in time.

productivity growth increase in productivity over the course of a defined period of time.

productivity improvement increasing levels of productivity either by increasing efficiency or by increasing output while maintaining present efficiency levels.

productivity improvement programmes special programmes designed to increase productivity.

productivity incentives pay bonuses and other rewards provided to workers to motivate them to increase productivity.

productivity investment investment in either greater efficiency or greater volume output so as to increase productivity.

productivity ratios ratios used to measure productivity, primarily those of input to output.

product launch the initial offering of a new product into a market for the first time.

product life cycle the 'lifespan' of a product, extending from its development and launch through various stages of acceptance and use by the market, finally ending with either market saturation or product obsolescence, when sales begin to decline and the product is abandoned.

product line group of products which are closely related (for example, the same basic product but sold in different volume packages) and which are marketed in a very similar manner.

product manager manager responsible for marketing a specific product or line.

product market market in which there is demand for a particular product.

product mix the range of products which a company offers to the market.

product orientation management philosophy that focuses on the products a firm makes, and on the innovation and improvement of those products.

product placement test market research technique whereby a product prototype is placed with a potential customer for a period of time; the latter uses the product and then reports on its positive and negative features.

product planning planning function which decides which products will be produced, in what volume, with what features and so on.

product plus in marketing, the selling features that give a product advantage over its competition.

product policy *see* product strategy.

product positioning in product strategy, the way a product is presented to the market, including pricing and promotional tactics and also a decision on which product features will be emphasized.

product–process fit extent to which present processes are suitable to produce a given product in an efficient and effective manner.

product proliferation increased product variety which leads to higher inventories.

product quality definition of the standards of quality required in a product.

product range the number of different products produced or sold in a given product line.

product standardization ensuring that products are of a uniform nature and can be produced through mass production.

product strategy subset of marketing strategy covering issues such as new product development, product positioning and marketing.

product test testing of a new product for such features as quality, utility, durability and appeal to consumers.

product weighted distribution in retail audits, adjustment made to raw data to account for factors such as the size of shops and the lines they are able to carry.

profession occupation or vocation, usually in a field which requires higher education or advanced training.

professional bureaucracy organizational structure with a highly autonomous core composed of trained, professional workers.

professional indemnity condition of some professional services whereby the service provider may be obliged to make good any loss or damage suffered by the client.

professional indemnity insurance insurance policy which provides compensation for professional indemnity payouts.

professional services general term for services where the providers are all qualified professionals, such as law, medicine, accountancy or consultancy.

professionalism the qualities expected of a professional.

professionalization 1 making an occupation into a profession by establishing standards and instituting requirements for training; 2 more generally, taking on the qualities of professionalism.

proficiency aptitude or ability at a certain skill.

proficiency test test which examines a person's proficiency at a certain task or skill.

profile 1 set of standard measures of characteristics exhibited by people or items in a group or set; 2 more specifically, detailed listing of the characteristics or traits exhibited by an individual.

profiling systems sets of techniques for developing profiles of individuals.

profit excess of revenue over all costs and expenditures over a given time period.

profitability extent to which a product or service makes a profit.

profitability analysis analytical measures used to determine profitability.

profitability measures ratios used to gauge profitability, such as profit to sales.

profit and loss account statement showing a company's financial performance over the course of a financial year; *see also* balance sheet.

profit centre any business unit to which profits are assigned and which is therefore entitled to draw up a profit and loss account showing business performance over time.

Profit Impact of Marketing Strategies (PIMS) widely used database which shows the characteristics of successful marketing strategies, products and brands.

profit margin profit expressed as a percentage of sales.

profit neutrality principle in historical cost accounting whereby the cost of acquiring an asset exactly matches the increase in value of the net assets of the firm.

profit-related pay wage scheme where part or all of workers' pay is related to levels of company profits.

profit sharing principle by which a portion of a company's profits are distributed to the workers.

profit squeeze situation where profits are declining, usually as a result of a combination of stable or declining income and rising costs.

profits tax tax on the profits of a business.

profit taking selling an investment that has increased in value in order to realize profits.

profit–volume chart graphic depiction of the profit–volume ratio.

profit–volume ratio sales revenue less variable costs, divided by sales revenue, showing which products are most profitable at which levels of volume.

pro forma standardized form or invoice.

program piece of consumer software designed for a specific task or function.

programme schedule of activities towards a desirable end, sometimes synonymous with project.

programmed decisions preplanned responses to problems which have been predicted and analysed in advance.

programmed instruction preset instructions, sometimes delivered through a computer terminal, which teach an employee how to perform a particular task.

programmed text texts used in programmed instruction.

programme evaluation and review technique (PERT) methods for analysing the content of programmes to see whether they have been effective and made efficient use of resources.

programming writing a computer application or software program.

programming language the computer language in which a program is written.

progress billing *see* staged payment.

progress chart showing current rates of progress on a particular project or programme.

progressive consumer consumer who is interested in and may be persuaded to buy new or more advanced products.

progressive tax income tax where the level of tax paid increases as income rises.

progress monitoring continuous analysis of activity on a project to determine the rate of progress.

progress payments staged payments made at points during a contract upon completion of certain stages towards progress.

project planned enterprise or undertaking.

project appraisal *see* appraisal.

project authority extent of authority given to project managers and their staff when a project is first established.

project champions individual managers who are willing to take responsibility for promoting a particular project within the organization and for securing the necessary resources to see it through to completion.

project costing systems for advance costing of projects.

project group team set up with the specific purpose of planning and implementing a project.

project implementation the carrying out of planned projects.

projection extrapolation of forward trends from current and past conditions.

project leader the manager responsible for project planning and implementation; *see also* project management.

project management management disciplines specifically relating to the management of projects, including planning, implementation, coordination and control, often on a fairly small scale in a short time.

project manager manager in overall charge of coordinating and managing a project from planning through to completion.

project milestone end of a particular stage of a project, when performance and costs are measured.

project purchasing the purchasing of all materials and components needed to facilitate a particular project.

project scheduling planning the sequence and timing of various stages of a project.

project value *see* net present value.

proletariat in Marxist economics, term for members of the working class employed in industrial occupations.

promissory note written document whereby one party promises to pay another a specified sum of money on a stated future date.

promotion 1 in marketing, one of the four elements of the marketing mix, the provision of information to consumers about available goods and services, along with incentives or motivations to buy, through advertising or other forms of communication; **2** advancement to a more senior position, usually with a corresponding increase in pay and responsibility.

promotional allowance payments made to an agent to cover the latter's promotional expenses.

promotional mix combination of promotional tools and communications media to be used in a particular marketing promotion.

promotional tool tactic used to promote goods and services to potential consumers.

promotion from within policy whereby senior management positions are filled by promoting more junior managers into positions of authority, rather than recruiting from outside the organization.

promotion planning the process of planning sales promotions, including media to be used, target audience identification and the design of the message to be sent.

promotion policy company policy on promoting employees and managers, typically covering issues such as requirements for promotion and length of service necessary for promotion.

prompt note reminder sent to a debtor by a lender, advising the former of when repayment is due.

proof of delivery signed document providing proof that goods have been delivered to their destination.

proof of loss acceptance by an insurance company that the insured has suffered a loss and that compensation may therefore be due.

propensity to consume *see* marginal propensity to consume.

property something which is owned by a person or organization, or by the state, including land, capital and other assets.

property market market in which landed property or real estate is bought and sold.

property to income ratio ratio of property costs to income earned by that property.

proportional tax tax which is paid at a constant rate even as income increases; as opposed to progressive tax.

proprietary company *see* holding company.

proprietor owner of a business, usually a small firm.

proprietorship the office and functions of a proprietor.

proprietory accounts accounts showing the assets and liabilities of an organization.

prospect advertising and sales term for a potential customer.

prospecting in marketing, the search for new customers and/or new market opportunities.

prospectus document which gives information about a company's present position and future prospects, sent to prospective share buyers or other parties whose support the company wishes to attract.

protanto increase *see* tapered increase.

protection in economics, government measures to influence markets in favour of domestically produced goods, such as increasing tariffs.

protectionism economic philosophy based on protection.

protective practice *see* restrictive trade practice.

protective tariff tariff introduced as part of a strategy of protectionism, forcing imported goods to carry artificially high prices.

Protestant work ethic theory first developed by Max Weber, that the success of northern European capitalism can be traced to historical and cultural factors.

protocol code of practice governing procedures or operations; necessary routine which must be followed.

provident benefit benefit paid out under a sickness or injury insurance plan.

provident fund fund from which pension benefits or sickness insurance benefits are drawn.

provision 1 money set aside to cover future losses; **2** alternatively, money written off in the annual accounts to cover losses already incurred.

provisioning the acquisition and storage of raw materials.

proximate cause original or initial cause.

proxy authority given to another party to vote on behalf of the proxy giver at a meeting or election.

proxy statement statement of information from parties engaged in share dealing required in some jurisdictions, stating the stock to be sold, the time of sale and other details.

prudence principle in financial accounting, the principle by which the lowest value in a series of values is always accepted as true.

prudential control controls, especially in banking and finance, which aim to ensure that resources are used wisely, to maximize benefit and minimize marginal consequences.

psychogalvanometer electronic equipment used in psychology, and sometimes also in market research, which can detect changes in human biological patterns which reflect reactions to things seen, questions asked and so on; also known as a 'lie detector'.

psychographics method of segmenting a market or group of people based on their individual psychological profiles.

psychological inventory *see* psychological test.

psychological price price which customers find acceptable, regardless of other factors.

psychological test general term for tests which look at different aspects of a person's psychological profile, such as intelligence, creativity, numerical aptitude and so on.

psychology, industrial *see* industrial psychology.

psychology, occupational *see* occupational psychology.

psychometric research research into measurable factors.

psychometric test test used to measure measurable factors.

psychomotor skills skills which require both mental and physical effort and coordination.

public accounting accounting techniques used in the public sector; accounting for revenues received and expenditures made by government.

public administration the management and administration of government departments and other public sector organizations.

public company company which has gone public and whose shares are publicly traded on stock exchanges.

public corporation corporation established and owned by government or some other public sector institution.

public holiday formally designated holiday which is designated by most companies and industries, sometimes also known as a bank holiday or statutory holiday.

public interest description of an action taken which is intended to result in greater good for society in general.

public issue offer of shares to the general public, by a public company.

publicity attracting or creating favourable public attention.

public management *see* public sector management.

public opinion view widely held by the general public on a certain subject or issue.

public ownership ownership of property by the state, rather than by private individuals.

public planning planning functions carried out by public sector organizations.

public policy policy set by government, usually intended to further the public interest.

public policy instrument technique used by government to carry out public policy, such as taxation or regulation.

public pressure expressions of public opinion, possibly accompanied by the threat of general public sanctions.

public relations means whereby companies seek to influence and shape the view held of them by the general public; used in marketing but more commonly employed to create a general favourable impression of the company.

public relations officer manager or executive working for a company in a public relations capacity.

public sale sale conducted through a private option.

public sector that portion of the economy which is in public ownership.

public sector administration administration and management principles and skills required for managing government departments or agencies.

public sector bureaucracy professionals working in the public sector charged with the planning and implementation of public policy.

public sector management general term for management skills and practices relating specifically to management of public sector organizations.

public sector market market for goods and services within and between public sector agencies and departments.

public sector organization organization providing goods, sometimes on a not-for-profit basis, in the public sector.

public service any service which is offered on a general basis to the population at large, usually on a not-for-profit basis.

public utility organization that provides basic infrastructure services such as water and electricity.

public works infrastructure projects such as roads or bridges, commissioned by the state for the purpose of general use by the public.

punt high-risk investment with a chance of large profits should the investment prove to be good.

purchase the act of buying a good; a good which has been bought and is now in the possession of the buyer.

purchase contract contract which sets out the terms of a purchase, including quantity and price to be paid.

purchase discount price reduction given by the seller to the buyer, for bulk purchases, prompt payment and so on.

purchase engineering designed techniques for increasing the likelihood that people will buy a product, service or brand.

purchase money money used to make a purchase.

purchase order statement made by seller to buyer, confirming a purchase and requesting delivery of goods.

purchase price price at which a good is purchased; price paid.

purchaser *see* buyer.

purchasing making a purchase; acquiring a good in exchange for money.

purchasing agent agent appointed by a company to handle purchasing activities, usually to purchase components or raw materials.

purchasing power amount of surplus income in an economy which can be used to buy goods.

purchasing power parity ratio of domestic price level to foreign price levels or, more practically, the amount goods and services which an equivalent amount of local currency would purchase in a foreign country.

pure competition market condition where there are many buyers and sellers, easy market access and full information available to all parties; *see also* perfect market.

pure interest charges levied on loans, credit and other forms of capital borrowing.

pure market economy *see* free economy.

pure monopoly *see* perfect monopoly.

pure profit profit remaining after all costs have been paid.

pure risk in insurance, the inherent risk present in such factors as fire, flood, death and so on, which it can be assumed will cause damage when they occur.

push money type of commission paid to agents or salespeople as an incentive to increase turnover.

push–pull strategy marketing strategy which aims to push goods through the channel of distribution while at the same time providing 'pull' through promotions to the end consumer.

put option option to sell a stated quantity of securities at a given price, within a given period of time.

puts and calls general term including both put options and call options.

put through situation in securities dealing where the buyer and seller are both clients of the same broker.

putting-out system form of contracting out of work whereby tasks are let out to self-employed contractors, often working from home.

pygmalion effect term for the influence which one individual in a group may have over the behaviour of others, who may try to mimic the actions of this dominant individual.

pyramidal organization strongly hierarchical organization with progressively smaller layers of management going up through the organization.

pyramid ratios method of analysing financial ratios and performance ratios which assumes a small number of ratios to be of key importance, calculates these and then proceeds to calculate those which are of less importance.

pyramid selling sales technique where sales people concentrate not so much on selling a product but on recruiting others to sell on their behalf, with the latter paying the recruiter a percentage of their profits.

Q

qualifications **1** skills or attributes which fit a person for a particular job or post; **2** modifications of or reservations about a position.

qualified accounts accounts where the auditor has expressed reservations about some of the statements or data in the accounts.

qualified endorsement statement whereby the party making the endorsement absolves themselves of any liability in event of subsequent accident or malfeasance.

qualified report report where a reviewer has expressed reservations about some of the statements made.

qualify to possess a required qualification; to express reservations or make alterations.

quality **1** attribute or degree; **2** in production, the achievement of a predetermined standard in terms of variances or defects; **3** in marketing, the extent to which a product or service meets customer expectations and needs.

quality assurance promise by the producer to the customer that a product or service is of a defined standard of quality.

quality at source ensuring manufacturing quality through inspection and checking during the manufacturing process.

quality circles teams of employees who have responsibility for maintaining and improving quality.

quality control procedures for ensuring quality standards during production.

quality control circles *see* quality circles.

quality management branch of management which focuses on quality issues.

quality market market where customers view product or service quality as their primary need.

quality movement management philosophy which focuses on quality as one of the most important management issues, seeking to build it into all processes and functions.

quality protection in quality control, measures specifically taken to prevent defects and preserve quality.

quango UK acronym for quasi non-governmental organization; para-statal organizations used to manage certain public sector activities.

quantitative methods methods of analysis using statistical or numerical data.

quantitative restriction restriction on the quantity of goods that may be traded, exported or imported.

quantity number of units in a given lot or set.

quantity discount reduction in price offered by the seller to the buyer in exchange of bulk purchases.

quantity theory monetary theory relating money income to the total quantity of money in an economy.

quartile unit of measurement consisting of one-quarter of the entire time or volume being measured.

quasi–market organization where market mechanisms are used to conduct transactions and transfers of resources but which is not in fact a free market.

questioning approach analytical method which focuses on the key questions in a situation, and on providing answers to them.

questionnaire set of previously defined questions put to respondents in order to gather information.

queue customers waiting in turn for service delivery, in situations where there are more customers than service staff who can help them.

queuing system systems developed by service firms to manage queues and reduce waiting times.

queuing theory academic theories relating to the behaviour of people in queues, with the object of developing more efficient queuing systems.

quit **1** to leave a job; **2** to terminate a contract; **3** to discharge another party from their obligations; *see* quit claim.

quit claim to discharge another party from their obligations.

quit rate rate at which workers leave employment.

quorum minimum attendance level necessary at a committee meeting for that committee to be able formally to take minutes and make decisions.

quota **1** quantity of goods required for a particular purpose; **2** in importing, the maximum quantity of a particular class of good that can be imported into a country.

quota restriction any quota which serves as an upper limit on the number of goods which can be sold, traded, produced, etc.

quota sampling form of random sampling of people, items, etc. in a particular quota.

quota system use of quotas to restrict imports.

quotation **1** range of buying and selling prices for a particular security at a given moment in time; **2** more generally, an estimate of price by a seller for a service or work to be performed.

quote *see* quotation.

quote sheet document providing details of a quotation.

R

R&D *see* research and development.

rack jobber wholesaler in consumer goods, dealing primarily with large retailers such as supermarkets.

rack rent standard commercial rate of rent.

raider *see* corporate raider.

rain check rights given by the seller to the buyer (e.g., during a special offer) to purchase the same product for the same price at a later date.

raise increase in wages.

rake-off share of profits, usually meaning an underhanded or illegal payment; *see also* kickback.

rally increase in share prices immediately following a decrease.

RAM *see* random access memory.

random access memory (RAM) computer memory which can be easily overwritten, used as a short-term memory to hold programs and data currently being run or used.

random access storage computer data storage capacity based on random access memory, where files can be easily retrieved, altered and replaced.

random process any process which proceeds without any apparent or easily predictable pattern.

random sampling choice of samples from a production batch or group of people according to no preset pattern or previously determined criteria.

random walk view in finance theory that share prices do not follow a determinable pattern, and that future share prices cannot be predicted by studying past performance.

rank position or grade in a sequence.

ranking establishment of rank, used in job grading or performance appraisal.

rapid prototyping techniques for generating models or prototypes of new products in a short space of time.

ratchet financial incentive offered to managers if they outperform targets.

rate 1 synonym for price or wage; **2** synonym for rank.

ratebuster worker on piecework who works faster than colleagues and produces at a higher rate, therefore earning higher wages.

rate cutting reduction in a rate or price.

rate discrimination *see* price discrimination.

rate fixing the setting of a rate or price at a certain level across a range of products, or across a range of different jobs.

rate of exchange *see* exchange rate.

rate of interest *see* interest rate.

rate of return *see* return on investment.

rating measure of performance, usually in the context of a rating scale.

rating accuracy measure of the accuracy of a given rating scale, that is, how well it reflects the real situation.

rating scale scale on which individual items, performances and so on are measured; rating scales usually span the possible results, from lowest to highest, worst to best and so on.

ratio number showing a relationship between two quantities; i.e. a ratio of two to one means there as twice as many of one quantity as the other.

ratio analysis use of ratios as a tool of financial analysis.

ratio–delay study study which examines the number and nature of delays in production processes.

ratio hierarchy method performance measurement technique using inter-locking ratios.

rational agents agents or causes which can be understood rationally or log-ically.

rationality **1** condition of being rational or logical; **2** that which is capable of being understood by reason; **3** synonym for efficiency.

rationality, bounded *see* bounded rationality.

rationalization **1** to explain or to make clear using rational methods; **2** making things more rational; restructuring or altering an organization so that it is more rational (i.e. more efficient).

rational working hours work system where hours worked vary according to the amount of work needing to be done.

ratio–trend forecasting labour planning technique which assesses future labour needs based on current activities and amounts of labour required for each.

raw materials unprocessed resources which are used in manufacturing processes.

raw test score basic score achieved in a test.

reach the total audience which a promotion or communication can reach.

reaction response of one to stimulus or to activity on the part of another.

reactive condition of responding to events as they happen rather than attempting to anticipate them; as opposed to proactive.

reactive management management philosophy which concentrates on dealing with events as and when they occur, rather than on forward plan-ning.

reader reply form printed form which is part of an advertisement, which readers are invited to fill out and return to the advertiser.

readership total number of people who read a magazine or journal; *see also* subscriber.

real earnings total earnings adjusted to take account of price changes or inflation.

real estate *see* landed property.

real income income measured in terms of purchasing power.

real income per head per annum in economics, the measure of the purchasing power available to each individual over the course of a year.

real interest rate rate of interest less the rate of inflation.

real investment expenditure or investment that results in the creation of a new capital asset.

realizable value the cash value of an asset if it were to be sold or otherwise disposed of.

realization the conversion of an asset into cash.

real learning time time required for a skill or technique to be learned to a level where it can be used effectively in practice.

reallocation **1** in accounting, transferring costs originally apportioned to one cost centre to another; **2** more generally, transferring resources from one business unit to another.

real options options which arise when making investments in real assets.

real price price measured in terms of the amount of labour required to earn a given purchasing price.

real time actual time as it passes.

real-time data data which is created and disseminated as the events they describe are actually happening.

real wages wages measured in terms of their purchasing power.

reapportionment *see* reallocation.

reappraisal a second examination of a project or property with the aim of confirming or looking for variances from the original appraisal.

reassignment transfer of an employee from one job or position to another.

rebate money paid back to the purchaser, usually as a form of incentive; any money returned to the customer.

recall situation where a manufacturer asks all distributors, retailers and customers to return products to the factory so that defects can be remedied.

recapitalization changing the capital structure of a firm, usually by increasing (or decreasing) the number of shares.

receipt written document acknowledging that one party is 'in receipt' of goods delivered by another party.

receivables money owed to or credit issued by a firm.

receiver third party who takes over the management of a bankrupt firm, with the aim of either making the firm solvent or terminating it and disposing of its assets.

receivership condition where a bankrupt firm has had its management placed in the hands of a receiver.

recession period when an economy is in decline, with falling levels of output and employment.

reciprocal causation situation where two or more factors simultaneously influence each other.

reciprocal trading trading agreement between two or more nations.

reciprocity trading agreement between two firms or countries whereby each buys goods of approximately equal value from the other.

recognition agreement whereby an employer accepts the presence of a union in the workplace and agrees to bargain with that union.

recognition dispute industrial dispute which occurs when an employer refuses to recognize a union and the union takes action accordingly.

recommendations suggestions or advice concerning a particular course of action.

recompense payment made as compensation or more generally to reward someone for services, usually on a one-off basis.

record 1 written, audio-visual or computerized statement of events and transactions which have occurred; **2** to make such a statement.

record date date on which a person or institution buying shares is registered as a shareholder with the company.

recourse the right to seek redress or payment from a defaulter or someone in breach of contract, or to use legal processes to obtain the same.

recovery 1 stabilization and increase in prices or value following a decrease; **2** compensation for losses received from another source.

recruitment general term for the process of attracting suitable employees and then hiring the most suitable into the firm.

recurring expense expense which is likely to be incurred again, often on a regular basis.

recycling the conversion of waste products back into raw materials, which can then be re-used in the manufacturing process.

redeemable bond *see* bond, redeemable.

redemption the liquidation of a debt or obligation before it reaches maturity.

redemption fund money set aside to redeem an outstanding obligation.

redemption price price at which a redeemable bond or security may be redeemed.

redemption yield 1 yield on an investment on redemption; **2** yield on fixed-interest securities calculated on the basis of the adjusted redemption price.

redeployment the transfer of resources, assets, employees and so on from one business unit to another.

red tape colloquial term for regulations, laws and bureaucratic delays which impede or prevent business activity.

reducing balance method method of spreading the cost of a fixed asset over a period of time.

reductionism analysis of complex things which attempts to reduce their complexity to a few simple concepts.

redundancy 1 laying off or dismissal of workers who are no longer required by the firm; **2** more generally, the condition of being redundant.

redundancy agreement agreed procedure between employer and employees by which redundancies will be announced and put into effect.

redundancy counselling counselling and advice provided to employees who have been made redundant, intended to help them cope mentally with the event of redundancy and to prepare to find a new job.

redundant surplus to requirements.

redundant worker employee who has been made redundant and is now looking for other work.

re-employment finding new work for an employee who has previously been made redundant.

re-engineering redesign of a system or process using engineering techniques; *see also* business process re-engineering.

re-export the export of goods which have previously been imported.

reference a letter or statement by a former employer as to the character and skills of a prospective employee.

reference currency currency in which a multinational company's worldwide earnings are ultimately disclosed.

reference group in consumer behaviour research, a group of people sharing certain common characteristics, whose behaviour is then studied in the context of the type of group to which they belong.

reference tariff scale of tariffs which can be applied in a given situation.

referral market in relationship marketing, market composed of existing customers or others who might provide referrals about the company's goods to new customers.

refinance to change the conditions of a loan or obligation, for example by changing the term of payment or the total of the loan.

reflation following a depression, the period during which prices return to previous levels.

refresher training training which updates and revises existing skills.

refund money repaid to a customer.

refundable interest portion of prepaid interest that is refunded if the loan is paid off early.

regional development government policies aimed at stimulating economic growth in certain regions of a country.

regional distribution centre distribution centre which serves retail outlets in a defined geographical area.

register general document containing a large number of records of specific events.

registered company company which has been registered according to local business law.

registered representative *see* agent.

registrar 1 person or agency who oversees the issuing of securities and ensures conformity with local law; **2** more generally, anyone charged with ensuring the records conform with legal requirements.

registration formal act of registering a company, share issue, etc. so as to comply with local law.

regression in statistics, method of examining relationships of variables by studying the functional relationships between them.

regression analysis research technique based on regression methods which tries to predict trends in one type of activity by examining trends in another, related type of activity.

regressive tax tax where the rate of tax decreases as the amount of income increases.

regret rule in decision making, technique whereby one chooses the option that would cause the least regret if it turns out to be the wrong one.

regulation rule or directive either prescribing or proscribing certain forms of action or behaviour.

reinstatement restoration of a person or thing to its former position.

reinsurance practice whereby insurance companies lay off large risks by placing them with reinsurers; in the event of a loss, the insurer can then claim back part or all of the compensation paid from the reinsurers.

reinsurance broker broker specializing in the reinsurance market.

related company 1 company which is partly owned by another company, though without the latter having majority control; 2 companies which are part of a conglomerate or group; *see also* affiliate.

relational database a collection of data organised into tabular files and related by one or more common fields.

relationship the presence and nature of contacts between two or more persons or things, usually suggesting the presence of causes or influence.

relationship banking banking business conducted on the basis of long-term relationships between banks and their most valued clients.

release process by which one party to a contract agrees that the other party need no longer be bound by the contract's terms.

relevance extent to which any other fact or concept has a bearing on the issue under consideration.

relevance analysis analysis of existing research programmes which attempts to rate them in order of their relevance to the company's main activities.

relevance trees graphic description of the nature and extent of the relevance of some concepts, ideas and issues to others.

relevant range range of data or items covered by a particular analysis.

reliability extent to which a product, machine, etc. is reliable and will not break down or malfunction.

reliability engineering engineering techniques for ensuring that systems perform as reliably as possible, with a minimum of breakdowns or malfunctions.

relocation movement of plant, people, etc. to another physical location.

remargining placing additional margin against a loan.

remedial maintenance maintenance of machinery or equipment undertaken to correct defects in either the machinery itself or the mode of its operation.

remittance *see* payment.

remuneration wages and other monetary benefits paid to employees.

renege to repudiate an agreement or contract.

renew to continue an agreement which is due to expire; to restore a thing to its original state.

renewable resources natural resources which can be replaced; as opposed to non-renewable resources.

rent money paid for the use of a good or property to which the user does not have title.

re-opener clause clause in a collective agreement providing that the agreement is subject to renegotiation upon certain conditions.

reorder level in inventory, the level at which stocks are automatically reordered to bring them up to a maximum level.

reorganization any alteration of organizational structure, processes and/or procedures.

reorientation to change one's direction or outlook.

repatriation 1 transferring income or profits from an overseas operation to the home country; 2 bringing employees who have been on overseas assignments back to their homes.

repeat demand frequent and recurring demand for goods or services, usually those which are consumed quickly.

repetitive problems problems which arise repeatedly during the course of ordinary business operations.

repetitive strain injury workplace injury caused by performing the same physical action on a continuous basis.

replacement the substitution of one product, service, good, etc. for another of identical nature.

replacement analysis analysis of existing plant, machinery and stocks with a view to determining the optimum time to replace them.

replacement chart an organization structure chart which shows which managers will replace which other managers in the event that the latter are absent or leave suddenly.

replacement cost cost of replacing assets or stocks.

replacement cost accounting accounting techniques for determining replacement costs and linking these to the value of the firm.

replacement demand demand for goods which need to be replaced over the medium or long term, usually as a result of wear and tear or obsolescence.

replacement method method of depreciation based on the replacement cost, rather than the original cost, of assets.

replacement price accounting accounting method that involves calculating the amount an organization would need to pay for its assets if it did not already possess them.

replacement theory theoretical concepts underpinning replacement analysis.

replacement value accounting *see* replacement cost accounting.

report written or verbal account summarizing events or activities, commonly used by a person, work group, business unit, etc. to supply information about their own activities or plans to others in the organization.

reporting the process of producing and delivering reports, sometimes to a preset schedule.

reporting by responsibility reporting procedures which require managers to report only on those issues for which they are directly responsible; *see also* management by exception.

reporting period scheduled period of time where a report is due at the end of that time.

repossession 1 reclaiming goods bought on credit when it is clear that the purchaser can no longer pay; **2** reclaiming landed property when the mortgage holder is in default.

representation 1 formal statements of a situation made to an authority in advance of a decision; **2** alternatively, condition where an organization or group of people are represented by an agent or delegate.

repressive tax tax which is so high as actually to discourage economic activity.

repudiate to set aside or refuse to be bound by the terms of an agreement or contract; *see also* void.

repurchase situation where the seller buys a good back from the buyer after a period of time, usually at a greatly reduced price.

reputation what others believe about a person, organization, good, brand and so on.

required return rate of return on investment required by an investor.

requirement 1 demand or need; **2** inputs required in order to conduct business, such as capital, labour, raw materials and so on.

requisition written record provided to a company's store keeping or inventory facility, requiring that materials or goods in store should be delivered to some other part of the organization.

resale selling of goods bought from another, without altering the condition of those goods.

resale price maintenance contractual condition whereby the original manufacturer controls prices and price increases at various stages in the channel of distribution.

rescheduling altering or amending a schedule, usually by changing the times of various tasks or processes.

research inquiry which tries to ascertain the facts of an unknown situation.

research and development (R&D) business function which seeks both to carry out research and apply the results of that research in practical form through new product development or product modification, changes in operating procedures and so on.

research culture proactive organization culture characterized by constant analysis and assessment of current practices and future prospects.

reservation price *see* reserve price.

reserve 1 money set aside as a contingency for future liabilities, depreciation and so on; **2** also, synonym for reserve price or reserve stock.

reserve price lowest bid at which a seller will be willing to sell.

reserves, discretionary reserves which can be used at the discretion of an individual department or business unit, without seeking approval from higher authority.

reserve stock stocks kept in inventory as a contingency against future shortages.

residual income income remaining after all taxes and expenses have been deducted.

residual income method performance analysis technique which measures the income, return on investment, cost of capital, asset valuation and so on of each division or business unit, comparing the resulting residual income figures of each.

residual interest equity remaining after all costs and liabilities have been deducted.

residual risk that risk that remains once all possible measures have been taken to reduce or avoid risk.

resignation process by which an employee voluntarily terminates his or her employment with a given firm.

resistance pressure against the introduction of new techniques or ways of working, carried out by people who do not wish to see change introduced.

resistance networks networks of employees or managers who have a common desire to resist change and use their network as a method of doing so.

reskilling training employees in new skills, usually in cases where their existing skills are no longer required.

resource anything which supplies raw materials, labour, capital, etc. which a business can use; *see also* natural resources.

resource allocation strategy strategic overview which defines which resources will be needed at which times and then designs the methods by which these goals will be achieved.

resource appraisal analysis of the company's present resources.

resource classes classification of resources into different types according to various criteria.

resource handler manager whose primary task is the management of physical and/or human resources.

resource planning planning function which determines what resources will be required in the future.

respondent 1 person who responds to a questionnaire or survey, providing information; **2** anyone making a response.

response answer or action as a result of stimulus, such as a question, promotion, etc.

response orientation ability of an individual to choose from among several options and make the correct response.

response rate in market research, the ratio of responses to questionnaires sent out.

responsibility the extent to which a person or organization is held accountable for their own actions or those of others.

responsibility accounting system for apportioning responsibility within an organization.

responsibility centre business unit where managers are given responsibility for productivity, costs, profits and so on.

resting order order to buy or sell which is not executed until a named condition is met.

restitution payment in exchange for goods or services taken, or for losses; *see also* compensation.

restraint of trade any activity which impedes market forces or which prevents a company from trading freely.

restricter employee whose productivity is below normal; in pay schemes where pay is related to productivity, the performance of these employees restricts the pay available to other members of the work team.

restriction limitation placed on action.

restrictive labour practice term for working conditions imposed by unions which impede or prevent production efficiency.

restrictive trade practice 1 term for business activities that interfere with or prevent fair or free trade; 2 in legal terms, any business practice that is against the public interest.

restructuring changing the structure of an organization; *see also* reorganization.

results 1 the outcome of any process or programme; 2 more specifically, general term for the outcome of a financial analysis, showing a company's profit and performance over the reporting period just finished.

results orientation philosophy of management that focuses on results of processes rather than the processes themselves.

resumé *see* curriculum vitae.

retail the sale of goods, individually or in small lots, to consumers or end users.

retail audit in market research, a study of retail outlets including the range and volume of goods sold in each.

retail banking banking business conducted with private customers rather than institutions; *see also* commercial bank.

retailer person or company engaged in retail business.

retail gravitation phenomenon whereby shoppers tend to congregate in or near certain types of retail outlet.

retailing the selling of goods on a retail basis.

retail life cycle the phases through which a product or service passes when sold through retail outlets, from introduction to mainstream acceptance and ultimately to decline; *see also* product life cycle.

retail management branch of management devoted specifically to managing and selling through retail outlets.

retail outlet physical location, such as a shop, where goods are sold on a retail basis.

retail price price at which goods are sold in retail outlets.

retail price support subsidy paid to a retailer by a producer or distributor, to allow the latter to sell goods at a price which would otherwise be unprofitable.

retained earnings money retained by the company after all expenses, taxes and dividends have been paid.

retainer payment made to another in exchange for services, covering a specific period of time.

retaliatory duty tariff on imports from a particular country, levied by government in response to perceived unfair trade practices in the other country.

retention keeping or maintaining assets rather than disposing of them; in marketing, the effort devoted to ensuring that customers remain loyal.

retention marketing marketing activity which focuses on existing or actual customers with a view to ensuring their loyalty and continued custom.

retention money in building and construction work, that portion of the contract price which is held back by the customer until the latter can be assured that the finished project has no defects and is functioning as design.

retirement 1 termination of employment on reaching a certain age, or because illness or injury mean the employee is no longer capable of work; **2** the removal from use of an asset.

retirement benefit scheme pension plan which provides an income upon retirement.

retirement income income provided to an employee in retirement.

retraining training which provides new sets of skills to workers and managers who may already have considerable skills and experience, but who need to learn new sets in order to be employable or to work more effectively.

retroactive condition which is declared to have existed in the past as well as the present and future.

retroactive pay increase pay increase which is extended to cover an agreed past period of time, meaning that the employee is owed arrears of pay for that time.

retrogressive consumer consumer who values economy and low price over quality and product features; as opposed to progressive consumer.

retrospective payment payment for services rendered at an earlier time.

return 1 money which is paid back, as for example in a return on investment, **2** document which provides a statement of taxable income to tax authorities; **3** good returned by the buyer to the seller after purchase, usually because the buyer is not satisfied with the good.

returned work finished goods which are sent back to the production line because they contain unacceptably high levels of defects.

return on assets managed measure of company performance, the ratio of profit to the value of assets currently under management.

return on capital *see* return on capital employed.

return on capital employed (ROCE) measure of company or investment performance, the ratio of the profit derived from an investment or activity to capital employed to establish or maintain that investment or activity.

return on equity (ROE) profit derived from equity currently held.

return on investment (ROI) measure of company performance, the ratio of profit to the value of the investment required to realize those profits.

return on sales ratio of total profit to total cost of sales.

return on total assets as return on assets managed, but takes into account all assets including those which are inactive or under other management.

revaluation new calculation of the value of an asset which has been subject to either an increase or decrease in shares.

revaluation reserve money held in reserve to anticipate changes in asset value created by revaluation.

revenue total of income received during a given time period, before any deductions for costs, taxation, and so on; *see also* income.

revenue account accounting record of all revenue received.

revenue neutral situation where the level of tax income received by a government remains essentially unchanged.

revenue passenger kilometres (RPKs) in passenger transport, an assessment of the amount of money earned per passenger per kilometre of distance travelled.

revenue reserves profits which are held in reserve as a contingency or in preparation for future activities.

reverse discrimination *see* positive discrimination.

reverse evaluation performance appraisal or evaluation carried out by subordinates on their manager.

reverse takeover takeover where a company that acquires another company then restructures itself so that the acquired company now manages the acquiring company.

revolving credit *see* revolving loan.

revolving fund fund which maintains a static balance, with money paid out being balanced by money paid in from other sources.

revolving letter of credit letter of credit that is automatically renewed upon expiry.

revolving loan loan that is automatically renewed upon reaching maturity.

revolving underwriting facility type of Euronote, which allows a firm to borrow capital at a predetermined interest rate.

reward 1 any return or recompense for services, including pay and benefits; **2** any benefit obtained from a good.

reward, extrinsic *see* extrinsic reward.

reward, intrinsic *see* intrinsic reward.

reward system the combination of methods by which employees are rewarded for their work, including pay, fringe benefits and so on.

re-work repeating work which did not meet quality standards when it was done the first time.

right *see* rights.

right first time quality management approach which aims to ensure that production processes accurately match specifications, reducing or eliminating the need for re-work.

right of recourse the right to seek recompense from another, either directly or through the courts.

right of way right to travel across property owned by another.

rights 1 claims which a person or organization may have over the property of another; **2** in securities trading, the right of existing shareholders to buy new shares when they are issued.

rights issue share issue where shares are offered to existing shareholders in amounts proportional to their current holdings.

right sizing euphemism for downsizing, term for the process in which a company adjusts the numbers of its workforce to fit supposed present requirements.

right to work movement which advocates the rights of non-union workers to be employed in unionized workplaces.

ring fenced 1 an activity that is treated completely separately from other business activities; **2** the maintenance of confidentiality about clients' affairs by an agent.

ringi in Japanese business, the system whereby decisions are made by consensus.

risk the chance that a venture will not meet expectations or result in a loss.

risk adjustment altering the weighted average cost of capital (WACC) to reflect a risk premium for the project in question; more generally, the process of altering rates of interest or return to reflect probable risk.

risk analysis techniques used to assess the likelihood of a certain event happening within a certain period of time, used to determine the level of risk inherent in an investment, or in a person or good being insured.

risk assessment general term for the definition and statement of levels of risk inherent in a given situation.

risk capital capital placed in investments which carry higher than usual levels of risk; *see also* venture capital.

risk economist economist who specializes in the measurement of risks associated with certain investments.

risk–free rate rate of interest which has not been adjusted to reflect the risk of lending.

risk management management techniques concerned with the assessment of risk, and the minimization or avoidance of risk.

risk manager manager involved specifically in activities connected with risk management.

risk, political *see* political risk.

risk sharing the spreading of risk through the assumption of various portions of an individual risk by different parties; *see also* reinsurance.

risk simulation modelling techniques used to determine the levels of risk inherent in various future scenarios.

risk spreading methods of reducing risk which cannot be avoided.

risk taker investor or manager who is willing to act in risky situations.

risky shift phenomenon whereby people's individual behaviour varies from norms of behaviour expected by the groups to which they belong.

ritual formalized and repetitive patterns of behaviour.

rivalry *see* competition.

robotics general term for computerized automated systems functioning under autonomous control.

ROCE *see* return on capital employed.

ROE *see* return on equity.

rogue product product which suffers very high rates of malfunction or spoilage.

rogue trader in securities trading, an individual trader whose unsupervised actions cause losses to his or her company or principals.

ROI *see* return on investment.

role function or position within an organization, defined in part by its relation to other roles.

role ambiguity situation where an employee is expected to perform two or more roles, and where there is no clear definition of which role is expected at which time.

role conflict situation where an employee is expected to perform two or more roles and where one role, if performed, will prevent the performance of some or all of the other roles.

role incompatibility situation where some elements of a role or job are not compatible with others, making it impossible to perform the role satisfactorily.

role perception how people perceive their own roles, or those of others.

role play training technique which involves the acting out of simulations, with each participant playing a particular role.

role reversal type of role playing where participants play roles opposite those they have in real life (for example, a shop-floor employee plays the role of a senior manager).

roll-back reduction of prices or wages to earlier levels.

rolling contract contract which is automatically renewed when it expires.

rolling plan long-term plan that is constantly revised and updated.

rollover renewing a loan which has matured and been fully repaid.

rollover bonus bonus which is paid in part during the period of earnings and in part at a specified later date (usually at the end of the period of earnings).

rota plan showing the times when certain workers will be present for work, or will perform scheduled tasks.

rotating strike strike which takes effect for short periods at different workplaces in succession.

route 1 the path that materials and components will follow through the manufacturing process; **2** the path taken by goods proceeding through the distribution channel.

route diagram graphic depiction of a route.

routine maintenance regularly scheduled maintenance which is intended simply to keep machinery or equipment in good operating order.

routing the process of laying out or mapping a route.

royalties payment made to the holder of a copyright, trademark, patent or other registration of intellectual property.

RPKs *see* revenue passenger kilometres.

rules regulations governing activity or behaviour.

rules of competition laws concerning competitive activity, aimed at preventing anti-competitive or unfair trade practices.

rules of procedure rules stating how a meeting should be carried out.

run the span of continuous production from the start of a process to the finish.

runaway out of control.

runaway inflation *see* galloping inflation.

running costs costs, either direct or indirect, incurred as a result of production processes and related to production volume; as opposed to fixed costs.

running yield *see* current yield.

run on the bank *see* bank run.

S

sabotage deliberate and usually illegal actions aimed to cause damage or hamper production.

safeguard action taken to prevent or reduce a particular risk.

safety stocks minimum level of stock which must be kept in inventory as a contingency.

salami code in computing, a form of malicious code that removes small amounts of data and diverts them elsewhere.

salary *see* wage.

salary administration management methods used to determine salaries for different jobs within the organization.

salary band range of salaries paid for a particular job.

salary bracket *see* salary band.

salary class as salary band, but also takes account of fringe benefits attached to each salary.

salary club employers' association which gathers information and discusses policy on salaries.

salary grade *see* grade.

salary increment planned regular increase in salary.

salary-men Japanese term for waged employees of large companies.

salary progression rate at which an individual employee's salary can increase within the bounds of their particular salary band or grade.

salary review review of salaries and benefits conducted with the aim of ensuring whether these are appropriate or adequate.

salary structure the bases on which salaries are determined for all jobs in a company.

sale **1** transfer of goods in exchange for a monetary payment; **2** retailer's advertised temporary reduction in price on some goods.

sales total of goods sold, and/or their monetary value.

sales analysis general term for the analysis of sales information with a view to determining trends.

sales audit analysis of sales over a given period in terms of volume, revenue, profit, customers and so on.

sales budget budget based on forecast sales, including both expected revenue and costs of sales.

sales chain channel of distribution along which goods pass from producer through intermediaries to the consumer.

sales costs costs incurred in the sales process, such as wages for sales staff, rent and overheads for retail outlets, and so on.

sales coverage ratio of salespeople to potential customers in a given geographical area.

sales effort economists' term for the activities of companies devoted to the selling of their products, to some extent synonymous with marketing.

sales engineer salesperson who is also a trained engineer and can provide technical advice and support to customers.

sales force all the employees or agents engaged by a company to sell goods.

sales forecasts projections of goods sold over a given future time period.

sales growth increase in the volume and revenue sales, not to be confused with increasing profits.

salesman *see* salesperson.

sales management branch of management concerned with sales, including managing the sales force, planning and directing sales efforts and so on; usually considered to be a branch of marketing.

sales manager manager specializing in sales management.

sales manual printed documents laying down procedures to be followed by the sales force, including preferred selling techniques for a given product or service.

sales mix **1** combination of products sold by a company in a particular market; **2** alternatively, the combination of selling techniques used in a particular market; *see also* marketing mix.

sales objectives the goals or targets for sales set for territories, sales teams and/or individual sales people.

sales order order placed by a customer with a salesperson.

sales order processing administrative support function which takes orders from salespeople and ensures they are filled, payment is made and the goods and services are delivered.

salesperson employee whose primary role is to sell goods or services to customers.

sales planning planning of sales activities including the definition of sales territories and sales targets.

sales promotion *see* promotion.

sales promotion planning *see* promotion planning.

sales revenue income received from sales.

sales staff *see* sales force.

sales target *see* sales objectives.

sales tax indirect tax levied on goods at the point of sale.

sales territory geographical region assigned to an individual salesperson or unit.

sales-wave research market research technique which aims to gauge the frequency of repeat purchases.

sales, year to date (YTD) total of all sales since the beginning of the financial year.

salvage the recovery and reclamation of damaged goods or assets.

sample example of a product or service which is provided for inspection, either by clients for information purposes, or by quality inspectors to check for defects.

sample size the number of units in a sample.

sample survey survey based on a selected sample of a given population.

sampling the process of selecting and testing a sample.

sampling error extent to which a selected sample is not representative of the larger population.

sampling error reduction techniques used to gauge whether sampling error has occurred and then to reduce or avoid it.

sampling frame information about the population as a whole which is used to select samples.

sampling order order of a small sample of a product which is used as a trial by the buyer prior to deciding whether to purchase larger quantities.

samurai bonds foreign bonds issued in Japan.

sanction action taken against a business by another party, including legal penalties imposed by government, industrial action by employees, and switching or substitution by customers.

satellite work centres work places located some distance from the main production facility, where particular tasks are carried out.

satisfaction condition of being satisfied, where the benefits received match or exceed the effort expended.

satisfaction factors **1** those factors which result in satisfaction; **2** in consumer behaviour, those consumer needs which must be met by a product or service.

satisficing in decision making, the selection of an alternative that will provide benefit.

satisfiers factors identified by Frederick Herzberg that lead to satisfaction in the workplace.

saturation market situation where the volume of goods available equals or exceeds market demand.

savings income not spent on consumption.

savings account bank account for customers who wish to accumulate money without regular withdrawals.

savings bank bank whose primary business is taking deposits.

savings bond *see* bond, savings.

savings rate in the economy, the proportion of income which is saved rather than spent on consumption.

savings ratio ratio of total savings to total income.

SBU *see* strategic business unit.

scab worker who goes to work in a picketed workplace, thereby breaking the strike.

scale measure of factors in order of magnitude; synonym for size.

scale economics *see* economies of scale.

scalogram research tool used for determining underlying patterns in very large arrays of data.

scanning the process of searching one's environment and collecting information which can be analysed for significance at a later date.

scarce resources resources where supply is outstripped by demand.

scarcity condition of being scarce, used of money or resources.

scarcity value increase in the value of a resource due to scarcity.

scatter diagram graphic depiction of the relationship between variables.

scenario description of a situation; projected future situation given current conditions and trends.

schedule 1 plan showing times when certain tasks will be carried out; *see also* rota; **2** in insurance, documents supporting a policy showing the types of risk covered and the additional premiums to be paid.

scheduled downtime downtime which is planned so as to allow maintenance or repairs to be carried out.

scheduled maintenance maintenance which is planned and built into schedules so as to allow machinery to operate at maximum efficiency.

scheduling the practice of planning and compiling schedules.

scheduling, batch *see* batch scheduling.

scheduling charts graphic depictions showing schedules.

scheduling methods techniques used for setting efficient schedules.

scheduling, production *see* production scheduling.

scheduling techniques *see* scheduling methods.

science systematic knowledge, usually gained as the result of systematic experiment and observation.

science park *see* industrial estate.

scientific management theory of production management developed by F. W. Taylor, based on the study of workflows and productivity and the relationship between management and the workforce.

scope economies *see* economies of scope.

scorecard record of ratings or scores as the outcome of a particular analysis.

scoring, credit *see* credit scoring.

screen–based systems computerized trading systems used in international securities trading, where price and other information is displayed on a computer screen.

screening 1 assessing candidates for a job so as to weed out those who are unsuitable; **2** more generally, the preliminary assessment of information, ideas and so on so as to discard those which are not relevant.

scrip paper document stating that the bearer is to be paid in money, shares and so on at a future date.

scrip dividends a form of dividend which allows shareholders to take their dividend in the form of money, additional shares, product, or other stated forms or reward.

scrip issue issue of new shares to existing shareholders on the basis of shares currently held.

search *see* executive search.

SEAQI *see* Stock Exchange Automated Quotation International

seasonal demand demand for a good which is based on seasonal fluctuations in the market (e.g., ski equipment in winter).

seasonal employee worker hired on a short-term basis during a particular time of the year (for example, agricultural labourers hired during harvest time).

seasonal forecast forecasted level of seasonal demand for future seasons.

seasonal unemployment unemployment which is derived from the seasonal nature of some types of work.

second penetration product high-technology products based on refinement and further development of the original technology concept.

secondary banking banking activities carried out by institutions which are not formally recognized as banks.

secondary boycott boycott extended to cover other firms associated with the firm that is the primary object of the boycott.

secondary distribution **1** distribution of stock by a firm which has purchased a large block of issued shares and is now selling these on in smaller lots; **2** more generally, any distribution activity carried out by agents on behalf of the principal wholesaler or distributor.

secondary labour market labour market for general or unskilled workers.

secondary picketing picketing by workers not directly involved in the main strike.

secondary strike during industrial action, a strike conducted by a union against another firm which does business with the company involved in the primary dispute.

secretary administrative worker who handles correspondence, filing and data management and other tasks on behalf of a manager or executive.

secured credit credit advanced where collateral has been offered; *see also* secured liability.

secured liability debt against which the borrower has pledged assets as collateral.

securities documents which provide legal ownership of commodities, assets or money.

securities dealer person or organization involved in buying and selling securities.

securities markets markets where securities are bought and sold.

securities trading selling or buying of securities through securities markets.

security **1** property or assets pledged as collateral against a loan; **2** measures taken to protect against risk.

security markets *see* securities markets.

security of tenure condition where a tenant has been confirmed as being in long-term possession of a property.

segmentation dividing a group of people into smaller subgroups based on certain identifiable characteristics; *see also* market segmentation.

segmentation analysis analysis of markets with a view to segmenting them; *see also* segmentation.

segregated trust *see* split-level investment trust.

selection the process of analysing job applications and interviewing applicants so as to choose the applicant most suited to a particular job.

selection consultant professional who provides advice on selection techniques.

selection test personality and skills testing which gauges a prospective employee's suitability for a job.

selective distribution distribution through only a limited number of available distributors or retail outlets.

self-actualization needs needs which relate to one's desire to improve oneself or to expand one's personal horizon.

self-administered fund pension scheme which is administered directly by a company on behalf of its employees.

self-assessment assessment method whereby one judges one's own abilities and performance.

self-completion questionnaire questionnaire completed by the informant and then returned to the researchers.

self-employed a person who is in self-employment.

self-employment working for oneself, with responsibility for one's own trading losses and profits, rather than working for another firm and drawing a salary.

self-esteem needs needs which relate to one's image or view of oneself.

self-fulfilment needs needs which relate to one's personal desires or ambitions.

self-instruction learning process whereby learners, perhaps using some aids, teach themselves a skill or ability.

self-insurance a system whereby firms set aside money as reserves to cover potential losses, rather than taking out an insurance policy.

self-liquidating any asset that is automatically converted into cash after a given period of time.

self-management management of one's own career, time, learning programme and progression.

self-perception a person's own view of themselves.

self-regulation regulation of an industry or business area by the companies and others involved in that area.

self-regulatory organizations independent organizations within an industry or business area set up to enforce self-regulation.

self-selection *see* self-service.

self-service sales operation where the customer chooses goods and performs most of the required service tasks himself or herself.

self-service outlet retail outlet based on the concept of self-service.

sell to dispose of an asset or good in exchange for money; as opposed to buy.

sell and leaseback *see* leaseback.

seller person or business selling a good or asset; as opposed to buyer.

sellers' market market where demand is greater than supply, giving sellers control over prices and conditions of sale.

selling the process of disposing of an asset or good in exchange for money; as opposed to buying.

selling costs *see* sales costs.

selling platform the product or service features which form the principal selling points.

selling price 1 the price for which a good or asset is sold; **2** the price named by the seller as that which he or she will accept.

selling short in securities markets, the practice of selling stocks in anticipation of a price drop, then buying them at a lower price.

sell out 1 to sell all of current stocks of a good; **2** also, colloquially, to betray one's cause to the opposition or competition in exchange for reward.

sell short *see* selling short.

semi-autonomous groups groups to which some degree of independence and responsibility has been devolved but which remain accountable in other areas.

semi-fixed cost *see* stepped cost.

semi-manufactured goods processed raw materials which are ready to be converted into finished goods.

seminar lecture or presentation to a small audience on a narrowly defined subject.

semiotics branch of linguistics concerned with signs, symbols and images.

semi-skilled worker worker who has some skills but still requires high levels of supervision.

semi-variable cost *see* mixed cost.

sempai-kohai in Japanese, 'elder brother–younger brother'; practice of mentoring of junior managers by their more experienced seniors.

senior debt debt which takes precedence over other existing liabilities.

seniority the length of time an employee has been in continuous service with a firm.

seniority wages additional pay increments granted to employees who have considerable seniority.

sensation sensory experience or consciousness.

sensitivity extent to which a subject will respond to an outside stimulus.

sensitivity analysis 1 in decision making, analysis which gauges the effect or consequences of any given decision; **2** in marketing, determination of the extent to which products or services are price-sensitive.

sensitivity training training which aims to improve interpersonal skills by making people more aware of the views and attitudes of others.

sensory those things which are received by the senses.

sensory perception the act of apprehending objects, sounds and so on using the senses.

separated manager term for a manager who places excessive emphasis on procedures and not enough on results.

separation rate rate at which employees leave a firm.

sequestered account bank account that has been frozen through a process of sequestration.

sequestration taking possession of another's assets (literally, separating these assets from their owner) where debts have not been repaid.

serial correlation forecasting technique which attempts to predict future trends on the basis of past trends.

serial interface interface between a computer and other computers or peripherals using a single wire or cable.

serial storage storage system where goods or information are stored in the order in which they arrive.

service non-tangible goods delivered to a customer either as adjuncts to a physical product or as stand-alone goods.

service charge in banking and financial services, a separate charge made for the administration of a loan or other service.

service cost cost of providing a service to the customer.

service cost allocation techniques for allocation costs of service provision to various cost centres.

service department part of a firm that exists to provide a service, either to external customers or to other parts of the organization.

service increments increases in pay which are related to length of service or employment with a company.

service industries industrial sectors which are primarily engaged in service provision, such as transportation and hospitality.

service mark brand or trademark associated with a service.

service pricing the techniques involved in setting prices for services.

service portfolio the range of services offered by a company to its customers.

service quality the extent to which a service meets the needs, expectations and demands of customers.

service sector general term for service industries; of limited explanatory use, since many sectors include a combination of goods and services.

services marketing marketing activities required to market services specifically, as opposed to those used to market products.

servuction system the system whereby services are simultaneously produced and delivered to the customer.

set a defined group of items or data.

setting up *see* setup.

settlement day date on which a purchase on credit must be paid for.

setup 1 process of configuring machinery to undertake a production run; **2** more generally, the establishment of the mechanisms needed for a particular process.

setup costs costs involved in setup.

setup time time required to complete a setup.

seven Ps in marketing, extension of the four Ps concept to include product, process, price, place, promotion, physical evidence and people in the marketing mix; *see also* four Ps.

severance termination of employment; *see also* dismissal; redundancy.

severance pay one-off addition to wages paid to an employee upon severance.

sex discrimination discrimination against someone on the basis of their sex or gender.

sex equality situation where there is no sex discrimination and both sexes are treated equally.

sexual harassment workplace behaviour in which workers of one sex intimidate or offend other workers, usually of the opposite sex, through sexually-oriented comments or behaviour.

shadow price *see* opportunity cost.

shakeout change in the structure of an industry or market, usually of a nature which causes weaker competitors to cease trading or to go bankrupt.

shamrock organization organization theory developed by Charles Handy, where a core of permanent workers are supplemented by shifting populations of temporary and part-time workers.

share single unit of equity issued by a company or mutual society and purchased by a shareholder.

share capital money raised through share issues.

share certificate formal document certifying ownership of shares.

shared option a form of real option where the value of the option can be affected (and in effect shared) by other parties beyond the owner of the option.

shared values values which are common to all members of a group or society.

shareholder someone who owns shares in a company.

shareholder monitoring maintenance of contact between a company and its shareholders, including updating of the shareholder register.

shareholder equity that portion of the equity of the firm which is owned by shareholders or stockholders.

shareholding position of being a shareholder.

share incentive scheme form of employee bonus or incentive whereby employees receive shares rather than money.

share index index showing the performance of registered shares against the market.

share loan loan granted by a mutual society, credit union, etc. where funds currently on deposit serve as collateral.

share of production plan wage bonus system whereby bonuses are paid based on departmental or company productivity rather than individual achievement.

share of the market ratio of a company's sales in a particular market to the total of all sales in that market, used to express that company's position in relation to its competitors.

share option the right to acquire shares within a stated period of time, usually also at a stated price.

shares plural of share; used commonly as shares are usually traded in multiple units.

shell commune company which exists only on paper, usually as one in a series of holding companies.

shift scheduled working time each day, usually of a fixed number of hours duration.

shift premium additional wages paid for working certain shifts, such as night shifts.

shift working workplace organization based on more than one shift; three or four shifts may be employed, so that work is done on a continuous basis over 24 hours.

ship **1** to send goods physically from one place to another; **2** a seagoing vessel carrying cargo or passengers.

shipment a specific lot of goods being shipped.

shipping **1** sending goods physically from one location to another; **2** more specifically, seagoing vessels used to carry cargo or passengers.

shipping and forwarding agent distributor who specializes in arranging the transport of goods to their destination.

shipping note *see* consignment note.

shop **1** a retail outlet; **2** trade union term for the workplace within a single company or plant.

shop audit *see* retail audit.

shop card *see* store card.

shop committee union members who represent the other workers in a shop.

shop control production control systems in operation on the shop floor.

shop floor the area of a factory or plant which is devoted to production and related activities.

shopping consumer activity which focuses on buying goods and services but which has a recognized social aspect as well.

shopping centre concentration of retail outlets with small stores built around one or more large supermarkets or department stores which serve as retail magnets.

shop steward union official who serves as the union's permanent representative on local matters.

short account account registering short sales.

shortage situation where there is not enough of a good in supply to meet demand.

shortfall **1** in accounting or inventory management, situation where the actual sums or numbers of items held are less than what the records show; **2** more generally, a failure to meet forecasted targets.

short interval scheduling scheduling of tasks and goals over a short period of time, these can then be rescheduled for a similar period of time at the end of each preceding period.

short of exchange in foreign exchange trading, position where a trader has sold more currency than he or she currently possesses.

short position broker or trader's position where securities have been sold short and acquisitions of securities to cover the sales have not yet been made.

short sale in securities trading, sale made by a trader or broker who does not actually own the security in question; usually takes place in a declining market.

short selling *see* short sale.

short-term debt debt which must be repaid in a short period of time, usually less than a year.

short-term investment investment which is expected to be realized in a short period of time, perhaps less than a year.

short-termism mode of thinking which focuses only on the near future and ignores longer term implications.

short-term pressures factors influencing the operations of a business at present and over the near future, but which are expected to dissipate over a longer period of time.

short-time working reduction in the number of hours worked per employee per week, usually because there is a shortage of work.

shrinkage tendency of stocks held in inventory to decline over time due to accidental damage or pilfering.

shutdown stopping a production line or plant from operating.

shyster colloquial term for a corrupt or dishonest professional service provider, used especially of the legal profession.

SIC code Standard Industrial Classification code; code assigned to a company under the SIC system developed in the USA, which indicates the activities and areas of business in which the company is involved.

sick building syndrome situation where the fabric and systems of a building have decayed to the point where they endanger the health of those working in the building.

sick leave time away from work an employee is allowed in event of his or her illness.

sickness and accident policy insurance policy which provides compensation for income lost due to either illness or accident, as well as some healthcare costs.

sick pay wage paid to employees on sick leave, usually comprising part or all of their standard salary.

sight bill bill which must be paid when presented by the holder.

signalling discretionary activity by firms which provides information and serves as an incentive to customers, shareholders and so on.

silent partner partner who invests in a business but takes no part in running it; *see also* dormant partner.

silicon brains *see* artificial intelligence.

simple debenture debenture issued against an unsecured loan.

simple interest interest calculated on the primary sum lent, and not on any further accrued interest; as opposed to compound interest.

simulation model of a process or situation which can be used to explore the consequences of alternative decision making.

simulation modelling creating simulations using mathematical techniques.

simulator device which simulates the operation of a machine or process, usually mechanically or computer assisted.

simultaneous movements in motion studies, instances where the worker must make two or more movements at the same time.

single capacity 1 ability to carry out only one function at a time; **2** in stock markets, the ability to act as either a jobber or a broker, but not both.

single currency resulting unified currency created by the merger of several previously existing currencies.

single-entry bookkeeping bookkeeping practice in which transactions are entered only once in the accounts; as opposed to double-entry bookkeeping.

Single European Market market which is the end result of the European Union's programme of economic and monetary union.

single line store retail outlet specializing in a single product type.

single payment loan loan which is to be repaid in a single payment consisting of principal and interest.

single premium costing pension plan, insurance policy, etc. where the beneficiary pays the required premium in a single lump sum.

single pricing policy in exporting, selling goods at a uniform price into all overseas markets.

single status philosophy in job evaluation, the assumption that all jobs are of roughly equivalent status, eliminating any difference between line and staff or between blue collar and white collar.

single task role role or job which requires the performance of only one task.

single transaction channel channel developed for the carrying out of only one transaction between supplier, intermediaries and purchasers.

sinking fund fund wherein a company sets aside money to repay debts or create a reserve for future use.

sit-down strike form of industrial action whereby employees enter the workplace but then refuse to work.

sit-in form of industrial action where the workers occupy the workplace but will do no work and refuse to leave.

situational interview interview consisting of questions focusing on a given assumed situation, for example, how a candidate for employment would handle certain aspects of the job if hired.

situation appraisal in problem solving, analysis of a given situation as a basis for exploring options and making decisions.

situation profile detailed analysis of a company's present situation and position; *see also* position statement.

six markets framework model which shows a firm's various relationship markets, including internal, referral, influence, recruitment, supplier and customer markets.

size-effect phenomenon whereby firms experience increasing levels of labour and industrial problems as they grow in size.

skewing biasing or creating asymmetry.

skill ability to perform a complex task effectively.

skill acquisition curve *see* learning curve.

skill-based pay pay system where bonuses are paid in order to recruit and keep highly skilled employees.

skill dissipation extent to which skills lose their value over time.

skills plural of skill; usually used to summarize either the skills possessed by a person, or the skills needed to perform a task.

skills, interpersonal *see* interpersonal skills.

skills inventory summary of the skills possessed by employees and managers within an organization.

skill testing examinations of employees or potential employees to determine which skills they possess and to what extent.

skills training training programmes which provide instruction in particular skills.

skills upgrading training programmes or other activities which enhance or update existing skills.

skillware in computing, people who are trained and skilled at working with computer systems.

skimming introducing a product to a market at a very high price and then gradually lowering the price so as to attract more customers once those willing to pay the high initial price have made their purchases.

slack 1 low level of business activity; **2** time in a production process which can be eliminated so as to speed up production.

slave unit mechanical or electronic device which is wholly controlled by another unit, usually known as the master control unit.

sleeper 1 product or service for which demand has been steady for some time, but which is now suddenly in increasing demand; **2** inactive management or organization.

sleeping partner *see* dormant partner.

sliding parity exchange rates exchange rates where any change value is controlled and spread over a period of time; *see also* moving parity.

slip chart scheduling chart which plots planned time or progress against actual time or progress.

slippage 1 time which has been lost or wasted; **2** extent to which a project or process is behind schedule.

slip system accounting system which uses copies of invoices rather than ledgers to record transactions.

slowdown 1 form of industrial action in which workers perform their tasks more slowly, leading to a decrease in output; **2** in economics, a decline in the rate of increase in output, though not an actual decrease.

slump decline in activity or output.

slumpflation economic condition characterized by declining output (slump) and rising prices.

slush fund 1 fund set aside for a particular purpose usually not connected with the main business activity; **2** also, a fund from which illegal payments or bribes are made.

small and medium-sized enterprises (SMEs) general term including all businesses except those which are categorized as large; exact definitions vary.

small business generic term for firms with small numbers of employees and low turnovers, often owner-managed and usually operating out of a single site.

small firm *see* small business.

small office–home office (SO–HO) office or business established in the worker's home.

small print detailed conditions of sale or credit contained in a contract, formerly sometimes printed in small and difficult to read script.

smart money colloquial term for investments made by experienced investors who are able accurately to judge both the value and risk of an investment.

smokestack industry general term for an industrial sector characterized by large plants and factories, usually engaged in mass production; the term is sometimes used pejoratively, as these industries are becoming less important in advanced economies.

smoothing, exponential *see* exponential smoothing.

snap time short break from work, usually for the purpose of taking meals.

social accounting evaluation of projects or programmes in terms of their impacts on and costs for society.

social audit analysis of the impacts which a proposed activity or project will have for society as a whole, and particularly for those members of the public who might be directly affected.

social benefits value to society which results from a business activity or project, beyond those values which derive directly from the products or services it sells.

social change long-term changes in the structure of society and in popular attitudes and values.

Social Chapter European Union legislation which provides Europe-wide guidelines on employment policy.

social class class of society (e.g. working class, middle class, upper class) to which an individual belongs.

social competence ability of a person to handle himself or herself in social situations.

social considerations the implications which a project or planned course of action has on society at large.

social contract theory of the relationship between individuals, organizations and society as a whole, wherein each is required to act in the interests of the others.

social control the ability to control or influence people's attitudes or behaviours.

social cost cost of a business activity in terms of its impact on society at large.

social cost–benefit analysis cost–benefit analysis applied to social costs.

social environment 1 the social aspects of a culture or locality; **2** society.

social factors factors which derive from some aspect of local society or culture.

social investment investment in the provision of social goods such as education and healthcare.

socialism political and economic philosophy which advocates the ownership of assets by society as a whole.

social isolation condition affecting some employees who work from home, who miss out on the social contact which can be derived from the workplace.

socialization the integration and acceptance of a person, product or concept into society.

social justice a result which is just and fair in social terms, which leads to the promotion of equity or the elimination of inequity.

social marketing subset of marketing which focuses on the marketing of socially useful goods or concepts; the latter do not necessarily have monetary value and or the ability to be traded in a marketplace.

social needs needs which derive from a person's position in society.

social policy government policy regarding the structure of society and such issues as the distribution of wealth.

social relationships relationships which exist between people or groups in society.

social responsibility the responsibility that companies have towards society at large, in particular, to conduct their activities and use their profits in ways that are of benefit to society.

social science the scientific study of science and human relationships.

social security financial assistance provided by the state to the unemployed or less well-off.

social stratification existence of classes in society.

social structure the organization and structure of society.

social trends long-term changes in society and in people's beliefs and values.

social welfare the well-being and security of society at large.

societal issues issues which concern all of society.

societal marketing the marketing of goods and services which, while profit-making, serve also to improve the quality of life for purchasers and for society at large; *see also* social marketing.

socioeconomic accounting accounting practices which take social consequences of actions and decisions into account.

socioeconomics discipline which merges economics and social sciences, focusing on both rational economic and societally induced behaviour and decision making.

socioeconomic status marketers' classification of society into different grades based on social class or situation and personal wealth.

sociology study of the development and nature of society.

sociotechnical system organization development theory which aims to maximize task efficiency and employee satisfaction.

soft currency currency which has only limited convertibility.

soft goods in marketing, term referring to clothing, fabrics and similar products.

soft loan loan offered at a low rate of interest, or under other conditions favourable to the borrower.

soft sales promotion *see* soft sell.

soft sell unaggressive sales techniques, usually relying on subtle forms of persuasion or motivation.

soft skills personal, interpersonal and communications skills; as opposed to hard skills.

software computer programs composed entirely of data stored in memory or on a disk which, when activated, can be employed by the user to carry out certain computer-based tasks; examples of software programs or applications are word processing programs, spreadsheets, databases, Internet browsers, graphic design packages, CAD-CAM and so on.

software piracy illegal copying and sale of software programs; *see also* piracy.

sole trader self-employed small businessperson who owns all the equity in his or her business.

solicitor UK term for a lawyer.

solus offer seldom-used term for the offer for sale of a single product or service.

solus position advertising space in a journal or magazine which is not near any other advertising.

solvency *see* solvent.

solvent the condition of being able to pay back all outstanding debts; as opposed to insolvent.

S–O–R–C behavioural thinking model used in organization development, the initials standing for stimulus–organism–response–consequence.

sound an investment or business proposition which is judged to be financially viable and to carry a relatively low risk of failure.

sound and voice recognition in computers, peripherals and software which enable a computer to recognize certain sounds including the voices of users, and to carry out commands given verbally rather than entered through a keyboard or touchscreen.

sourcing searching for and maintaining sources of supply of components, raw materials, labour, capital and so on.

span of control **1** limits of control which a person or organization has on their environment; **2** more specifically, the defined limits of authority which are attached to a managerial position.

span of managerial responsibility *see* span of control.

spatial aptitude test tests designed to measure spatial awareness.

spatial awareness **1** extent to which a person is aware of the space around them and can put into context the events going on within that space; **2** more generally, human awareness of space and shape.

special deposits money which UK banks are required to deposit with the Bank of England.

special drawing right in effect, an overdraft which individual countries maintain with the International Monetary Fund, allowing them to borrow limited amounts of money without special authority.

special order order placed by a customer for a good which is not presently available but which can be produced; in some cases, customization of existing goods is required.

specialist skills skills possessed by a limited number of people and which are essential to carry out certain tasks.

speciality stores retail outlets carrying only a few specialized lines of products; *see also* single line store.

specialization concentration on a particular task or function.

specialization of labour concentration of labour efforts on particular tasks or functions; *see also* division of labour.

special situation condition of shares where major developments (such as merger or takeover) are expected in the short term.

specification definition of the type of work to be done, or of the dimensions and qualities of a good to be produced.

speculation investment in relatively high-risk investments in the hopes of making a large profit in a short time.

speculative purchasing buying goods or securities when the price has declined in the hopes that prices will shortly rise again, allowing the buyer to sell at a profit.

speculative risk risk inherent in a business proposition, contingent on the future conduct of the business and the possibility that it might fail.

speculator one who invests on a speculative basis; *see also* speculation.

speech processing system computer system which can recognize and act upon verbal commands.

speed-up attempt to increase the speed of production or the rate of progress on a project.

spider-web diagram graphic representation of reference points, used in decision making.

spin-off secondary product or service derived from research aimed at developing a different product or service, usually an offshoot of new technologies or processes.

split in securities trading, the multiplication of the number of shares in a company; in effect, each outstanding share 'splits' into two or more shares, each having the same properties as the original.

split capital investment trust investment trust whose value is based in part on the value of its investments and in part on the value its own shares command in the market.

split level investment trust investment trust offering two kinds of shares, one which earns dividends only and one which represents a share of the trusts capital and can therefore appreciate in value.

split order a large order for goods or securities which is then broken up by the buyer and resold in smaller quantities.

split run copy in advertising, the process of running two or more similar or identical advertisements at different places in the same publication.

split shift in shift work, situation where an employee's working shift is split into two separate parts, with time off between them; often used in restaurants and hotels.

spoilage damage suffered by goods in transit or while in store.

spokesperson representative of a group or organization who is authorized to speak on behalf of the whole group or organization.

sponsorship provision, usually on a charitable basis, of funds and support required for some social or non-profit-making activity.

spot term used to describe goods, commodities, securities and so on where money and ownership change hands immediately the sale is concluded; *see also* spot market.

spot contract contract concluded in a spot market, where goods are delivered immediately to the buyer.

spot delivery immediate delivery of purchased goods to the customer.

spot exchange rate exchange rate available in the market at a given point in time.

spot interest rate current interest rate.

spot market market where goods and money change hands as soon as the sale is concluded; as opposed to forward market.

spot payment payment made immediately upon a sale being concluded.

spot price price of goods, commodities, securities etc. in a spot market.

spread 1 the difference between two prices; **2** in securities trading, the difference between asking and offering prices, that is, between what the buyer is willing to pay and the seller is willing to accept.

spreadsheet 1 graphical depiction of accounting or other data in multi-column form; **2** a computer software program that arranges data in spreadsheet form.

Square Mile colloquial term for the area of the City of London where the bulk of its trading and financial services institutions are concentrated.

stability economic condition characterized by low and steady growth.

stabilization policy government policies aimed at stabilizing economic performance so as to avoid either inflation or recession.

stabilized exchange rates exchange rates where government intervention has succeeded in maintaining rates at or about a particular level.

staff general term for employees; sometimes also used to refer specifically to employees not directly involved in the production line.

staff appraisal *see* appraisal.

staff association *see* employee association.

staff management management of administrative or support functions, as opposed to line management.

staff status the definition that a particular activity is a 'staff' rather than a 'line' function.

stag colloquial term for an investor who buys and sells shares rapidly, taking a profit from each sale.

staged payment payment made at equal intervals until the sum outstanding is paid off.

stagflation economic condition which combines unacceptable levels of inflation with stagnation.

staggered working day work day with hours timed to start/finish earlier or later than normal.

stagnation very low or zero rate of economic growth.

stakeholder persons or organizations who contribute to or are affected by a business, and are therefore assumed to have the right to express views on how the business conducts itself; typical stakeholders include customers, employees, government, suppliers and members of the general public.

stamp tax *see* transfer tax.

stamp trading use of trading stamps as a method of payment.

standard norm of behaviour to which people are expected to adhere; the level of quality required in a product or service.

standard costing system techniques used to establish standard costs.

standard costs assessment of costs which will be incurred under ordinary operating conditions, used as a tool for comparison with actual costs.

standard deviation measure of the extent to which individual figures vary from the average; in effect, an average of the average.

standard error 1 measure of the likelihood that data contained in a given sample or analysis are likely to be correct; **2** probability of error.

standardization 1 the elimination of variance; **2** the setting of standard product types, quality levels and so on to which all products made must then conform.

standardization, advertising *see* advertising standardization.

standardized product industries industries which produce highly standardized products, usually using mass production or batch production techniques.

standard of living measure of the relative wealth of the population of a country, in particular on the extent to which they enjoy the possession of certain consumer goods.

standard performance rate of productivity which can be expected under normal conditions.

standard profit earnings per unit of production under standard costing.

standards plural of standard, used to describe a set of norms or conditions to which adherence is required.

standard time time taken to complete a task under normal conditions.

standby situation where workers are available for work and can be called in at short notice.

standby pay special rate of pay paid to workers on standby.

standing committee committee which is established on a permanent basis.

standing cost *see* fixed cost.

standing order 1 fixed procedures by which meetings are conducted; **2** order given to a bank by a customer to make regular payments to a named party.

staple basic commodity.

start-up business newly established business, usually small.

start-up costs costs incurred in establishing a new business.

state general term for government in its role as representative of the people at large.

state aid *see* state subsidies.

stateless corporation *see* stateless globalism.

stateless globalism condition of very large multinational corporations which in effect are operating worldwide and are no longer dependent on any one company.

statement record of financial transactions; *see also* financial statement.

statement, financial *see* financial statement.

state of the art most advanced and sophisticated design or technology currently available.

state pension pension provided by government from a state-run pension scheme.

state subsidies payments made by government to individuals or companies with a view to encouraging certain kinds of economic activity.

station *see* workstation.

statistical modelling general term for the use of statistical techniques in modelling and forecasting.

statistical process control computerized process control systems based on statistical programming.

statistical quality control quality control system based on statistical measures of the quality of goods produced; statistical stock control; *see* stock control.

statistics data collected and present in numerical form.

status situation; rank or authority.

status agreement agreement as to whether a particular job should be designated as either line or staff.

status quo 1 position as at present; **2** unchanged position.

status symbol product or good which serves to confirm or enhance the user's prestige and status among peers.

statutory audit audit of a firm's accounts which is required by local law.

statutory company company established and owned by the state.

statutory minimum wage minimum wage which must be paid to all employees, as required by local law.

statutory pension scheme pension plan to which all must by law contribute.

statutory reporting reporting of financial and other data which is required by local law.

statutory undertaking *see* statutory company.

steady state a condition whereby economic conditions, market performance, output, etc. are neither declining or rising; an assumption, in planning, that there will be no large fluctuations in currently existing conditions.

stepped cost costs which increase incrementally in proportion with increases in production, trading and so on.

stepped increase pay increase which results in different rates of pay increase for different grades of employee.

stewardship accounting recording and monitoring of business transactions with a view to oversight rather than analysis.

stimulus external factor which provokes a response.

stochastic process decision-making process where, in conditions of uncertainty, decisions are based on best probabilities of what will occur or is occurring.

stock 1 merchandise, components or materials held in inventory; **2** shares in a particular company.

stockbroker broker who buys and sells shares on behalf of clients.

stock certificate *see* share certificate.

stock control general term for the management of goods and materials held in inventory, including the monitoring of stock levels, reordering and distribution to other parts of the organization.

stock cover length of time current stocks will last at the present rate of consumption.

stock dividend *see* dividend.

stock exchange the formal institutions which comprise a stock market.

Stock Exchange Automated Quotation International (SEAQI) London-based market for shares in companies listed outside the UK.

stockholder's equity *see* shareholder equity.

stockholding the shares in a company owned by an individual or institution.

stock index *see* share index.

stocking agent agent who carries stocks of goods in a warehouse, rather than ordering goods purchased directly from the manufacturer.

stock in trade a firm's primary business activity.

stockist retailer who carries a certain product or brand in stock and offers it for sale.

stock jobber jobber who trades in bulk lots of shares.

stock loss decrease in the value of stocks or shares.

stock market the market in which shares are bought and sold.

stock options reward or incentive given to top managers whereby they are offered the right to purchase shares in the company at a favourable price, if they so wish.

stockout situation where all stocks in inventory have been sold or consumed.

stockpile large reserve of goods, materials, merchandise and so on held in inventory in anticipation of demand.

stock purchasing purchasing of stock to maintain or increase stock levels.

stocks plural of stock; synonym for shares.

stock shortage situation where stocks are in short supply.

stock transfer change of ownership of shares which takes place as a result of transactions in a stock market; the transfer involves the issuing of new share certificates and the recording of the name of the new owner.

stock turnover rate at which merchandise or other goods held in inventory are sold or consumed and must be replaced.

stop loss form of reinsurance that is activated once the insurer's losses reach a certain level.

stop order order given to a broker to buy or sell a given security once it reaches a specific price.

stoppage 1 any halting of a process or programme; **2** in industrial action, general term for stopping work, including strikes, sit-down strikes and so on.

stoppage time time lost due to stoppages.

stop payment order given to a bank to cancel or refuse to pay a cheque which will shortly be presented.

stop price price at which a stop order is activated and the broker proceeds to conduct the desired transaction.

store 1 a retail outlet; *see also* shop; **2** a place where goods, merchandise, materials and so on are held, such as a warehouse or depot.

store audit analysis of the merchandise currently in stock in a retail outlet; can also include analysis of the sales performance of each product or line.

store card credit card issued by a retailer to its customers.

storming *see* brainstorming.

straight line depreciation simple form of calculation of depreciation, whereby deprecation is calculated in terms of uniform amounts at regular time intervals.

straight loan loan which is not backed up by collateral.

straight time basic rate of pay for standard tasks conducted in normal working hours.

stranger group in market research, reference group composed of people who do not know each other and have never met before.

strategic alliance arrangement whereby two companies cooperate to reach a common objective but without formally merging.

strategic assets those assets which enable a company to succeed in its chosen strategy, or which are necessary for such a strategy in the first place.

strategic audit survey conducted as part of the strategy-making process, which assesses an organization's current strategies and their appropriateness and fit.

strategic business unit (SBU) distinctive business activities conducted within a large company or corporation, which can be defined as a separate sub-organization and given responsibility for planning, strategy and so on.

strategic change the adaptation of a company, its goals and policies, structure, organization and systems in order to proceed in a new strategic direction.

strategic choice the choices made by a company's leaders which then dictate a company's strategy, organization and so on.

strategic competence the accumulated knowledge and skills within a company which serve as a source of competitive advantage.

strategic decision decision between one or more strategic options, which sets a company's strategy towards a particular goal or path.

strategic direction general statement of the way in which a company intends to progress and develop, without naming specific targets.

strategic goods goods exempted from GATT rules because they have military significance for the importer, exporter or both.

strategic groups groups or teams who are charged with developing strategy and generating strategic options.

strategic imperatives driving forces that shape strategy, or cause strategies to be defined.

strategic management management task, usually performed by senior executives, for defining and setting company strategy.

strategic marketing planning long-term marketing planning which defines when and where a company will seek its markets and how it will reach them.

strategic planning planning process whereby a firm establishes how it will attempt to meet its long-term goals and the direction in which it will proceed.

strategic posture the relationship between a firm and its markets, competitors and so on; the basis from which the firm attempts to carry out its strategy.

strategic reorientation change in direction of an existing strategy in order to focus on new goals or new methods of reaching goals.

strategic resources those resources which are deemed necessary for the successful implementation of a strategy.

strategic transformation widespread change within the firm and its organization, systems and structures in order to deal with environmental changes and develop new strategies.

strategic turnaround recovery of an organization from a position of decline or near failure, returning it to a position of growth and success.

strategy planned approach to the achievement of long-term goals, including the activities a firm will undertake, the resources it will require, the markets where it will do business and so on.

strategy implementation the putting into practice of the concepts outlined in a strategy.

strategy making the overall process of defining, developing, planning and implementing a strategy.

stratification *see* segmentation.

stream flow of information or materials.

street broker broker who is not a member of a formal exchange.

street-name stocks stocks held in the name of a stockbroker for trading purposes.

stress 1 condition where excessive physical and psychological pressure on an employee can lead to exhaustion, impaired judgement or even problems with mental and physical health; **2** in engineering, excessive pressure placed on a piece of machinery which causes damage over the long term.

stretch finance additional loan capital provided to a business which is failing to meet its financial targets.

stretch out redefinition of jobs to take on more tasks or responsibilities.

strike in industrial disputes, a situation where employees stop work and refuse to report for work until the dispute is settled; may be accompanied by other action such as picketing.

strike benefits money paid by unions to striking workers as compensation for lost wages; *see also* strike pay.

strikebreaker a worker who continues to report for work when strike action has been called by the union.

strikebreaking working during a strike in defiance of the union; also sometimes used to mean forcing workers to end a strike.

strike fund *see* defence fund.

strike pay partial or entire equivalent to wages paid by unions to members who are on strike.

striker worker who is on strike.

striker-days days per employee of work lost due to strike action.

striking price price at which buyer and seller agree to complete a transaction.

string diagram diagram showing work-flows, often using pieces of coloured string to trace material and product flows.

structural adjustment programme economic recovery programmes instigated in developing countries, aimed at reforming or improving the economies of these countries.

structural determinants environmental or organizational factors that influence behaviour.

structural inertia the in-built tendency of organizations towards inertia, often leading to resistance to change.

structural principles basic theoretical principles of organizations, defining the structures around which they should be built.

structural unemployment long-term unemployment created when the skills demanded by employers are not the same as those possessed by prospective workers.

structure the manner in which an organization is constructed, including such aspects as hierarchy, lines of communication and spans of control.

structure chart graphic depiction of the structure of an organization.

structure–conduct–performance paradigm the theory that market structure is the basic determinant of the behaviour and profitability of firms within the market.

structure tree *see* structure chart.

structured interview *see* interview, structured.

structured query language interface used to access information held in a computer database, usually designed as part of the database program.

study planned programme of research or inquiry into a specific subject.

style 1 in design, a distinctive shape or pattern; **2** in management, the philosophy or approach used by different managers, formed of a combination of personal attributes, skills and beliefs about themselves and their work.

subcontracting offering work on a contract basis to another person or organization rather than doing it oneself.

subculture subordinate culture within a larger culture.

subject population population being studied or analysed.

subjective test test where the results are scored by an examiner based on the latter's own opinion or knowledge of a subject.

subliminal advertising advertising which seeks to create an impression in the mind of the consumer without the latter necessarily being aware of the advertising at all (illegal in some jurisdictions).

sub-network network which is in itself a part of another network.

subrogation assignment of rights in a legal case to another party.

subscriber anyone who subscribes to a share offer; *see* subscription.

subscription formal offer to purchase shares when they are issued.

subsidiary organization which is owned or controlled by another organization.

subsidization the practice of granting subsidies.

subsidy payments or rebates by government to businesses with the aim of encouraging certain forms of business activity.

subsistence theory of wages view by the classical economists that personal earnings tend to equal the minimum level of income necessary for subsistence.

subsistence wage minimum wage required if the worker and his or her family are to be able to pay for necessities such as housing and food.

substandard below the required or acceptable standard.

substantive agreement agreement which resolves most or all of the issues under dispute in collective bargaining, but which must still be ratified by all parties.

substitution using one product or service in place of another.

success factor general term for factors which, if controlled and directed, lead to the success of a project.

succession 1 the transfer of rights, property, etc. from one person to another; **2** in management, the replacement of one executive with another.

succession management specific aspect of human resources management which ensures that senior or particularly valuable employees are replaced quickly without loss of effectiveness.

succession planning aspect of succession management which involves planning future succession needs.

successive approximation succession of approximately true statements or results which gradually bring the researcher close to the truth.

suggestion award reward by employer to employees who make valuable suggestions through a suggestion scheme.

suggestion scheme formal scheme for gathering employee views as to how the company could become more efficient or effective, increase productivity and so on.

suite a group of associated computer software programs.

sunk capital capital which has already been allocated or expended on a project and which cannot be recovered.

sunk cost cost that has already been incurred.

sunlight test in business ethics, rule of thumb by which actions can be judged as desirable or undesirable, the criterion being whether the action in question would result in embarrassment or sanctions should it come to public notice.

sunlighting re-entering paid employment after retirement.

'sunrise' industries industrial sectors judged to be at the forward edge of technological advancement and having considerable potential for growth; in advanced economies, examples include biotechnology and electronics.

'sunset' industries industrial sectors judged to have little capability for growth or rejuvenation, and where long-term performance looks set to decline.

superannuation pension benefit payable after retiring; synonym for pension.

supermarket large retail outlet specializing in selling foodstuffs.

supernumerary employee who is in excess of the minimum labour requirements.

superstore very large retail outlet located in an out-of-town location, sometimes specializing in a relatively limited number of product lines.

supervisor low-level manager responsible for supervising the work of others.

supervisory board in Germany, the more senior of the two boards of directors that all public companies are required to have.

supervisory staff managers responsible for supervising the work of employees.

supervisory training training for employees recently promoted to supervisory posts.

supplement additional or extra quantity.

supplementary training additional training which complements training programmes already completed.

supplier company or individual supplying materials, goods or services to another company.

supplier association association of companies involved in the supply of a particular type of raw material or component.

supplier base in manufacturing, general term for the firms and organizations which serve as suppliers of components or raw materials.

supplier credit credit granted by suppliers to companies buying from them.

supplier relationship relationship developed between a manufacturer and its suppliers in order to ensure an adequate and timely flow of materials and/or components.

supply materials, components, goods, services and so on which are required in order to conduct business operations.

supply and demand in economics, the two primary forces affecting markets.

supply chain management integrative management approach which seeks to control or influence all elements within the supply chain in order to ensure an adequate and timely flow of materials, components and finished goods.

supply price lowest price which will be accepted by a seller.

supply-side economics economic theory that supply, rather than demand, determines economic output; the most notable proponents of this theory are A. Laffer and Milton Friedman.

support activities processes and functions which support the main production and marketing activities, such as administration, accounting, human resources and so on.

support buying buying of currency by a central bank in order to help maintain present exchange rates.

supportive leadership management philosophy which emphasizes encouraging and supporting employees rather then directing and controlling them.

support staff staff involved in administrative and other activities rather than directly involved in production; *see also* staff.

surcharge 1 additional charge levied on a good; **2** additional tax levied as a penalty for late payment, etc.

surety a separate bond or guarantee confirming that a person or organization will carry out their part of a contract, specifying penalties should they fail.

surplus excess or overage.

surrender value cash value of an insurance policy should the holder wish to cancel the policy and return it to the insurer.

surrogate market *see* quasi-market.

surtax additional tax imposed over and above normal limits.

survey study of a given area of land, or of a defined population, noting all relevant characteristics.

surveying conducting a survey.

suspended trading cessation of trading on a stock exchange in the face of extraordinary events; may affect a particular stock, or the entire exchange.

suspense account account used to hold items temporarily before they are allocated permanent status within another account.

suspension temporary cessation of business or employment; in the case of the latter, suspension is sometimes used as a disciplinary measure.

sustainable development in developing countries, economic policies that are designed to promote growth without undermining the country's ecology or resource base.

sustainable economic growth *see* sustainability.

sustainability economic conditions whereby output can continue at a steady or growth state without exhausting resources.

swap transaction which involves an exchange of goods, commitments, liabilities, etc. rather than money.

swap fund fund whereby investors pool their investments and each take a share of the resulting income.

swaption option to enter into a swap contract.

sweated labour underpaid workers who work long hours, often in poor working conditions.

sweatshop working environment where employees are paid very low wages and often work in poor or hazardous conditions.

sweetheart deal agreement of mutual advantage to all parties directly involved (though not necessarily to the advantage of all parties affected).

swing shift working shift where workers actually work a variety of different shift hours rather than a regular shift.

switching consumer or buyer behaviour which involves ceasing to purchase or disposing of one product or good, instead buying another product or good which is now preferred.

switch selling sales technique which first offers one product to a buyer and then, on acceptance, withdraws the offer and offers a second product instead.

SWOT analysis analysis of a firm's competitive position in terms of strengths, weaknesses, opportunities and threats.

syllogism logical deduction.

symbol sign or image which represents a larger and more complex thing or concept; *see also* logo.

symbol groups voluntary associations of retailers trading under a single brand name but remaining independent.

symbolic information information which is used rationally rather than intuitively.

symbolic pricing pricing so that the price set helps to create an image of the product or service in the minds of consumers.

symbolic simulation simulations built using symbols, including mathematical representations; *see also* mathematical model.

sympathy strike strike action conducted by workers in a different location and/or different union in support of other workers already involved in an industrial dispute.

symposium meeting or conference devoted to a specific subject.

syndicalism left-wing political movement which advocated the seizure of control by the workers of the means of production and the state through strikes and industrial action.

syndicate association of people or organizations for the purposes of making an investment or carrying out a business activity.

syndicated lending loan made by a syndicate or association of banks.

syndicated research large-scale research projects conducted by a syndicate of companies.

synergism *see* synergy.

synergistic takeover unopposed takeover of one firm by another which allows them to combine their efforts and resources to greater effect.

synergy additional strength or energy achieved by combining the efforts of more than one person, business unit, company, etc., so that the whole is greater than the sum of the parts.

syntax construction of written or verbal commands, or the order in which they must appear, of particular importance when writing computer software programs.

syntax error error in computer program which occurs when commands do not follow each other in the proper sequence.

synthetic standards work and productivity standards created through the observation and measurement of work.

system process or organization by which things are done.

system design the process of designing a physical system or network.

system dynamics the application of systems thinking to industrial systems; in practical terms, a set of techniques for modelling systems, organizations, markets, etc. in dynamic form, often used in forecasting.

systems analysis analysis of systems or methods currently in use.

systems design *see* system design.

systems engineering use of engineering techniques to design and maintain systems.

systems of production systems and processes used to produce goods.

systems selling selling a package of related or dependent services and goods.

T

tachistoscope device used in market research for determining the optimum length of time that an advertisement should be displayed.

tactics methods used to achieve immediate, short-term goals.

tainted goods goods which are presently subject to boycott.

take colloquial term which can mean either revenue or profit.

take-home pay employee earnings after tax and other deductions.

take-off 1 in economics, stage where an economy begins to grow rapidly towards industrialization; **2** in marketing, stage where a new product, service or brand, having been introduced, begins to find widespread acceptance among customers.

take-off period time during which take-off takes place.

takeover the acquisition of another firm through purchase; *see also* acquisition.

takeover bid offer to purchase outstanding shares in an effort to gain a controlling interest in a company.

takeover, hostile *see* hostile takeover.

takeover, synergistic *see* synergistic takeover.

take stock 1 to survey and make a record of current inventory; **2** colloquially, to assess a position or situation.

talking shop conversation about professional matters.

tally count or number.

tangibility condition of assets or goods which have physical existence and can be apprehended through the senses.

tangible assets asset which has a physical existence; as opposed to intangible assets.

tangible property property which exists in physical form.

tapered increase pay increase which gives proportionally more to lower paid workers than to the higher paid.

tare weight of transported goods, or of an empty transport vehicle.

target 1 synonym for goal; **2** stated level of performance, production, productivity, etc. which a company wishes to achieve.

target audience people at whom a particular communication or promotion is aimed.

target customer consumers who have been identified as potential customers and at whom promotional efforts are then aimed.

targeted marketing marketing programmes aimed at a specific market or segment.

target management the management of a company which is the target of a takeover bid or merger proposal.

target market the group of customers at whom the seller directs promotional and other marketing efforts.

target population population which is the subject of a survey or other research effort.

target price price set for agricultural products under the European Union's Common Agricultural Policy.

tariff a tax, especially on imported or exported goods.

tariff barrier tariff imposed at a rate which discourages imports.

tariff, preferential *see* preferential tariffs.

tariff war form of trade war in which nations levy high and discriminatory tariffs on each others' goods.

task a specific piece of work, carried out with an immediate objective in mind.

task analysis analysis of the nature of a particular task and the effort required to complete it.

task-based appraisal appraisal of employee performance which focuses on the employee's ability to carry out assigned tasks.

task-based participation form of worker participation whereby workers or work groups are given considerable autonomy in terms of defining tasks and determining how they should be carried out.

task dependency situation where one employee or work team is reliant on the efforts of others to complete their own tasks.

task description formal statement of the activities required to complete a task.

task force team or group of workers given responsibility for completing a particularly complex task.

task orientation management philosophy which focuses on tasks, including task definition, assignment and completion.

task uncertainty situation where employees are uncertain as to what tasks they should perform, or in what order.

tax income-raising mechanism used by government; taxes can be levied on income (direct taxes) or on activity (indirect taxes).

tax abatement temporary decrease in the amount of tax levied, usually in recognition of the special circumstances of the party being taxed.

taxable income portion of income on which tax is assessed and must be paid.

tax accountant accountant who specializes in preparing tax returns and calculating tax to be paid.

taxation *see* tax.

taxation, corporate tax levied on business profits.

taxation domicile the country in which a company is considered to be resident for the purposes of tax assessment.

taxation law systems of laws and regulations on which the tax system is based.

taxation, personal tax levied on personal income.

taxation reform amendment to the tax system with a view to creating a more efficient or more equitable system of taxation.

taxation shield *see* tax shield.

taxation system *see* tax system.

tax avoidance methods used, sometimes illegally, to avoid being assessed for tax; *see also* tax evasion.

tax credit tax reduction or rebate on tax paid, usually granted in order to stimulate certain types of business activity.

tax dodge method, usually illegal, of avoiding or evading tax.

tax evasion methods used, usually illegally, to avoid paying tax which has been assessed; *see also* tax avoidance.

tax exemption special condition where a particular type of transaction or income is exempt from tax assessment and payment.

tax haven country or territory which offers very low tax rates to residents.

tax holiday temporary tax exemption or reduction in the rate of tax paid.

tax-option corporation US form of corporation which pays no income tax, with tax instead being paid individually by the owners.

tax planning plan for the distribution of income into various forms of tax-exempt or low tax investment in order to minimize the amount of tax paid.

tax rate amount of tax which is paid, usually expressed as a percentage of the value of the income, goods or transactions being taxed.

tax reduction lowering the rate of tax being paid.

tax schedule documents required by taxation officials as a statement of income and taxable income.

tax shelter legitimate device by which some portion of income or transactions is exempt from tax assessment and payment.

tax shield depreciation or losses charged against income, thereby lowering the total of taxable income.

tax system governmental mechanisms for assessing, levying and collecting tax income.

tax year twelve-month period used by tax authorities as the basis for calculating income and tax due.

Taylorism synonym for scientific management, the system of management developed by Frederick Winslow Taylor.

team group of people working together and joining their efforts to reach a common goal.

team building the process of establishing effective teams and work groups.

teamster driver of a lorry or truck; in the US, member of a teamsters' union.

teamwork work that is performed by people working in teams, usually with the aim of achieving greater effectiveness than could be achieved by the same people working individually.

technical change *see* technological change.

technical manager manager whose work focuses on some technical aspect of production or delivery.

technical position summary of the factors affecting a firm's position, including both internal and external forces.

technical progress *see* technological change.

technical risk risk which can be calculated to exist but which in fact may not be present.

technical skill skill required to handle certain technical tasks, particularly those involving machinery or electronics.

technician worker who has a high level of technical skill in one or more fields.

techniques methods by which a task is carried out.

technological change advances in technology which offer opportunities for new markets, new products, new processes, new ways of operating and so on.

technological development any change in technology which leads to technological change.

technological forecasting the anticipation of changes in technology and their likely results or impacts.

technological trend in technological forecasting, the identification of certain areas of technology that are in rapid development and the logical outcomes of these developments.

technological unemployment unemployment created when jobs formerly done by hand can now be done more cheaply by machinery, and workers are made redundant as a result.

technological university institute of higher education specializing in teaching subjects related to engineering and technology.

technologist person with high levels of skills in fields requiring the use of technology.

technology mechanical or electronic devices which are used in production, are built into products, or are used to make systems more efficient; application of science to business and industry.

technology agreement agreement between management and employees concerning the introduction of technology into a workplace.

technology-based training training methods which use technology aids such as simulations, interactive video, computer-aided training and so on to impart primary learning.

technology investment investment in acquiring new technologies.

technology management management techniques specifically related to the use of technology to perform work.

technology, new *see* new technology.

technology, paradigmatic *see* paradigmatic technology.

technology strategy element of a firm's strategy which sets out which technologies it wishes to acquire and when, and the uses to which these will be put.

technostructure that part of the structure of an organization within which technical activities take place.

telecommunications communications using the worldwide system of satellite communications and land lines including telephone, video, fax, e-mail and so on.

telecommuting *see* teleworking.

tele-conferencing conference using audio or video telephonic links, putting all participants in real time communication with each other.

telecottage place where teleworking is carried out.

telemarketing direct sales technique using the telephone rather than personal visits.

teleprocessing data processing using computers in remote locations, with commands sent and data received over telephone lines.

teleshopping purchasing goods or services using telecommunications links, either by telephone or by computer using the Internet.

teleworking working from home, and sending and receiving data across telephone lines using telephones, faxes and computers connected to the Internet.

temporary exports goods which are taken abroad on a short-term basis for a specific purpose other than sale, and which are thus exempt from export or import tariffs.

temporary staff workers hired on a short-term basis only, often to cope with unusual or seasonal demand.

temporary worker worker hired on a short-term basis only, whose employment terminates as soon as the specific purpose for which he or she was hired has been accomplished.

tender in contracting out, a formal offer or bid for the work being contracted, usually accompanied by an estimated price for completion.

tender, issue by *see* issue by tender.

tender offer bid for shares issued by tender.

tenure period of secure employment during which an employee will not be dismissed.

term stated length of time, often used to describe the time between the granting of a loan and its final repayment.

term bill *see* time bill.

terminal 1 final; 2 in computing, a workstation where commands can be input and data received, usually consisting of a monitor, keyboard and mouse.

terminal arbitration arbitration aimed at overcoming remaining differences and reaching a final agreement.

terminal market market dealing in futures.

terminal qualification qualifications received on completion of a training programme.

terminal value value of an investment when it is terminated or matures; future value of an investment allowing for interest and/or depreciation.

termination ending of a contract, particularly a contract of employment.

term loan a long-term loan, often with a term of ten years or more.

term policy insurance policy valid for more than one year.

terms and conditions specific clauses in a contract specifying what is to be performed and by which party.

term shares shares which are held under the condition that they cannot be resold for a specified period of time.

terms of sale statement of the conditions of a sale, including the price, delivery terms and any credit advanced.

terms of trade measure of international trade performance.

term structure of interest rates the relationship between fixed interest securities with differing maturity dates, which is reflected in their differing interest rates.

territorial dispute 1 dispute between two unions as to which has the right to recruit employees in a particular workplace; 2 dispute between two nations as to which has title a particular piece of territory.

territorial taxation system tax system within a particular jurisdiction, usually either a country or a portion of a country such as a state/province or city.

terrorism political action involving violence causing destruction and death, aimed at causing widespread fear and destabilizing the local government and economy.

test battery range of tests used for a particular purpose.

test in depth detailed check or test.

testing experimental examination of a product, system, etc. in either laboratory or field conditions.

test marketing experimental marketing of small quantities of a product or service in a limited market so as to gain more information.

tests experimental examinations; *see also* testing.

theoretical requirements forecasting forecast of future requirements in terms of resources, labour and so on.

theory 1 set of ideas about how a system, process, people, etc. will function or behave in practice; 2 conceptualization of something that may exist but has not yet been proven to exist.

theory of concentration Marxist economic theory that, with the passage of time, more and more capital will become concentrated in fewer and fewer hands.

Theory X and Theory Y concept of human motivation formulated by Douglas McGregor, describing people's actions and behaviour in the workplace.

thin market market in which there is very little activity by either buyers or sellers.

third market securities which are officially listed on an exchange but are actually traded on the over-the-counter market.

third party intervention action by a party not involved in a dispute to resolve the dispute and bring the conflicting parties together.

Third World general term for the underdeveloped countries of Africa, Asia and Latin America.

threat anything which could cause a company to suffer a loss, either in real terms or of its competitive position.

threat matrix matrix chart which classifies potential threats according to their seriousness and probability of occurrence.

threshold lowest acceptable limit.

threshold price minimum price for grain and cereals set under the European Union's Common Agricultural Policy.

threshold worker worker entering employment for the first time.

throw-away disposable product which is used once and then discarded.

tied indicators performance indicator which is linked other similar indicators.

Tiger economies the rapidly industrializing nations of East and Southeast Asia, usually including Taiwan, Singapore, Malaysia, Indonesia and Thailand, which through most of the 1980s and 1990s were characterized by very high rates of growth; *see also* Dragon economies.

tight credit *see* tight money.

tight money situation where interest rates are very high and borrowing is difficult.

tight rate work situation where productivity bonuses are difficult to earn; as opposed to loose rate.

till in retail outlets, cash register or drawer where money is kept and transactions are recorded.

time and motion study work study which focuses on the physical movements made by employees and the time taken to make each.

time bill bill of exchange which is due to be paid on a specified date.

time buyer advertising agency manager who purchases advertising space from television and radio stations.

time loan loan which must be repaid after a specified number of days.

time management planning tasks and processes so as to use time in the most efficient manner possible.

time note promissory note which is due to be paid on a specified date.

time period principle in financial accounting, the setting of the length of time to be covered by each accounting cycle.

time preference 1 economic measure of the value of present consumption versus future consumption; **2** the decision as to whether to invest or spend funds available.

time rate wage paid for work for a specific period of time; *see* hourly rate.

time-related payment scheme pay system where wages are paid according to a previously determined time rate.

time server worker who does the minimum amount of work possible.

time sharing system where the same piece of equipment is used to carry out two operations simultaneously.

time study work study which focuses on the time required to perform certain tasks or run certain processes.

time to market time elapsed from the conception and prototyping of a new product until it can be introduced into the market on a commercial basis.

timework work for which wages are paid on a time rate.

tip 1 gratuity given to service personnel in exchange for prompt or good quality service; **2** in securities trading, private or unofficial recommendation to buy or sell.

title ownership of property.

tokenism hiring practice where a small number of people from minority groups are hired in an effort to appear to be conforming with equal opportunities policies.

token order very small order for a product or service, placed in order to test the product or service or to comply with some other requirement.

tolerance the extent to which a product or service may deviate from the specification.

toll form of taxation most commonly levied on the use of infrastructure facilities such as roads and bridges.

tools mechanical or electronic devices used to carry out a task.

top-down approach philosophy of management whereby all key decisions are made at the top of the organization and then communicated down to subordinates.

top-down training training programmes where senior echelons of the company receiving training before lower levels.

top hat pension scheme special pension scheme designed for senior executives.

top management the uppermost level of management, usually consisting of the board of directors and the senior departmental or divisional managers.

top-out peak period of demand.

total constructive loss situation where the damage to an asset exceeds its total insured value, even though it may still be possible to salvage the asset and use it again at a later date.

total cost sum of all fixed and variable costs.

total debt sum of all obligations and liabilities.

total income sum of all revenue from all sources.

total loss situation where an asset has been damaged to the point where it is no longer usable; *see also* total constructive loss.

total loss control programmes designed to minimize loss or damage to assets.

total quality control quality control systems applied across an organization.

total quality management (TQM) comprehensive approach to quality which focuses first on customer definitions of quality and then on orienting the entire production function towards achieving products and/or services of this quality.

total productive maintenance maintenance policy designed to yield maximum effectiveness over the lifetime of a firm's machinery or equipment.

total remuneration sum of all wages and fringe benefits received as a reward for work performed.

total retirement benefits sum of all benefits received by an employee upon retirement.

total revenue *see* total income.

touchscreen system of computer control whereby the user touches panels that appear on the monitor; the computer senses the pressure of the touch and interprets the commands accordingly.

tourism management management techniques and skills specific to management in the tourism industry.

Toyodaism management philosophy behind the Toyota production system.

Toyota production system production system developed by the Toyota corporation, including elements such as just-in-time production, *kaizen* and teamwork.

TQM *see* total quality management.

track record past performance.

trade commerce or exchange between businesses or countries.

trade association association of companies engaged in the same or similar lines of business, formed to help advance the mutual interests of all member companies.

trade barrier *see* tariff barrier.

trade deficit negative balance of trade.

trade discount discount for bulk buying, usually offered to companies buying on a wholesale basis.

trade dispute *see* industrial dispute.

trade fair event where a large number of manufacturers and distributors gather to exhibit their products to potential buyers.

trade magazine journal carrying items of news of interest to managers in a particular industry.

trademark image, logo or other graphical material associated with a brand and which, if registered as such, may not be reproduced or copied without the permission of the trademark holder.

trade mission excursion by politicians and business people to another country for the purpose of promoting trade links.

trade name name which a business uses when trading in order to identify itself to customers; may be different from the official registered name.

trade-off selection of an alternative which provides the largest number of advantages even though this may mean giving up some other advantages.

trade promotion promotions of products or services by manufacturers or distributors and aimed at retailers rather than end consumers.

trader person engaged in trade, particularly in both buying and selling.

trade reference report attesting to a company's creditworthiness.

trades council council of representatives of trade unions.

trade union association of employees who combine in order to engage in collective bargaining with management over issues such as pay, working conditions and so on.

trade union federation association of national trade unions.

trade union recognition *see* recognition.

trading buying and selling of goods, commodities, securities, etc.

trading area geographical area in which firm trades; *see also* market.

trading down marketing strategy which attempts to reach a larger audience by means such as changing the image of a product, reducing the price and altering promotional strategies.

trading estate *see* industrial estate.

trading floor *see* floor.

trading name *see* trade name.

trading post particular place on the floor of an exchange where deals can be made.

trading profit profit.

trading stamps stamps or coupons which can be collected or traded by consumers and redeemed against the purchase of certain goods or services with participating retailers.

trading up marketing strategy which attempts to reach a high-income market segment by means such as changing the image of a product, increasing the price and altering promotional strategies.

tradition custom or way of doing things which has become part of standard practice or beliefs.

traffic **1** flow of goods or merchandise; **2** flow of people through a retail outlet.

train to instruct someone in a new skill or procedure.

trainability extent to which someone can be trained.

trainee person being trained, or undergoing a training programme.

trainer person who leads a training programme and ensures that training is delivered to trainees.

training the process of instructing or educating people so that they learn new skills and/or procedures

training agency company or institution specializing in providing training programmes.

training audit analysis of a company's training needs and/or ability to conduct training programmes for employees.

training design design of training programmes so as to provide the most effective and efficient training to employees.

training economics analysis of the costs and benefits of training programmes.

training function aspect of human resources management, which includes the identification of training needs, the sourcing and delivery of appropriate training programmes, and the evaluation of the effectiveness of these programmes.

training, in-company *see* in-company training.

training loop process whereby training needs are assessed, training is delivered and the effectiveness of training is assessed.

training officer manager responsible for assessing training needs and providing training programmes for employees where needed.

training plan overall programme of training to be delivered to employees.

training specification definition of training required by an employee or group of employees.

training time time required to deliver a training programme.

training transfer extent to which knowledge gained through training is diffused and spread to other employees.

tranche portion or section.

transaction trade or business deal between two parties; any agreement between two parties.

transaction analysis analysis of dealings and relationships between parties.

transaction cost costs associated with exchanges or transactions in a market; literally, the cost of making a transaction.

transaction cost economics economic theory first developed by Ronald Coase which focuses on the role played by transaction costs in economic behaviour.

transfer to move goods from one location to another; to move employees from one job or location to another.

transfer costs costs incurred during the transfer of goods between departments of an organization.

transfer pricing notional price charged by one department to another when goods are transferred within an organization.

transfer tax tax levied whenever goods change ownership.

translation 1 rendering speech or written documents from one language into another; **2** more generally, synonym for conversion.

transnational corporation *see* multinational corporation.

transportation methods of conveying goods or people from one location to another.

transportation matrix graphic depiction of transportation requirements at a given time and place.

trans-shipment transfer of goods or people being transported from one carrier to another (for example, from road to rail).

travel-to-work area geographical region from which a company recruits employees, defined as the distance employees are willing to commute to and from work.

travelling salesman salesperson who personally visits prospective customers within his or her geographical sales area.

treasury bill government security issued and traded on the open market.

treasury stock stock which has been issued by a company and then bought back or otherwise reacquired by that company.

Treaty of Rome original treaty, signed in 1957, which established the European Economic Community (EEC), the forerunner of the European Union.

trend direction or tendency.

trend bucker someone who goes against prevailing trends.

trend setter influential person whose activities and behaviour are widely copied, thereby establishing a wider trend.

triad 1 as described by Kenichi Ohmae, the three most important trading and industrial centres, namely Japan, the USA and Western Europe; **2** also, the term for a Hong Kong-based criminal organization.

trial 1 initial use of a product or service by a customer, during which time the quality and benefits provided are evaluated; **2** alternatively, synonym for probation.

trial balance preliminary listing of all account balances.

trial period *see* probationary period.

trickle down in economics, the theory that wealth earned by large enterprises eventually results in increased prosperity for individuals.

trigger event which in turn sets off other events.

trigger price mechanism price level which, when reached, activates certain pre-planned actions.

troubleshooter manager whose primary function is to solve problems and deal with crises as and when they occur.

troubleshooting dealing with unexpected problems in production or distribution systems.

trough lowest point of a cycle.

truck system payment in kind rather than in cash; *see also* barter.

trust assets, money, etc. which is handed over to another party to manage on the owner's behalf; alternatively, a business culture in which employees and managers have confidence in each other and feel secure.

trust company company which manages trusts held for others, usually investment trusts.

trustee person nominated to manage funds or assets held in trust for others.

trusteeship the office of trustee.

trust fund 1 fund managed by trustees; **2** money held in trust.

turnaround reversal of a decline in profits or profitability, thus restoring the position of a declining company.

turnkey contract contract whereby the seller agrees to act as the single point of sale for a wide variety of goods and/or services sourced from other divisions and/or other countries.

turnkey system personal computer sold with a full suite of software, which is ready to be operated immediately the power is switched on.

turnover 1 frequency with which goods are sold, requiring inventory to be replenished; **2** frequency with which employees join and leave a company.

turnover ratios ratios of turnover to other business factors, such as profits, as an indicator of business activity and profitability.

turnover tax tax levied on goods at each stage of production or distribution; *see also* value added tax.

tutorial 1 training or learning session guided by a tutor; **2** anything which teaches or provides learning (e.g. manual, video, etc.).

twilight area region of a country which has suffered prolonged economic decline, characterized by high unemployment and by low wages and productivity.

twinning partnerships between business and educational establishments to provide training and research services.

two-bin system method of stock control in which a portion of stock is held in reserve, sometimes literally in a second bin.

two-tier board German management structure whereby each public company has two boards of directors, a management board responsible for the day-to-day running of the company, and a supervisory board with oversight powers.

two-tier monetary system exchange control system whereby a country sets two different rates of exchange for its currency, for use in different circumstances.

U

ultimate consumer the person who actually consumes or uses the goods purchased; not always synonymous with customer or buyer.

ultra vires beyond legal power or authority; to act 'ultra vires' is to go beyond what one is permitted to do.

unabsorbed cost overhead costs not allocated to a particular cost centre.

unadjusted rate of return in investment decisions, the ratio of future income required to future investment needed.

unbalanced growth situation where different parts of an economy grow at different speeds.

unbundle to separate products or services which were formerly delivered as a single package or bundle.

uncalled capital share capital which has not yet been called up.

uncertainty situation where the facts or issues are not clear; situation where only partial knowledge is available.

unclaimed balance funds left in inactive bank accounts which are eventually closed.

unconstitutional that which violates the agreed operating principles of an organization, particularly a labour union.

uncontrollable costs costs which cannot be controlled in terms of when they are incurred and/or their total amount.

UNCTAD *see* United Nations Conference on Trade and Development.

UNCITRAL *see* United Nations Commission on International Trade Law.

underemployment situation where an employee is not working to his or her full potential, usually because the tasks he or she is performing do not require the employee to use all of his or her skills.

undermanning situation where a company does not have enough employees to carry out all available tasks.

underselling setting prices at levels lower than those of competitors.

underwriter person or organization who determines the nature of insurance policies, including whether the insurer will accept the risk and the level of premiums and compensation.

underwriting the act of defining an insurance policy; *see also* underwriter.

undifferentiated marketing marketing which uses virtually the same marketing mix to market to all segments; *see also* mass marketing.

unearned income income derived from investments or capital gains, rather than directly from productive work.

unearned increment increase in value which is not directly due to any effort or investment by the owner of the asset.

unearned premium premium income which has not yet been paid in.

unemployable person who is unable to find work by reason of his or her lack of skills, physical or mental disabilities and so on.

unemployed person person who is not presently in work.

unemployment 1 condition of not being in work; **2** in economics, the total number of potential workers not in work.

unemployment benefit state benefit paid to workers who are unemployed to allow them subsistence.

unemployment rate ratio of unemployed workers to total number of workers available for work.

unfair competition competitive practices which take undue advantage of either the seller's own position or the lack of information among buyers in a market.

unfair dismissal situation where an employee is removed from his or her job without due cause.

unfair industrial practice *see* unfair labour practice.

unfair labour practice practices by employees which violate existing labour laws or regulations.

unfunded pension plan where no advance premiums have been paid before the scheme begins to pay benefits.

uniform 1 exactly similar; **2** alternatively, clothing worn by employees which identifies them as members of a particular firm.

uniform accounting accounting practices or systems which are adopted by a large number of different firms.

unilateral arbitration condition where, in a dispute, either party can refer the issue to a third-party arbitrator without reference to the other.

unilateral strategy strategy which is designed and implemented by top management with little or no reference to lower levels of the organization.

union *see* trade union.

unionized belonging to or member of a trade union.

union label mark attached to a product label specifying that it has been produced by unionized workers.

union rate hourly wage set by unions for particular kinds of work.

union recognition *see* recognition.

union shop workplace where a union is recognized and where all employees must be members; *see also* closed shop.

unique-product production production system dedicated to providing one-off or customized products, as opposed to batch production and mass production.

unique selling point (USP) feature of a product, brand or service which distinguishes it in the market, for example, by providing a bundle of benefits not available elsewhere in the market; this feature then becomes the focus of promotion and marketing tactics.

unit item or quantity of one; a small subgroup within an organization.

unitary (U-form) firm organization structure which is not divisionalized; instead, a single hierarchy encompasses the entire firm, and all management functions concentrate on the production of a single product line.

unitary perspective single view of a subject or issue, often to the exclusion of other possible views.

unitary system managerial system in which control is concentrated at a single point at the top of the organization.

unit billing invoice which lists all items or units purchased.

unit control inventory control method which involves listing all items currently held in inventory.

unit cost cost of producing, distributing and selling one unit of a good or service.

unit cost indicator cost factor (input or output) used in calculating unit costs.

unit cost ratio ratio of input costs to output costs.

United Nations Conference on Trade and Development (UNCTAD) United Nations agency which deals with problems of trade between advanced and less developed or developing countries.

United Nations Conference on International Trade Law (UNCITRAL) UN body which acts to arbitrate and resolve trade disputes on an international basis.

unit pricing price per unit of a good or service.

unit trust a form of mutual fund established for the purposes of making investments.

unity of command organization principle whereby all command functions emanate from a single leader.

unity of direction management principle whereby all parts of the organization must have the same strategic direction and goals.

universal design theory theory that there are universally applicable design principles that can be used to design organizations.

universalism social value in which people are seen as individuals within the framework of a larger society, but where individuality is the dominant focus; as opposed to collectivism.

universe in research, the total population or data which can possibly be surveyed or analysed.

unlimited accounts account where the account holder is eligible for an unlimited amount of credit.

unlisted security security which is not listed on a formal stock exchange, but is instead traded over the counter.

unloading sale of goods or securities rapidly in large volume to avoid losing money in times of price decline.

unofficial that which has not been formally directed or required; that which is outside the bounds of official control.

unofficial action **1** activity by a member of an organization that is a result of their own initiative, rather than as directed by their organization; **2** alternatively, action which is not formally reported or accountable.

unpaid balance portion of the purchase price that remains to be paid after any downpayment has been made.

unpaid dividends dividends that have been declared but have not yet been paid out.

unproductive time working time which is not directly devoted to production or support functions and which is essentially wasted.

unrealized profits profits which exist in theory but are not actually realized until goods, assets, securities, etc. are sold.

unrecorded expenses expenses which have been incurred but have not been formally recorded in the company's accounts.

unrecorded revenues revenues which have been received but have not been formally recorded in the company's accounts.

unregistered not formally registered or recognized in law.

unregistered union trade union whose existence has not been formally registered with government authorities.

unsecured creditor creditor who has not been offered any security or collateral.

unsecured debt debt which has been assumed without any collateral being offered.

unsecured loan loan where the lender does not require collateral from the borrower.

unskilled worker worker who possesses no significant skills and is fit only for simple manual work.

unsocial hours working hours beyond the normally defined working week, such as evenings and weekends.

unstructured interview *see* interview, unstructured.

updating bringing up-to-date.

upgrading improving to a higher standard.

upkeep *see* maintenance.

upscale above average.

upset price *see* reserve price.

upward appraisal appraisal of superiors by players.

upward delegation referring a problem or issues to a senior member of the organization.

upward feedback information about the outcomes of processes which is received by lower-ranking members of the firm which is passed up to more senior managers.

useless quality quality standards or features which are in excess of what is demanded or needed by customers.

user person who uses or consumes a product or service; *see also* consumer.

user benefit benefit derived from the use or consumption of a good.

user cost cost which the user of a good may incur in the course of acquiring, consuming, using or disposing of that good.

user expectation the expectations of benefits to be received which a user may have before purchasing or acquiring a good.

user friendly product, especially one featuring high levels of technology, deliberately designed to be easy to use with a minimum of instruction.

user value value placed on a good by its users.

USP *see* unique selling point.

usury interest, particularly very high levels of interest charged where the borrower has little choice but to pay.

utilities, public *see* public utility.

utility the extent to which a good performs the function for which it was designed.

utility theory theory used in risk analysis to determine how people assess utility in the context of risk.

V

vacation time off allowed to employees for rest and recreation.

vacation pay pay which employees continue to draw while on vacation.

validation **1** confirmation of validity; acceptance or confirmation that a certain action, thing, issue, etc. is relevant and true at a given time; **2** ratification.

VALS *see* values and lifestyles.

valuation setting a value on an asset or good; *see also* appraisal.

value **1** the worth which is assumed to be inherent in an asset or good; *see also* cost; price; **2** that which people hold to be important.

value added value which is added to materials or goods as they pass through various stages of the production and distribution process.

value added tax (VAT) indirect tax levied on goods when they are sold; *see also* sales tax.

value analysis analysis of business operations to ensure that each is efficient and is providing value to both the company and the customer.

value approach decision-making approach which takes account of people's ethical values.

value chain concept devised by Michael E. Porter, that logistics can add value to products at each stage of transfer.

value chain analysis analysis of existing value chains to see if they do provide value; *see also* value analysis.

value constellation value inherent in relationships with stakeholders, competitors, customers and so on.

value engineering use of engineering techniques to build value into a product.

values plural of value, used mainly in the context of what people hold important in a social context.

values and lifestyles (VALS) market research technique which segments customers by their personal attitudes, motivations and behaviour in social situations.

value satisfaction in marketing, satisfaction by a customer that a purchased product or service is offering an appropriate level of value.

value set common values held by members of a particular group or culture.

value system interlocking sets of common values held by members of a society.

vandalism random destruction or damage to property for its own sake.

variable annuity annuity where payments can vary depending on the amount of money invested initially.

variable budget budget for variable costs.

variable cost cost that varies according to the total volume of production.

variable expense expense that varies according to the volume of production or activity.

variable factor programming scheduling technique which seeks to vary individual workloads in order to increase productivity.

variable factors factors which can be altered, either through controlled processes or at random.

variables factors which can change as the situation changes, over which the manager or business may have limited or no control.

variable working hours *see* flexible working hours.

variance difference between two sets of figures; difference between forecast or expected results and actual results.

variance analysis analysis of the nature and causes of observed variances.

variance reduction techniques techniques for standardizing costs in order to reduce variances and thereby overall costs.

variety diversity or choice.

variety reduction rationalization of stocks or products in order to reduce warehousing and distribution costs.

variety store retail outlet selling a wide range of different products and lines.

variety wars competition based on the rapid introduction of new products aimed at displacing competitor products from their positions in the market.

variometer *see* tachistoscope.

VAT *see* value added tax.

VDU *see* visual display unit.

Veblen effect economic phenomenon noted by Thorsten Bunde Veblen, whereby high levels of consumption lead to higher prices and/or increased demand.

velocity of circulation rate at which money circulates in an economy.

vend to sell.

vending machine automated machine which sells small products upon receipt of payment.

vendor person making a sale to another.

vendor rating measure of reliability, cost, etc. applied to a supplier or seller in comparison with others.

vendor reliability ability of a vendor to meet the conditions agreed with the buyer.

vendor's lien the rights of vendors to take possession of the goods of a buyer should the latter fail to pay for goods purchased.

Venn diagram graphic model using interlocking circles or other geometric shapes to show the relationship between factors.

venture enterprise or business activity.

venture capital money invested directly in businesses, rather than through loan or equity capital.

venture capital fund mutual fund set up to make venture capital investments.

venture capitalist person who invests surplus private money in the form of venture capital.

venture teams project teams set up to establish and manage new ventures.

verbal aptitude test test which measures the ability to communicate verbally or orally.

verbal communication communication through spoken words.

vertical integration acquisition of other companies involved in other stages of the production and sales process, for example, the acquisition of retail outlets by a manufacturer.

verticalization *see* vertical integration.

vertical merger *see* vertical integration.

vertical promotion promotion to a higher level or grade of job; advancement to a more senior position.

vertical relations relations and communications between different levels of an organization.

very large scale integration (VLSI) electronic circuit design which integrates a very large number of circuits, processors and other components, required to support modern computer technology.

vested interests those interests which people have in a property or organization by right of ownership or other legal attachment; alternatively, those interests which people have in either maintaining or changing a situation so as to protect their own interests and benefits.

vested rights right of access to money in a pension fund by employees once they have left the firm.

vestibule training in-company training which is provided in a space set aside for this purpose, rather than on the shop floor.

veto power right of a person to veto or refuse to ratify any proposal put before them.

vetting checking the references and credentials of a prospective employee.

vicarious liability extent to which an employer is liable for the actions of employees.

video-conferencing *see* tele-conferencing.

virtual corporation organization structure based on a highly integrative use of information technology, encompassing both suppliers and customers, and eliminating the need for much infrastructure and physical space as a result.

virtual library *see* on-line library.

virtual office term for the automation of office functions and their links to information technology which allow office work to be carried out in dispersed locations.

virtual plant manufacturing concept whereby different production functions are carried out in different places, sometimes by suppliers and customers, all linked together by information technology.

virtual reality computer simulation which allows users a near-real experience of a place, situation, design concept, etc.

virus in computers, malicious code which has the capacity to replicate itself whenever it encounters another computer program; *see also* logic bomb.

visible exports tangible products exported to other countries; as opposed to invisible exports.

visible imports tangible products imported from other countries; as opposed to invisible imports.

visible management management philosophy which encourages managers to maintain a high profile among workers through constant personal contact; *see also* management by walking about.

visible trade international trade consisting of visible items, rather than services; *see also* invisibles.

vision quality of being able to foresee events and trends and determine strategy accordingly, highly prized in senior executives and leaders.

visual abilities test test which measures employees' ability to comprehend and understand things seen.

visual aid general term for technologies used to present visual and graphic accompaniments to lectures and presentations.

visual display unit visual device used to display computer data, also known as a monitor.

VLSI *see* very large-scale integration.

v-mail *see* voice mail.

vocation occupation or profession.

vocational education training for a particular profession.

vocational guidance counselling given mainly to younger people which aims to advise them of the vocation or profession for which they are best suited.

vocational training *see* vocational education.

voice the ability of a member or stakeholder of an organization to make their views known and taken seriously.

voice mail computer-based system for storing, sending and receiving spoken messages, usually linked to a telephone system.

voice recognition system computer peripherals and software which can recognize and interpret spoken commands.

void no longer valid.

voidable contract contract that can be declared void by either party under certain conditions.

volume quantity or content.

volume checking large-scale audit involving a detailed check of all of an organization's records.

voluntary arbitration in collective agreements, clause whereby a dispute can be referred to arbitration only by the consent of all parties involved.

voluntary assumption of risk concept whereby it is assumed that employees or others in potentially risky situations are aware of the risks and assume responsibility for them.

voluntary bankruptcy bankruptcy which is declared by a person or company without being forced to do so; as opposed to involuntary bankruptcy.

voluntary groups *see* symbol groups.

voluntary organization organization, usually in the not-for-profit sector, made up largely of unpaid volunteer workers rather than paid employees.

voluntary redundancy situation where redundancies are required and where some employees volunteer to be made redundant, in exchange for compensation.

voluntary restraint restraint which is self-imposed.

volunteer worker worker who agrees to provide labour without being paid; found most commonly in voluntary organizations.

vostro account account maintained by a bank with another bank in a foreign country; as opposed to nostro account.

voting rights rights vested in shares which allow shareholders to vote at annual general meetings.

voting trust arrangement whereby shareholders hand over their voting rights to others; *see also* proxy.

voucher written document showing that the bearer is entitled to a specified quantity of goods or services.

vulture capital colloquial term for investment in distressed or damaged assets which are then restored to full working condition and subsequently resold.

W

wa 'harmony', a key value in Japanese organization culture.

WACC *see* weighted average cost of capital.

wage money paid to employees in exchange for their labour.

wage and price controls government measures to curb or prevent increases in both wages and prices.

wage bracket wage paid for a particular occupation or class of work.

wage compression situation where the range of salaries between the highest and lowest grades is reduced, for example, by giving lower paid workers larger increases than higher paid workers.

wage control measures to curb or prevent wage increases, usually by government or company.

wage coordination principle by which workers doing equivalent tasks are paid equivalent amounts.

wage determination the process of setting wage levels.

wage drift tendency by which pay increases at a rate above the national average.

wage freeze prohibition of wage increases for a specified period of time.

wage inflation inflation which is in part driven by rapidly increasing wages.

wage rate the specified amount of money to be paid in wages for a given period.

wage stabilization government policies aimed at preventing excessive levels of increase or decrease in wage rates.

wage structure the overall pay structure of a firm within which individual wages are determined.

wage, subsistence *see* subsistence wage.

wage–work bargaining in collective bargaining, the relating of wages paid to the amount of work done.

waiting-line theory *see* queuing theory.

waiting time length of time a customer must wait in a queue before being served.

waiver statement by one party that they will not enforce any rights or dues which they are owed.

walk-in prospective employee who literally walks in the door to apply for a job.

walking the floor management practice of spending time on the shop floor to communicate with managers and see production work at first hand; *see* management by walking about.

walkout *see* strike.

Wall Street the financial services and trading centre of New York City.

want scarcity of lack of commodities or money.

wants motivating forces that lead consumers to demand products which, though not necessarily essential, are nonetheless desirable; *see also* needs.

warehouse physical location where goods and materials are stored.

warehouse clubs wholesale businesses which also sell on a retail basis to consumers who must first become members of a customer club.

warehousing the process of storing goods in a warehouse.

warrant document authorizing another to act on one's behalf.

warranty certification that a product meets certain quality standards, usually guaranteeing recompense or replacement should the product in fact fail to do so.

wastage proportion of products or materials which are spoiled, damaged or lost during production and distribution.

wastage rate speed or frequency at which wastage occurs.

waste useless or superfluous materials, often created as a byproduct during the production process.

waste control strategy strategy for reducing levels of waste and thereby increasing efficiency.

waste, environmental *see* pollution.

wasting assets assets whose value is gradually depleted through constant use.

waybill transport company's own statement identifying goods being shipped and their destination.

weak market market where there is little demand for products or services being sold.

wealth the total of a person's property and assets.

wealth tax tax levied on personal wealth.

web browser computer application which enables the user to search for websites on the World Wide Web.

weighted average calculation of an average in which each item in the series is weighted to reflect its importance; the average is then calculated on the basis of the total weights.

weighted average cost of capital (WACC) weighted average of the costs of debt and equity.

weighted points plan method of assessing suppliers or vendors by scoring them according to important factors such as cost and reliability.

weighted sample sample deliberately selected to fit a particular profile; as opposed to random sample.

welfare 1 the well-being of people and society at large; **2** benefits paid to people to ensure their basic needs are met.

welfare economics branch of economics which deals with achieving the maximization of welfare.

welfare officer company or union official who has the function of ensuring that employee welfare needs are met.

welfare state political and social construct which aims to provide for the welfare needs of all citizens.

wheeler-dealer colloquial term for a trader or dealer, very often meaning an unscrupulous trader or one with low ethical standards

whipsaw situation where a trader suffers a loss when buying goods and then a further loss when selling them.

whistleblowing practice whereby employees inform their managers when they witness corrupt or illegal practices by their colleagues.

white-collar worker office worker or other not directly involved in production.

white elephant asset whose costs outweigh any profits.

white goods consumer durable electrical appliances such as kettles, refrigerators and washing machines.

white knight in takeover situations, a friendly bidder who acts to counter a hostile bid.

whole-job ranking job grading technique which compares jobs with each other in order to grade them in appropriate order.

wholesale dealing in goods in bulk as part of the distribution process; as opposed to retail.

wholesaler company involved in wholesale trade.

wholesaling the sale of goods in bulk by the manufacturer or a distributor to retailers.

wide area network computer network linking a number of computers and terminals over a large geographical area.

wildcat strike strike action which is called without warning, usually by local groups of workers in individual plants.

winding up *see* liquidation.

win–win bargaining bargaining result whereby all parties achieve most of their major objectives.

WIPO *see* World Intellectual Property Organization.

withdrawal 1 removal or taking away; **2** selling all equity and withdrawing from ownership of a company; **3** in marketing, the abandonment of a particular market.

withholding tax *see* pay as you earn.

without dividend *see* ex-dividend.

work labour; the carrying out of tasks and functions in the workplace.

workaholic person who works excessively, and who may have difficulty detaching himself or herself from work.

work audit observation and analysis of the tasks carried out by workers.

work cycle individual tasks involved in doing a job, usually on a repetitive basis.

work day hours per day when an employee is required to be at work.

worker person who is engaged to do a job.

worker control principle in Marxist political economy that the means of production should be controlled by the workers who provide their labour.

worker participation management philosophy which encourages workers to give their views and be involved in decision making.

work ethic belief in some cultures that work has an inherent value and is a moral and social good.

work experience experience gained through working.

work-flow *see* production flow.

workforce *see* labour force.

work group *see* team.

work group compatibility extent to which an employee can fit into a work group in terms of technical and interpersonal skills.

work group output total productivity from a given work group.

working area physical location within which a worker performs his or her duties; *see also* workstation.

working capital excess of current assets over current liabilities, leaving a sum which the company can employ for investment or other purposes.

working capital cycle process by which working capital is constantly expended and replenished.

working capital ratio *see* current ratio.

working days lost measure of time lost due to breakdowns, industrial action and other unforeseen causes.

working from home *see* teleworking.

working-time flexibility *see* flexible working hours.

work in progress work which is currently in the production system and has not yet been completed.

workload the quantity of work which each worker or manager must perform.

work measurement techniques used to establish the time required for a worker to perform a particular task or set of tasks.

work organization the structure of the workplace, including how tasks are carried out, who will carry them out where and when, and so on.

workplace physical location where work is conducted.

work sampling work measurement techniques carried out on a random sample of work, used to generate standardized values for work times.

work satisfaction extent to which workers derive satisfaction from the work they do.

works council organizations set up in the workplace which allow communication and consultation between management and workers.

work sharing distribution of available work among employees; more generally, the sharing of tasks between two or more employees.

workshop production facility where small-scale engineering or technical work is carried out.

workstation place where a worker performs his or her various tasks.

work structure *see* work organization.

work study general term for research on how workers carry out their tasks and perform their roles.

work-to-rule in industrial disputes, action whereby workers perform the minimum demanded of them, refusing to take on extra work or overtime.

work unit group or team of workers involved in carrying out the same or related tasks.

work week the number of hours worked in the course of a normal week, excluding overtime.

World Bank officially, the International Bank for Reconstruction and Development, established to provide financial assistance to developing or needy nations.

World Commission on Environment and Development international organization established to investigate the issues surrounding sustainable development, resulting in the Brundtland Report of 1987 and the United Nations Conference on Environment and Development in 1993.

world economy *see* global economy.

World Intellectual Property Organization (WIPO) international body set up to promote and harmonize intellectual property law worldwide.

world-system in economics, the integrated global economic and political system.

world trade total trade conducted between nations around the world.

World Trade Organization (WTO) worldwide trade body formed of countries that have acceded to the General Agreement on Tariffs and Trade, and which ensures that members abide by the principles of that agreement.

World Wide Web (WWW) network of locations, known as websites, connected by the Internet which provide information, advertise services, etc.

worry factor problem of insurance which is inadequate to cover a forecast loss.

worst case scenario the worst possible outcome that can be envisaged.

worth value.

wound up past tense of winding up, used to describe a company that has been liquidated.

write-off an asset that has been written off.

writing down reducing the book value of an asset.

writing down allowance amount that may be deducted from taxable income to account for depreciation.

writing off the assumption that an asset has been wholly consumed or destroyed, and its removal from the company's books.

written down value *see* net book value.

wrongful dismissal dismissal of an employee from his or her employment without due cause.

WTO *see* World Trade Organization.

WWW *see* World Wide Web.

WYSIWYG acronym for 'what you see is what you get'.

XYZ

X-11 time series technique widely used in forecasting.

X-axis the horizontal axis on a graph.

Yankee bonds bonds issued by the US government.

Y-axis vertical axis on a graph.

yield return on an investment; generally synonymous with profit.

yield rate rate of return on an investment.

yield to maturity yield gained from an investment when that investment matures.

yield variance difference between calculated or forecast yield and the actual yield on an investment.

zaibatsu in Japanese business culture, large groups of businesses connected by horizontal links including some co-ownership; *see also keiretsu.*

Z-chart graph showing total production on three dimensions: periodic, cumulative and moving annual totals.

zero balance account balance that is neither in credit nor in deficit.

zero-based budgeting budgeting technique which recalculates needs from the beginning for each budget, rather than simply adding an increment to the preceding budget.

zero base review review and analysis technique which sets aside present structures or processes and recalculates needs from a beginning basis.

zero defects quality control philosophy which aims to produce products without defects of any kind.

zero implementation computer software programs and applications which can be used immediately on installation; *see also* plug and play.

zero rating good that is liable for a zero rate of income tax; in effect, it is not taxable.

zero sum game situation whereby gains by one party are offset by losses to another.

zip code US term for postal code.

zone curve chart graph which uses zones depicting the full range of data, represented by maximum and minimum points, to represent trends rather than narrow lines which reflect averages or means.

Z-scores credit scoring technique against a standard compiled from the financial ratios of healthy and failed companies; the company being scored is compared with this standard.